THE ART OF COLLABORATING WITH AI

We are at a momentous inflection point in our evolutionary history: generative AI is becoming mainstream, transforming the world of work, and specifically that of knowledge workers. This book helps you to navigate your upskilling journey to remain relevant and to add value in the workplace.

Knowledge workers must face up to the fact that there is a need to urgently reboot their skill set to survive and thrive in the new AI era. Many of the historic competences and points of differentiation that employees could offer are being challenged with AI technology. This book is all about building the power skills that knowledge workers will need to develop to maintain a competitive edge and work effectively alongside AI. It's a future where AI will now do a lot of the heavy lifting and one in which employers will increasingly be looking for people to add value in areas where AI is weak. In particular, this puts the spotlight on the need for workers to dial up their potential as polymaths. These are people who can see the big picture from different perspectives and who can add that extra layer of innovative thinking and creativity to everything they do. Importantly, the book provides a framework for understanding how AI is likely to reshape the fundamental structure of the workforce, and how knowledge workers can strategically position themselves to enhance their value.

This book provides an essential guide to developing new skill sets for knowledge workers in the AI era. Not only does it ensure that you don't fall behind, it will also enable you to succeed and thrive.

David VL Smith founded the business research agency, DVL Smith Ltd, over 30 years ago and is a visiting professor at the University of Hertfordshire Business School. He holds a PhD in organisational psychology from the University of London. He is a former vice president of ESOMAR, the worldwide marketing intelligence association, and a fellow and past chairman of the UK Market Research Society.

Adam Riley started his career in London-based market research agencies in the early 1990s before becoming a global marketing strategist in the Chairman's office of Samsung in South Korea, after gaining an MBA from the London Business School. Returning to London, Adam joined the marketing strategy practice of Monitor Company (now Monitor Deloitte) before founding Decision Architects consultancy in 2006.

David and Adam founded Polymathmind.ai in 2023 to help organisations collaborate with AI and develop the power skills needed to grasp the opportunities it presents for the future.

THE ART OF COLLABORATING WITH AI

Harnessing the Power of Diverse Thinking

David VL Smith and Adam Riley

Routledge
Taylor & Francis Group
LONDON AND NEW YORK

Designed cover image: designbypie.net

First published 2025
by Routledge
4 Park Square, Milton Park, Abingdon, Oxon OX14 4RN

and by Routledge
605 Third Avenue, New York, NY 10158

Routledge is an imprint of the Taylor & Francis Group, an informa business

British Library Cataloguing-in-Publication Data
A catalogue record for this book is available from the British Library

Library of Congress Cataloging-in-Publication Data
Names: Smith, D. V. L. (David Van Lloyd), author. | Riley, Adam (Marketing strategist), author.
Title: The art of collaborating with AI : harnessing the power of diverse thinking / David VL Smith and Adam Riley.
Other titles: Art of collaborating with artificial intelligence
Description: Abingdon, Oxon ; New York, NY : Routledge, 2025. | Includes bibliographical references and index.
Identifiers: LCCN 2024043639 (print) | LCCN 2024043640 (ebook) | ISBN 9781032847610 (hardback) | ISBN 9781032839851 (paperback) | ISBN 9781003514879 (ebook)
Subjects: LCSH: Employees—Effect of technological innovations on. | Artificial intelligence.
Classification: LCC HD6331 .S59 2025 (print) | LCC HD6331 (ebook) | DDC 650.1/3028563—dc23/eng/20250217
LC record available at https://lccn.loc.gov/2024043639
LC ebook record available at https://lccn.loc.gov/2024043640

ISBN: 978-1-032-84761-0 (hbk)
ISBN: 978-1-032-83985-1 (pbk)
ISBN: 978-1-003-51487-9 (ebk)

DOI: 10.4324/9781003514879

Typeset in Joanna
by Apex CoVantage, LLC

CONTENTS

PREFACE

The motivation to write this book arose from the realisation that our lives as business consultants were radically changed almost overnight by the arrival of generative AI, specifically ChatGPT, in November 2022. We had always been aware of AI's ongoing development in the background, but it was an epiphany moment when we first used ChatGPT. We then fully recognised AI's immense speed and power. We knew it would transform our work as consultants and that of other knowledge workers in a way that no one could have envisaged a few years ago.

We began to observe that many knowledge workers quickly seized the opportunities presented by generative AI, but others seemed slower to recognise the need to upskill. Therefore, we decided to write a book that clarifies the pace at which AI is changing the world of knowledge work, maps out the new skills humans should cultivate to work alongside AI, and outlines the likely long-term direction of AI.

ACKNOWLEDGEMENTS

In writing this book, we benefitted enormously from the advice and professionalism of Jo Smith, who helped us determine the overall tone and content to best meet the needs of our audience.

We would also like to thank Anne Scott for her meticulous sub-editing and advice on effectively conveying our message. Additionally, we acknowledge the encouragement, support and first-class feedback from the Routledge Press team, which was instrumental in helping us complete and publish this book.

INTRODUCTION

AI represents an inflection point in history – a genuine paradigm shift. Like many, we had long suspected that machine learning and related technologies would be the latest in a long line of technological advances to impact and shape our world of knowledge work, but as soon as generative AI arrived in November 2022, it became clear to us that AI is not merely a new supportive tool but a transformative force poised to recast our professional lives as business consultants. We realised that AI would be able to undertake many tasks at breathtaking speed, tasks we previously thought were unique to experienced business consultants.

However, we adopted a positive stance, recognising that AI's superiority in many business-related tasks does not diminish the value of human workers. Instead, it redefines our roles. By embracing AI's capabilities, we could allocate our cognitive and creative resources to areas where we naturally excel, thus complementing AI rather than competing with it.

We anticipated a rollercoaster ride, acknowledging that working with AI would transform our cognitive processing skills, advancing the way we

DOI: 10.4324/9781003514879-1

think at a staggering pace. Writing this book was our way of understanding and sharing with fellow professionals how to begin collaborating with AI.

The aims of the book

In shaping this book, we first had to define our aims:

- **Awareness of AI's impact:** The primary aim is to ensure that readers fully understand where AI is taking us. They need to grasp the significant changes AI is bringing and find ways to complement, not compete with, AI.
- **Identifying power skills:** The second aim is to pinpoint the essential skills professionals should focus on – those that highlight the enduring value of human skills versus those that AI performs more efficiently. Here we map out practical frameworks to help professionals incorporate this new way of thinking into their daily work.
- **Future outlook:** The third aim is to provide readers with a road map to the human future as AI advances. Forewarned is forearmed, and this will help them continually adapt to the relentless march of AI.

Focusing on knowledge workers

Drawing from our experience as business consultants, we decided our expertise would be valuable to a wider group – knowledge workers.

The term 'knowledge worker' was coined by management theorist Peter Drucker[1] in his 1966 book, *The Effective Executive*. Drucker noted that the most valuable asset of 21st-century institutions, whether business or non-business, would be knowledge workers and their productivity.

Our aim is to focus on knowledge work and knowledge workers (an area of the economy where we have spent our entire careers). These are individuals who allocate knowledge to productive use, performing roles in the knowledge economy including anticipatory imagination, problem-seeking, problem-solving and generating ideas and aesthetic sensibilities. It's worth noting that there are approximately one billion knowledge workers worldwide, about 30% of the global workforce.

Our core unifying idea: Diverse thinking

The core message underpinning this book is that we believe that knowledge workers need to focus on key power skills to work constructively alongside AI. We see bringing together these disparate skills to achieve a goal as analogous to developing the qualities of a modern-day polymath.

Polymaths, with their interdisciplinary abilities, act as wide-angle lenses, making sense of various information sources, drawing them together into coherent pictures. While AI can assimilate massive amounts of data, humans excel at connecting the dots in a broader context. Humans can make subtle and compassionate observations about the human condition, which AI cannot replicate.

Additionally, humans' ability to apply abductive reasoning – making informed decisions under uncertainty – surpasses conventional deductive and inductive thinking, where AI now performs the heavy lifting. Finally, the creative and leadership skills of a polymath enable humans to tell compelling stories and inspire action with empathy and compassion.

An overview of knowledge worker power skills

We have distilled the skills the knowledge worker of the future will need into these seven key areas:

- **AI-Human Interface:** Proficiency in working with AI tools and understanding their robustness and validity is crucial.
- **The Sensemaker:** The ability to synthesise diverse information sources to understand and solve complex problems.
- **The Critical Thinker:** Handling uncertainty, complexity and imperfect information and interpreting and applying AI-provided data correctly.
- **The Audacious Creator:** Generating novel ideas and innovating – areas where human creativity excels.
- **The Forward Thinker:** Envisioning future scenarios and making decisions based on emotional intelligence together with ethical and societal understanding.
- **The Inspiring Communicator:** Conveying complex ideas through compelling narratives that bridge data and action.
- **The Galvanising Leader:** Fostering collaboration and building a culture based on empathy, emotional intelligence and interpersonal skills.

Mapping out the knowledge worker's AI journey

Having clarified the book's aim, target audience, central theme and the skills knowledge workers need, we begin by setting the scene for knowledge workers about what is happening to their world and provide them with the context they need to understand the importance of the power skills and prepare for the future.

We start the book with a chapter that reinforces AI as a genuine inflection moment in history and the importance for knowledge workers to respond seriously. Following this, we discuss the power and potential of AI and then explore various perspectives on AI's impact from governments, organisations, experts and society at large. We then reflect on how AI could fundamentally change society and the workplace, introducing the concept of the newly advantaged and disadvantaged. Following this, we discuss diverse polymath thinking as the way forward for humans to collaborate with AI.

After this scene-setting, in the remainder of the book, we put the spotlight on the seven power skills introduced above that will elevate knowledge worker capabilities and enable a successful collaboration with AI. We conclude with a look at future developments and the next steps in our journey with AI.

This is not a book on AI per se; our focus is on the human side of the human-AI equation. We do not claim to be experts on the technical details of AI, beyond being interested users, but we are great advocates for the power of human intelligence and how this must develop. We hope this book helps you understand the importance of taking action to work alongside AI, benefits from our practical frameworks for cultivating essential power skills in the AI era, and gives you a sense of the journey ahead with AI.

Note

1. Drucker, P. (1966). *The Effective Executive*. New York: Harper & Row.

1

AN INFLECTION POINT IN HISTORY

In this chapter, we examine what lessons can be learnt from preceding industrial revolutions and upheavals, particularly the impact on the way we collectively approached work and the repercussions for labour.

We explore techno-optimist and techno-pessimist positions since the late 18th century and illustrate that historically when human labour has prevailed over technological progress, the underlying reason has been an ability to develop, evolve and acquire new skills – but not withstanding, we test the hypothesis that our latest technological inflection point may be so profound that staying ahead of the curve may become increasingly difficult. We conclude the chapter by examining the wider impact that technologically driven change has had on society more broadly.

Artificial intelligence (AI) is going to change all our lives, for the better or for the worse. Sundar Pichai, CEO Alphabet Inc, has been widely reported as saying that 'AI is one of the most profound things we're working on as humanity. It's more profound than fire or electricity' (2020).[1]

DOI: 10.4324/9781003514879-2

The aim of this book is to encourage the reader to begin reflecting on the skills that they are now going to need to thrive in the AI era. But first it's important to set the context and register exactly why it is so important for knowledge workers to recognise that AI is transforming the labour market and to realise that we're entering unchartered territory for knowledge workers.

Our economics training doesn't go much beyond a single A-level between us, and so while we touch on some important areas of economics and labour market dynamics, we come at this as interested commentators rather than skilled practitioners.

Looking back to look forward

In 1954 Martin Luther King, Jr. told his congregation that 'we are not makers of history, we are made by history', perhaps reflecting Shakespeare's assertion in *The Tempest* that 'what is past is prologue'. They are both observing that history sets the context for, and shapes, our present and future.

History is the basis for all empirical decision-making. This has parallels with the observation of Spanish writer and philosopher George Santayana, who authored the aphorism that 'those who cannot remember the past are condemned to repeat it' (1905)[2]. Our current adventures with AI seem to be marking a new era and ushering in a new paradigm (an overused and oft-misused phrase, but perhaps this is one of the few instances when it is truly appropriate), and so maybe now is a good time to consider what we can learn from the past.

This is not a history book, and whilst industrial history can be fascinating, we will not dwell too long on what we can learn from the past. But given that the widely repeated axiom that 'AI will create more jobs than it destroys' leans heavily on historic precedent – that is, technology has always created more jobs (in the aggregate) than it destroys – it is worth investing a chapter on the historical context and considering the historical inflection points so characteristic of each 'industrial revolution' – that have sign-posted profound changes – and what implications have flowed from there. They might give us clues to what the future may hold.

> The longer you can look back, the farther you can look forward.
>
> (Winston Churchill, 1944)[3]

In a 2023 MIT Technology Review interview[4] Fei-Fei Li, Sequoia Capital professor of computer science at Stanford University and co-director of Stanford's Human-Centered AI Institute, argued that 'This moment in AI is an inflection moment'. By providing concrete applications and tools, the latest generative AI models have been the catalyst for widespread adoption of AI amongst the general public. In turn, businesses have woken up to the opportunity of applying AI to improve the efficiency of work processes, generate revenue and reduce costs, rolling these technologies out in more products for the real world. 'Because of that, [AI] impacts our world in a more profound way', Li says.

Lessons from the original industrial revolution

In his 2010 book *Why the West Rules – For Now,*[5] historian and archaeologist Ian Morris sets out 'the patterns of history and what they reveal about the future'. In our presentations we like to reference one of Ian Morris's charts (reproduced in Acemoglu & Johnson's book *Power & Progress – Our Thousand-Year Struggle Over Technology and Progress*).[6] Morris shows graphically that human progress is slow – almost invisible – until it isn't. Morris uses a Human Social Development Index construct in his analysis which captures four attributes:

- Energy capture (per person calories)
- Organisation (using size of the largest city)
- War-making capacity
- Information technology – tools for sharing and processing information

He argues that the introduction of the Boulton and Watt steam engine in 1776 proved to be a critical inflection point in the development of human society. See Figure 1.1 on the next page. Watt's was not the first such engine. Thomas Newcomen's 1700 engine was its progenitor – developed to pump water out of mines – but when asked to repair one of these early Newcomen engines, Watt realised just how inefficient it was and set about designing a better machine. The Newcomen steam engine needed 15 kilograms of coal per horsepower hour, but Watt's engine would only need 3.5 kilograms.

Working with industrialist John Roebuck, Watt patented his machine in 1769, but it wasn't until Mathew Boulton replaced Roebuck as Watt's partner that the Boulton and Watt steam engine became commercially

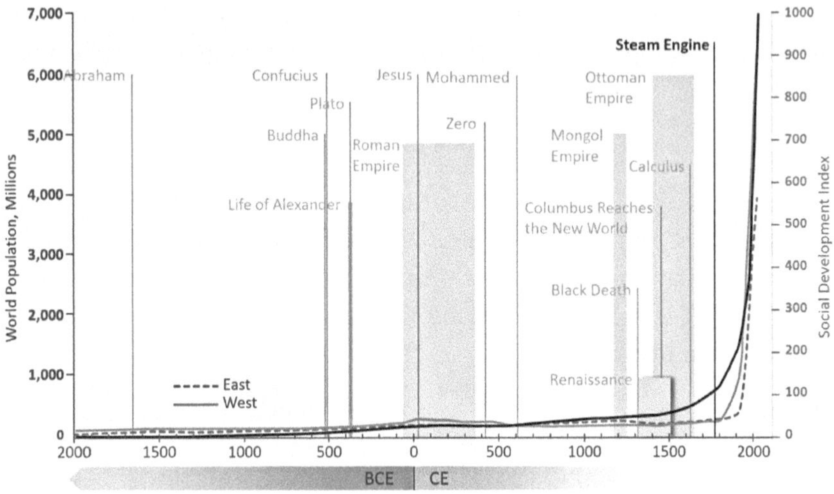

Figure 1.1 World Population and Social Development Index

successful. The cost of steam power continued to fall, and from the initial 'raison d'etre' as mine equipment, these machines were quickly repurposed by cotton cloth manufacturers (and others), and the mechanisation of traditional processes, pushing out craft and artisan production, has become a key part of the founding narrative of the first industrial revolution.

> In 1700 a spinster with a pedal-powered wheel needed two hundred hours to produce a pound of yarn; by 1800 extraordinary devices – Hargreaves' 'Jenny', Arkwright's 'Throstle', Crompton's 'Mule' – were doing the same work in three hours.
>
> (Ian Morris, 2010)[7]

These new technologies replaced human (and animal) muscle power and dexterity with mechanised substitutes. The post-industrial revolution economy grew in the aggregate, but well-established sectors and a way of life disappeared, never to return. The technology of the new steam engine jumped from industry to industry as new (what we now call) 'use-cases' were developed – the steam engine became an enabling technology with broad application. New work was found for displaced workers but not immediately. Conditions worsened, and it took time for labour laws to catch up, but eventually real wages for those in employment grew.

> If you go back to 1800, everybody was poor. I mean everybody. The Industrial Revolution kicked in, and a lot of countries benefited, but by no means everyone.
>
> (Jeffrey Kluger, 2014)[8]

November 2022 felt like another 'steam engine' moment, and what we are seeing now is the application of AI barrelling its way through our industrial landscape – a new transformational technology jumping from industry to industry. Historical precedent suggests industrial revolutions always winnow out industries and sectors ill-prepared for the future they bring, and we have no reason to believe that what we are experiencing now will be any different.

The economic debate about technological change and resultant job losses has raged ever since the dawn of the first industrial revolution (and actually long before). There is a famous anecdote that detailed Queen Elizabeth I's reaction to a patent application in the 16th century by one William Lee of Nottingham. He had invented the first mechanical knitting machine used in the textiles industry. The Queen was 'not amused'.

> Thou aimest high, Master Lee. Consider thou what the invention could do to my poor subjects. It would assuredly bring them to ruin by depriving them of employment, thus making them beggars.
>
> (Gravenor, 1831)[9]

Techno-optimist versus techno-pessimist

The interaction between Queen Elizabeth I and her subject Master Lee reflects this observation from author James Branch Cabell that 'The optimist proclaims that we live in the best of all possible worlds; and the pessimist fears this is true' (1926).

One of the greatest economic theorists of his time (all time?), David Ricardo moved from a position of techno optimism – espousing the benefits of mechanisation to conserve scarce resources, improve efficiency, increase output and lower production costs – to one of techno pessimism.

Observing the impact of mechanisation and a period of labour unrest (including the now famous Luddites), in 1821, Ricardo constructed a model to demonstrate that workers should fear technological change.

> All I wish to prove is that the discovery and use of machinery . . . will be injurious to the labouring class as some of their number will be thrown out of employment, and the population will become redundant, compared with the funds which are to employ it.
>
> (Ricardo, 1821)[10]

Speaking in the House of Commons in May 1823, Ricardo reiterated his proposition that 'the use of machinery was prejudicial . . . to the working classes generally. It was the means of throwing additional labour onto the market, and thus demand for labour generally was diminished'.

Ricardo's evolving position didn't go unchallenged at the time, but it was 100 years later that Swedish economist Knut Wicksell refurbished Ricardo's model and challenged his underlying assumptions. Where Ricardo ended up as a techno pessimist, Wicksell was an optimist. The techno optimist argument is that technological advances lower production costs. Lower costs equate to lower prices, which in turn extend the market, stimulating demand for consumption goods. It is profitable for firms to expand to satisfy demand.

Extra output requires more people alongside the machines, which absorbs the initially laid-off workers; so in addition to lowering prices, technology creates more jobs than it destroys. The long-term growth in employment seen during the first and subsequent revolutions relied heavily on the presence of latent demand for consumer goods that could be unlocked by lower prices driven by mechanisation.

> In early times, the products of skilled industry were for the most part luxuries intended for the few, whereas now the most exquisite tools and engines are employed in producing articles of ordinary consumption for the great mass of the community.
>
> (Samuel Smiles, *Self Help*, 1859)[11]

With the benefit of hindsight (and to this point in time), Wicksell has been proved correct, but the debate does give us some food for thought. It is also interesting that both Ricardo and Wicksell argued that technological advances were irresistible, with both recommending that governments did not seek to discourage innovation, whether it destroyed jobs or preserved them. Trying to limit technological advances was futile – like trying to hold back the tide.

Wicksell made the distinction between labour-saving, labour-using and labour-neutral innovations, namely those that lower, raise, or leave unchanged the marginal productivity of labour relative to capital. He believed labour-saving innovation would be the outlier with labour-using and labour-neutral technology being the norm. Does this still hold true? We will explore the extent to which AI will act as an enabler of or substitute for human endeavour later in the book.

There is also a failure to distinguish between the short-term and long-term effects of technological innovation. Technological unemployment was a term popularised by John Maynard Keynes in the 1930s – being a temporary phase of adjustment brought about by the 'discovery of the means of economising on the use of labour outrunning the pace at which we can find new uses for labour' (1933). Transitions engendered by revolutions are not seamless. Initially, innovation may hurt workers possessing specific skills or experience, but history suggests that these workers will invest in acquiring new skills that will equip them to operate in the new economy; however, this is not a painless or necessarily quick transition. There is also no guarantee that the new roles are as well paid or rewarded as the old job, now redundant.

The second industrial revolution

The world experienced its second industrial revolution, dated roughly from the middle of the 19th century to the outbreak of World War I. It is characterised by the association of science, technology and industrialisation, and concepts such as economies of scale and 'throughput', described for the first time as 'mass production', were introduced. Breakthroughs in steel production, chemicals, electricity etc. saw advancements in manufacturing and production technology that in turn enabled the widespread adoption of new systems and applications in transport and communications, as well as agriculture and food processing (Mokyr, 1998).[12]

US industry surged in the second half of the 19th century and placed greater emphasis on increased efficiency and higher worker productivity. The high cost (and relative scarcity) of skilled labour meant that American inventions often prioritised not just automation but also ways to boost the productivity of low-skilled workers (Acemoglu and Johnson, 2023).

> The labouring classes are comparatively few in number, but this is counter-balanced by, and indeed may be regarded as one of the chief causes of, the eagerness with which they call in the aid of machinery in almost every department of industry.
>
> (Sir Joseph Whitworth, 1851)[13]

Between 1815 and 1860, the real stock of equipment per capita in the US grew at 2.8% annually – this jumped to 4.5% between 1860 and 1900. In 1830, there were 30 miles of railroad tracks in the US, rising to 2,808 in 1840 and 30,000 in 1860. The aggregate capacity of US steam engines more than quadrupled between 1840 and 1860 – from 760,000 hp to 3,740,000 hp. By 1870, this was up to 5,590,000 hp (Mokyr, 1998).

Skilled workers such as engineers, fabricators, machinists, boilermakers and so on saw their wages rise significantly relative to common labourers. But whilst these skilled workers were creating the machines that drove industrial progress, other developments sought to level the playing field. In their 2017 paper, Frey and Osborne[14] observed that mechanisation and the factory system developed and refined over the course of the late 18th to late 19th centuries led to a general deskilling – work was decomposed into smaller, highly specialised sequences, requiring less skill.

A key development on the road to successful mass production was the introduction of interchangeable parts – standard pieces that could be used in different ways, making it easier for unskilled workers to produce complex products, from bicycles to sewing machines to guns (and much more). Another inflection point with present-day parallels. Eli Whitney Jr, scion of the Whitney family which was heavily involved in earlier waves of industrialisation and who took over the running of the Whitney Armory in 1842, commented that '[The objective was to] substitute correct and effective operations of machinery for that skill of the artist which is acquired only by long practice and experience' (Eli Whitney Jr, 1842).[15]

Increased mechanisation and improvements in worker efficiency increased productivity whilst undercutting the need for skilled labour. Mechanisation saw greater use of unskilled labour performing simple, repetitive tasks under the direction of a few experienced overseers. Ford's new assembly line that began operation in 1913 was specifically designed for machinery to be operated by unskilled workers – thus capital complemented unskilled workers whilst substituting for skilled artisans.

We see the same dynamic emerging with the current raft of AI applications. A recent 2023 study[16] from Stanford's Human-Centered Artificial Intelligence group ('HAI') and the Massachusetts Institute of Technology (MIT) reported that gains from AI mostly accrued to novice or less able workers and that there were fewer positive effects for the highest skilled or most experienced members of the company. Valuable expertise/experience is no longer as valuable as it was. In benefitting less experienced and less skilled staff, AI boosts their productivity, and in parallel it is marginalising skilled workers who may find that this AI-driven 'levelling up' is taking away some of their former comparative advantage.

The dawn of the information age

There is some debate about when the third industrial revolution began. Some argue that it started in the early 1970s with an era of further and rapid technological progress associated with the development of information technologies; however, one might point to a date 20 years earlier. In 1954, George Devol filed US Patent No. 2988237 for a 'Programmed Article Transfer System' for a robotic arm describing 'an autonomous machine that could store commands and move parts'. In 1956, in partnership with Joseph Engelberger, Devol created Unimation Inc (a combination of 'universal' and 'automation'), the world's first industrial robotics company.

In 1961, the two-tonne Unimate 1900 was the first mass-produced robotic arm deployed in a factory. Its most distinct feature was a grip on a steel arm that eliminated the need for a man to touch car parts just made from molten steel. Few workers wanted to operate the dangerous old equipment for moulding car parts. At General Motors's Ternstedt Division plant, it was an automated die-casting mould that dropped red-hot door handles and other car parts into pools of cooling liquid on a line that moved them along to workers for trimming and buffing. The Ternstedt die-caster worked around the clock for more than ten years alongside the plant's 3,000 men and women.

> There was very little opposition to robotics from American labor. . . . It helped with working people that the first robots were put to work doing hot, hazardous and dull labor.
>
> (Paul, Mickle, 1998)[17]

The Unimate is now on display at the Smithsonian Institution in Washington and in 2003 was inducted into the Robot Hall of Fame.[18]

Robotic automation was just one element of this third revolution; the other key factor was the coming of the information age, and we have all lived through the development of this information age economy. Signposts to the birth of the information age are many and varied; in 1959, Robert Noyce invented the first monolithic integrated circuit (made of silicon); in 1969, the first message was sent over ARPANET (a conceptual precursor to the internet); in 1971, the first microprocessor, Intel's 4004, was released; also in 1971 John Blankenbaker's Kenbak-1 was the first personal computer, followed in 1973 by Micral, the first PC to use a microprocessor. Microsoft was founded in 1975, followed by Apple in 1976.

The cost per computation declined at an annual average 37% between 1945 and 1980. During the 1980s and 1990s, it declined at an even more rapid 64% per annum. Were these early digital technologies aimed at primarily enhancing or augmenting human capabilities, not replacing them?

In a 1993 article in *Fortune* magazine,[19] Thomas Stewart argued that in the midst of a revolution induced by emerging information and communication technologies, [these] knowledge technologies were altering the cost–benefit equation for competing organisational arrangements, the information age is placing a premium on 'the ability to adjust and learn' that applies to both individuals and organisations. He gave an example which encapsulated the impact of the information age on business:

> Robert Immerman is the founder of InterDesign, a private company in Solon, Ohio, with annual sales above $10 million. InterDesign sells plastic clocks, refrigerator magnets, soap dishes, and the like.
>
> There's not a high-tech item among its products, but computers have changed the business. In the past twelve years, InterDesign's employment has tripled, total space has quintupled, and sales have octupled, but its megabytes of computer memory have gone up thirty-fold.
>
> Seven years ago (1986) Immerman dug deep and found $10,000 to buy a used disk drive that had 288 megabytes of storage – capacity that costs about $350 today (1993).
>
> Says Immerman: 'In the 1970s we went to the Post Office to pick up our orders. In the early 1980s we put in an 800 number. Late

> 1980s, we got a fax machine. In 1991 we added electronic data interchange'. Now, just two years later, more than half of InterDesign's orders arrive via modem straight into company computers. Staffers who used to man phones taking orders now track sales by product, customer, region – valuable information that Immerman once couldn't afford to collect.

To note, in 2024 you could buy a 5TB portable hard disk drive for less than $100 – that is 5m megabytes. By 1980, there were 1.13 times as many information workers as production workers, compared to just 0.22 in 1900. IT can do much of this information collection and processing more efficiently than workers can, eliminating the need for battalions of clerks, pools of secretaries, scores of purchasing and sales agents, and layers of supervisors and administrators (Greenwood, 1999).[20]

The downside to all this progress

In his 1970 book *Future Shock*,[21] American Futurist, Alvin Toffler warns us that 'our technological powers increase, but the side effects and potential hazards also escalate'. We are all familiar with how the information age has developed since Thomas Stewart wrote his article. But what impact has it had on skills and jobs? We can clearly now create more output with less labour.

Some research (Autor and Dorn, 2013)[22] suggests that computerisation erodes opportunities and wages for labour performing routine tasks, resulting in workers moving to low-skill service occupations. The outcome is an increasingly polarised labour market with growing employment in high-income cognitive (or knowledge) tasks and low-income manual occupations, accompanied by a hollowing out of middle-income routine jobs (Frey and Osborne, 2017).

Where human labour has prevailed over technological progress, the underlying reason has been an ability to develop, evolve and acquire new skills. But as new waves of technological advance creep into more cognitive areas (the domain of the knowledge worker), we may find staying ahead of the curve increasingly difficult. In recent years, there is evidence (Beaudry et al., 2013)[23] of higher skilled workers dropping down the occupational ladder, taking on work previously performed by lower-skilled labour and in turn pushing these workers even further down.

Acemoglu and Johnson (2023)[6] argue that American workers used to have access to good jobs, which, in addition to paying decent wages, provided job security and career-building opportunities. But with the advent of industrial automation, robotics and computerisation, American non-college graduates found it harder to get secure, well-paid jobs. People without a college education in the US have seen their real earnings decline since 1980. This led to feelings of economic isolation and points to the link between technology and advancement starting to leave behind certain strata of society. They became the post-war 'dispossessed'.

Politicians in the US recognised the challenge of people getting detached from the mainstream. In 2016, Bill Clinton suggested that 'Make America Great Again' (MAGA) used as a campaign rallying cry was a message that promised the dispossessed to 'give you an economy you had 50 years ago, and . . . move you back up on the social totem pole and other people down'. This phenomenon is not restricted to the US. There is a rise in populism/nationalism in Europe, South America and beyond that taps into the same dissatisfaction. And let's not talk about Brexit!

So what does history tell us about the coming wave of AI disruption? Optimists like artist Emmanuel Alonge (2021)[24] believe that,

> Technology is a liberation . . . the information age probably is the best thing to happen to the human race in human evolution. Now you have the equal opportunity to equip yourself through information and knowledge and express yourself as an independent mind.

But change is never seamless nor painless. There will be winners and losers. Looking at impact in the aggregate (which has historically been very positive) hides a lot of localised hardship.

Historically, the winners are those who can update their skills and capabilities to stay relevant in the new environment – but this will become harder and harder to do.

Summary

In this chapter we explored the historical evidence that technology has always created more jobs than it destroys and what clues to the future we can glean from the past. History has shown us that industrial revolutions always winnow out industries and sectors ill-prepared for the future that they usher in, and we have no reason to believe that what we are experiencing now will be any different. Trying to limit technological advance was and is futile – like trying to hold back the tide.

The good news is that evidence from the earliest industrial revolutions suggests that whilst innovation initially has a negative effect on workers possessing specific skills or experience, they will eventually find employment; however, this transition is not painless or quick, AND the net effect was general deskilling that resulted from the drive to more efficient processes. There are parallels in the latest technology-led revolution.

Recent research has reported that gains from AI have mostly accrued to novice or less able workers and that there were fewer positive effects for the highest skilled or most experienced members of the company. Valuable expertise/experience is no longer as valuable as it was. In benefitting less experienced and less skilled staff, AI boosts their productivity, and in parallel it is marginalising skilled workers who may find that this AI-driven 'levelling up' is taking away some of their former comparative advantage. As waves of this technological advance creep into more cognitive areas of work, we may find staying ahead of this curve increasingly difficult.

Notes

1. Pichai, S. (2020). Interview by Klaus Schwab. The World Economic Forum, Davos, Switzerland, January 22, 2020.
2. Santayana, G. (1905). The Life of Reason: The Phases of Human Progress. C. Scribner's Sons.
3. Churchill, W. (1944). "Speech to the Royal College of Physicians," March 2, 1944.
4. Li, F.-F. (2023). www.technologyreview.com/2023/11/14/1083352/ai-is-at-an-inflection-pointfei-fei-li-says/
5. Morris, I. (2012). *Why the West Rules – for Now: The Patterns of History and What They Reveal about the Future*. Cambridge University Press.
6. Acemoglu, D., & Johnson, S. (2023). *Power and Progress – Our Thousand-Year Struggle over Technology and Prosperity*.
7. Morris, I. (2010). *Why the West Rules—For Now: The Patterns of History, and What They Reveal About the Future* (Chapter 11, pages 496–497). Profile Books (UK).
8. Kluger, J. (2014). "Bill Gates Talks to TIME About the Three Myths of Global Aid." Time Magazine.
9. Gravenor, H. (1831). *History of the Framework Knitters*. https://conversableeconomist.com/2019/03/13/the-story-of-william-lee-and-his-knitting-machine/

10. Ricardo, D. (1821). *On the Principles of Political Economy and Taxation* (Chapter 31 'On Machinery'). John Murray.
11. Smiles, S. (1859). Self-Help. London: John Murray.
12. Mokyr, J. (1998). *The Second Industrial Revolution, 1870–1914*. Northwestern University.
13. Whitworth, J. (1851). https://en.wikipedia.org/wiki/Joseph_Whitworth
14. Frey, C. B., & Osborne, M. A. (2017). *The Future of Employment: How Susceptible Are Jobs to Computerisation?* Technological Forecasting and Social Change, 114(C), 254–280.
15. Whitney Jr, E. (1842). www.eliwhitney.org/museum/eli-whitney/family
16. Lynch, Shana. (2023). "Will Generative AI Make You More Productive at Work? Yes, But Only If You're Not Already Great at Your Job." *Stanford HAI*. https://hai.stanford.edu/news/will-generative-ai-make-you-more-productive-work-yes-only-if-youre-not-already-great-your-job.
17. Mickle, P. (1961). "A Peep into the Automated Future." The Trentonian. http://www.universelle-automation.de/1961_Trenton.pdf
18. *The First Robot*. (1961). www.capitalcentury.com.
19. Stewart, T. (1993). *Welcome to the Revolution*. Fortune Magazine, 128(15), 66–80.
20. Greenwood, J. (1999). *The Third Industrial Revolution: Technology, Productivity and Income Inequality*. Economic Review, Q2, 35(2), 2–12.
21. Tofler, A. (1970). *Future Shock*. (Chapter 18, '*The Strategy of Social Futurism*'). Random House (New York).
22. Autor, D. H., & Dorn, D. (2013). *The Growth of Low-Skill Service Jobs and the Polarization of the US Labor Market*. The American Economic Review, 103(5), 1553–1597.
23. Beaudry, P., Green, D. A., & Sand, B. M. (2013). *The Great Reversal in the Demand for Skill and Cognitive Tasks*. National Bureau of Economic Research.
24. Alonge, E. (2021). "A Quick Glance at the Professional Works of Ai Weiwei, Chris Ofili, and Andy Warhol." Art 152A: Artist Reports.

2

THE POWER AND POTENTIAL OF AI

In this chapter, we explore the speed, scope and potential impact of the AI revolution and consider the impact of AI on those roles that historically relied on human intelligence. We examine the question of just how far AI will invade the cognitive space of the knowledge worker and challenge the notion that AI will be good for everyone. We will test the jagged frontier of AI capabilities and use an example of the legal professional to investigate where hype and inflated expectation meet the hard reality of AI's impact on industry.

We conclude the chapter by considering AI as an enabler, or co-pilot, to AI as a substitute for human endeavour and the implications of this.

We've established that AI is a unique event in history, and we now move on to look in more depth at the sheer power of AI and the potential that it has to transform the world of work. Specifically, we focus on the rate at which AI will move from an enabler to a substitute for human endeavour.

DOI: 10.4324/9781003514879-3

Will AI raise all boats?

In this third decade of the 21st century, a new phase of industrial evolution is swirling about us. This centres on technologies that capture, optimise, utilise and deploy data. The speed of change, its scale, scope and complexity have no historical precedent and will disrupt every industry to a greater or lesser extent due to the confluence of connectivity, passive data gathering, computational power, advanced analytics, machine learning and AI that each gives rise to existential questions. This fourth industrial revolution promises to bring about (is bringing about) another period of profound change. Our relationship with technology will no doubt change, but as Carl Sagan observed, 'We live in a society exquisitely dependent on science and technology, in which hardly anyone knows anything about science and technology' (1989).[1]

Will technological change empower us? Will it free us from mundane things? Or does it become another weight on our shoulders?

> Technology is supposed to make our lives easier, allowing us to do things more quickly and efficiently. But too often it seems to make things harder, leaving us with fifty-button remote controls, digital cameras with hundreds of mysterious features and book-length manuals, and cars with dashboard systems worthy of the space shuttle.
>
> (James Surowiecki, 2007)[2]

The lesson from history – so far – is that innovation and change (industrialisation and capitalism) has had a hugely net positive effect, albeit accepting that the benefits were never uniformly distributed. But can this continue? Will the advent of the AI age 'raise all boats'? Whilst the idea that AI 'will raise many (but not all) boats' is an interesting one and might not be without merit, to borrow a financial services disclaimer 'past performance is not a guarantee of future results'.

The picture is building of how AI is likely to transform our lives, and it offers both utopian and dystopian perspectives. In his book *Co-Intelligence*,[3] Wharton Professor Ethan Mollick states that 'early studies of the effects of AI have found that it can lead to a 20% to 80% improvement in productivity across a wide variety of job types, from coding to marketing' (2024) and compares this to our old friend the Boulton and Watt steam engine that, he contends, improved productivity by 18% to 22%.

A widely reported Goldman and Sachs 2023 study suggests that global ten-year GDP will rise by 7% due to the economic gains anticipated from AI and that their 'expectation is that generative AI will have a measurable macroeconomic impact'.[4] The study also anticipated a lift in US productivity of 1.5% if widespread adoption were achieved over the next ten years. In parallel, McKinsey researchers (2023)[5] reported that 'generative AI's impact on productivity could add between $2.6 trillion to $4.4 trillion annually to the global economy', and commented:

> Generative AI could enable labor productivity growth of 0.1 to 0.6 percent annually through 2040, depending on the rate of technology adoption and redeployment of worker time into other activities. Combining generative AI with all other technologies, work automation could add 0.2 to 3.3 percentage points annually to productivity growth.

McKinsey also estimates that 8% of work hours could be automated by 2030 but that this push to automation will continue well beyond that, as, McKinsey suggests, historical precedent suggests that it will take up to 27 years to reach an adoption plateau. In his role as Institute Professor of Economics at MIT, Daron Acemoglu suggests a boost of 0.2 percentage points over the next decade with 5% of tasks profitably augmented or replaced by AI. Although there is some debate as to whether all these forecasts really take into account the 'game-changing' nature of AI and whether the application of historic evidence is relevant to what is a true paradigm shift. Is the past a good predictor of the future?

At what point does the optimism of productivity gains morph into something more troubling? We can contrast the optimistic view of AI with the dystopian vision of the future that offers us algorithmic bias, misinformation and widespread job displacement, with the societal polarisation and unrest that might stem from this. There are projections of 80% of the US workforce, seeing at least 10% of their role being taken over by AI, with some reports suggesting 20% of the workforce will have half of their job substituted by AI.[6]

The same Goldman Sachs economists estimated that AI 'could ultimately automate roughly 25% of work tasks' in major developed markets like the US, and greater automation will 'drive labor cost savings'.[7] Famed venture capitalist, and major OpenAI investor, Vinod Khosla goes further;

he believes 80% of work functions that comprise 80% of economically valuable jobs will be able to be done by AI (2023/24).[8]

Vivienne Ming, American theoretical neuroscientist and AI expert recently reported that 'Beyond hiring, some employers are toying with systems to automatically fire low-productivity workers. Other companies are developing machine learning-based personality assessments that screen out applicants predicted to agitate for increased wages, support unionisation or demonstrate job hopping tendencies' (2023).[9]

In his 2019 Congressional testimony on Artificial Intelligence and the Future of Work, Erik Brynjolfsson (Professor and Senior Fellow at the Stanford Institute for Human-Centered AI) reminds us that 'There's no economic law that says that when technology advances everybody necessarily benefits. Some people, even a majority of people, could be made worse off'.[10]

Will AI make your skills and experience redundant?

In 2017, Oxford academics Carl Benedikt Frey and Michael Osborne[11] explored how susceptible different jobs and roles are to displacement by technology. They concluded that even those jobs that once were considered safely human-centric will be at risk. The computer/automation revolution of the 20th century had led to polarisation of the labour market, reflected in rising employment in high-income cognitive jobs and low-income manual occupations with a 'hollowing-out of middle-income routine jobs'. Back in 2017, they concluded that 47% of total US employment is in the high-risk category, meaning that associated occupations are at risk of displacement by technology over the next 10–20 years.

Frey and Osborne noted a discontinuity between the industrial revolutions of the 19th, 20th and 21st centuries in the impact of capital deepening on the relative demand for skilled labour. Whilst 19th-century-manufacturing technologies largely substituted for skilled labour through the simplification of tasks, the computer revolution of the 20th century saw the substitution of many, more routine, middle-income jobs. Frey and Osborne went on that as technology develops 'lower skilled workers will relocate to tasks that are non-susceptible to computerization i.e. tasks requiring creative and social intelligence. For workers to win this race, however, they will have to acquire creative and social skills' (2017).

Now fast-forward a few years, and we find that whilst computerisation has historically been confined to routine programmable tasks and rule-based activities, the algorithms associated with AI are now rapidly entering domains reliant upon pattern recognition and higher-order cognitive functions and are beginning to substitute for labour in a wide range of non-routine cognitive or knowledge-based tasks.

The release of ChatGPT 3.5 in November 2022 changed the nature of the discussion in terms of what AI models could achieve but also dialled up the urgency. The 10-to-20-year job displacement horizon that Frey and Osborne suggested now looked very out-of-date. LLMs were proving unexpectedly capable in those human-centric tasks, and the abilities of AI models overlapped with the most creative, most educated and most highly paid workers. Ethan Mollick noted that 'something unusual happened . . . ChatGPT started to show abilities that no one expected or programmed into it . . . and however remarkable ChatGPT 3.5 was, its successor CHATGPT 4 was even more impressive' (Mollick, 2024).[3]

ChatGPT 4 achieved perfect scores on advanced calculus, physics, history, biology and chemistry and aced every creativity test it was given. It scored in the 90th percentile on the legal bar exam, passed the qualifying exam to become a neurosurgeon, and passed the written examination to become a certified sommelier.

LLMs are proving to be capable of significantly increasing the quality of outputs and productivity of staff or completely automating some tasks in their entirety. New applications are being found daily, and the potential extent of these capabilities is not immediately obvious, even to producers of large language models themselves. But we do know that they will continue developing rapidly as model size and quality improve.

We have also seen how surprisingly rapidly these capabilities have been adopted, improving the performance of workers who use these systems – often the less skilled or experienced workers – without the need for substantial training or investment.

A Harvard Business School (HBS) paper, *Navigating the Jagged Technological Frontier* (Dell'Acqua, McFowland, Mollick, et al., 2023)[12] details an interesting experiment conducted with 758 strategy consultants working for the Boston Consulting Group. Half the group were given a series of tasks where they were prompted to develop new product ideas, focusing on aspects such as creativity, analytical skill, persuasiveness and writing skills. The other half engaged in business problem-solving tasks using quantitative and qualitative data.

Initially – to establish a baseline – participants undertook a task without the aid of AI and were subsequently assigned to one of three groups to assess the influence of AI on their tasks.

- The control group worked without AI support.
- The GPT-only group had the assistance of an AI tool based on GPT 4.
- The augmented GPT group utilised the same AI tool but also benefitted from supplementary prompt engineering which increased their familiarity with AI.

An 'inside-the-technological-frontier' experiment focused on creative product innovation and development, while an 'outside-the-technological-frontier' experiment involved a business case with data across different formats and media (spreadsheets, interview transcripts etc.). The frontier represents a dividing line between routine/less complex consulting tasks and more complex, multifaceted analytical tasks conducted by more experienced consultants.

The exercise showed that within the frontier AI significantly improved human performance:

- Speed of task completion was 25% better.
- Performance as rated by humans was higher by more than 40%.
- Task completion was higher by more than 12%.

And furthermore, it operated in a way that benefitted bottom-half performers the most. The HBS team identified two modes of human–AI working or interaction, which they called Centaur and Cyborg. Cyborgs seamlessly integrated AI and human capabilities, whilst Centaurs delegate between human and AI tasks – there is a delineation between human-centric and AI-centric tasks.

Outside the frontier, humans relied too much on the AI and were more likely to make mistakes and that the shape and position of the frontier are vital to understanding the impact of AI on work. The research also found that the utility of AI can fluctuate over the course of a professional's workflow, with some tasks falling inside the frontier while other tasks fall outside. Not all users navigated the jagged frontier with equal adeptness, and understanding the characteristics and behaviours of participants who performed well versus those who performed less well may prove important as organisations think about ways to identify and develop talent for effective collaboration with AI tools (Dell'Acqua, McFowland, Mollick, et al., 2023).[12]

The HBS research (2023)[13] confirmed the capabilities of AI in high knowledge work tasks such as fast idea generation, writing, persuasion, strategic analysis and creative product innovation and found that,

> It was difficult to design a task outside the AI's frontier where humans with high human capital doing their job would consistently outperform AI. Even for experienced professionals engaged in tasks akin to some of their daily responsibilities the demarcation, AIs jagged capability frontier, was not always evident.

What the Harvard team described as Centaur or Cyborg mode, MIT's Thomas Malone called 'superminds' in his book of the same name (2018).[14] In thinking about how humans and AI can create a symbiotic 'Supermind', we must consider what the optimal model of collaboration should be, what human skills should we develop, and how these should be organised. And whilst the idea of a capability frontier is important, we should understand that such things are never static. As AI models develop, then so this capability frontier shifts, and more tasks that were previously heavily human-centric fall into the domain of AI expertise.

Building it up and knocking it down

What can we say about the pace of AI development and the speed with which this frontier will move? Well, step aboard the 'AI expectation roller-coaster'! We can characterise the development of AI capabilities as 'discontinuous' (sometimes called hyper-evolutionary), that is to say that they will not gently arc upwards. There will be large leaps forward and maybe backward steps. We won't experience a smooth evolutionary trajectory. This speed of change means that we will be in danger of constantly fighting yesterday's battles. So the question is how can we (individuals, organisations, regulators, politicians, society, etc.) get ahead of this curve rather than be reactionary and maybe letting complacency kill us (in terms of job displacement)!

The Gartner Hype Cycle depicts the lifecycle stages technology passes through from initial development to commercial availability and adoption. The 'Trough of Disillusionment' is not a topographical feature on the moon nor a nihilist 1970s punk band but rather what faces us as we come to terms with what AI can and cannot do for us.

As far as the latest generative AI is concerned, today we are at, or heading towards, the peak of inflated expectations (of course it is hard to call the peak until we are over it and careening down the other side). The peak is characterised by excitement about and enthusiasm for the technology and often unrealistic expectations of what it will do. There are some sure signs – not least the valuations placed on some AI start-ups – that the AI sector is inhaling its own exhaust – and that we are likely heading for a 'recalibration'. Telecoms sector valuations – back when the internet was going to transform the world (before it actually did) – assumed that the transformation would happen almost overnight. These valuations were unsustainable, and the telecom boom-to-bust cycle took just four years, which was much faster than the internet took to actually change our lives.

> As with the early days of the internet, broader enterprise adoption of AI remains some way off. The transformation triggered by AI may take many years longer than today's stock prices and funding expectations suggest. Hype and overinvestment are a dangerous combination.
>
> (June Yoon, 2024)[15]

So the Gartner Hype Cycle would suggest that enthusiasm will rapidly wane as hype meets hard reality, and we will drop into the trough of disillusionment as limits to the technology become clearer and as people question its viability and potential applications.

There are people (and we have come across them presenting at different conferences) who have always argued that this AI thing is just overblown and that worries about the future of work and the need for a paradigm shift in education are overdone. In the depths of the trough, they are likely to take comfort in their own foresight and claim the future will be business as usual.

However, as more realistic expectations emerge or as the technology evolves and develops in terms of capability, we will collectively become more knowledgeable about what it can achieve, allowing for more effective and widespread implementation in different scenarios and in different use cases. This is the slope of enlightenment, which finally leads us to the sunlight uplands of the plateau of productivity – where the technology reaches maturity and enjoys widespread market adoption. Higher productivity results as organisations become more proficient at leveraging their capabilities for their benefit.

Sentenced by algorithm

To see the Hype Cycle at work in the real world, we need look no further than the law. At the 2017 LegalTech conference, Monica Bay, Fellow at the Stanford Law School, posited that 'As computational technology and artificial intelligence matures, more people will be able to have better access to justice'.[16] But the way the process of the law and lawyering works will inevitably change. Frey and Osborne (2017) reported that paralegals and legal assistants, for which computers were already beginning to substitute, were the high-risk category – that is, at high risk of being substituted by technology. At the same time, lawyers, who relied on labour input from legal assistants, were in the low-risk category. Thus, for the work of lawyers to be fully automated, hurdles to creative and social intelligence would need to be overcome, implying that the computerisation of legal research will complement the work of lawyers in the medium term. But fast forward six years.

In a 2023 FT article, *Generative AI: A Legal Revolution is Coming – Eventually*,[17] senior lawyers were asked about their opinions on generative AI. Their reactions were almost uniformly positive (or grim, depending on your point of view).

> For the first time we have serious disruptive technology . . . firms who do not embrace the opportunity AI poses now will not see the erosion going on around them until it is too late.
>
> [Generative AI] is not just a tool, it's a game-changer.
>
> 60% to 70% of the current work in real estate [law] will eventually disappear.
>
> Generative AI will replace a lot of what lawyers do . . . that is revolutionary for lawyers and not just another technological advance.

These views reflect how people felt at the time. Maybe we can call this 'peak expectation'. We should then expect a steep fall in these expectations over the next few months/years, feeding disillusionment, as generative AI fails to live up to the hype. We begin to realise that imagined applications have come into contact with reality in terms of what the technology can actually do in its current state. In January 2024, a study from Stanford's Centre for Human-Centered Artificial Intelligence (HAI) reported its findings on hallucination, testing more than 200,000 legal queries against each of GPT 3.5, Llama 2 and PaLM 2.[18] It found:

- Performance deteriorates when dealing with more complex tasks that require a nuanced understanding of legal issues.
- In tasks measuring the precedential relationship between two different cases, most LLMs do no better than random guessing.
- In answering queries about a court's core ruling, models hallucinate at least 75% of the time.
- Case law from lower courts is subject to more frequent hallucinations than case law from higher courts, showing a tendency to perform better with more prominent cases due to them being more frequently cited and discussed and thus better represented in training data.
- Hallucinations are most common among the Supreme Court's oldest and newest cases, and least common among later 20th-century cases, suggesting LLMs' peak performance may lag several years behind current legal doctrine, failing to internalise case law that is old but still applicable and relevant.
- Models are susceptible to 'contra-factual bias', that is the tendency to assume that a factual premise in a query is true, even if it is wrong – likely due to their instruction-following training.

So, with inflated expectations and its revolutionary credentials increasingly under the microscope, in the trough of disillusionment, legal AI applications may be struggling under the weight of over-promising and under-delivering.

> Although [Generative AI] is a remarkable development, [most] short-term claims being made about its impact on lawyers and the courts hugely overstate its likely impact.
>
> (Richard Susskind, technology advisor to UK's Lord Chief Justice & President of the Society for Computers and Law, 2023)[17]

It is here that we find out what future impact it will have – expectations are tempered, and the focus moves to addressing weaknesses (which are just a usual part of the development cycle) and refining or improving its application in practical terms. Here developers will identify real world added value and hence onto the slope of enlightenment. It is just a natural progression – technology has to go through the discipline of the trough before we actually reach realistic, widely commercialised applications.

So we would expect legal AI systems to address their tendency to hallucinate (and other drawbacks) coming off the peak of expectations and through the trough of disillusionment. They would demonstrate a more nuanced understanding of legal issues, do a better job at integrating the complete body of caselaw, and identify contra-factual bias.

Roy Amara – American researcher, scientist, futurist and president of the Institute for the Future – is best known for coining Amara's law, popularised in the 1970s and 1980s, which contends that 'we tend to overestimate the effect of a technology in the short run and underestimate the effect in the long run'. Amara's law would suggest that the long-term plateau of productivity actually settles at a higher level than perhaps projected earlier in the lifecycle of the technology. It just hasn't happened as quickly as early enthusiasts had hoped, predicted, or expected. In the famous words of science fiction writer, William Gibson, 'The future is already here – it's just not evenly distributed' (although nobody seems able to pin down if or exactly when he said it).[19]

As one UK-based lawyer talking to the FT in 2023 put it, '[Generative AI] will mean fundamental changes to the law firm model . . . eventually'. Or from the managing partner of a NYC-based firm, 'Lawyers are predisposed to underappreciate the impact or potential impact of technology [and] overvalue things that they are good at'.

Enabled or substituted?

At the heart of this debate is the distinction between AI as an enabler and AI as a substitute. Are we to be masters of our tools or closer to what Henry David Thoreau envisaged when he said 'Men have become the tools of their tools' (1854)?

The reality is that all companies see employees as a cost AND a resource, and if costs can be cut without the loss of capability, then this is what they will do.

> I would say that a key distinction is whether you see your workers as a cost or a resource. If they are a cost, you are going to try and cut costs. If they are a resource, then businesses can try and flourish whilst increasing productivity, providing better tools for their workers [and] improving their training and their skills.
>
> (Barbara DeLollis, 2024)[20]

The rather glib idea that people who use AI will replace people who don't hides the reality that the AI-enabled workplace may need far fewer people or less skilled/experienced people on the human side of the human–AI equation. There is a lot of talk about the future belonging to those who will 'upskill'. But what doesn't seem to be happening is for people to engage with precisely/exactly what this upskilling means.

> The impact of AI on jobs was not going to be 'an employment apocalypse', but that reskilling, upskilling and lifelong learning would be key to managing the transition to augmentation.
>
> (Whiting Kate, 2024)[21]

With 23% of job classifications expected to change in the next five years, according to the Future of Jobs Report (2023),[22] millions of people will need to move between declining and growing jobs. We are in the foothills of this technology, and while Generative Pre-trained Transformers may reach the edge of their capabilities, the focus, entrepreneurial energy, and resource now being directed at AI and ML means we should expect lots of movement in this space.

Are we collectively over-egging the AI pudding? In the short term, yes we probably are. Is AI a more profound technology than fire or electricity? At the time of writing, no, it isn't, but it may become so. Will AI have a greater long-term impact on our lives and jobs than we currently realise? Amara's law suggests it will. Should we be retooling our own capabilities to prepare for this future? Absolutely, and the sooner we start the better.

Summary

In this chapter we explored the idea that AI optimism does not mean that necessarily we will all be better off – some of us, even a majority of us, may be worse off. Evidence has shown that earlier bouts of technological progress hollowed out a lot of mundane middle-class jobs, and now even those jobs that we once might have considered 'safely human-centric' will be at risk from AI.

As AI progresses, the technological frontier – representing the dividing line between those jobs effectively done by AI and those that are still in the domain of human intelligence – will not be static. As the frontier moves forward, the human domain will be reshaped.

We should expect the development of AI capabilities to be discontinuous – there will be leaps forward and a few dead-ends, but we should keep in mind Amara's law, which suggests that while we may overestimate the effect of technology in the short term, we have a tendency to underestimate its long-term impact. We should start considering the role of AI as a substitute for human endeavour rather than just an enabler and what this might mean for the skills and capabilities that we humans need to develop to prepare for this future.

Notes

1. Sagan, C. (1989). "Why We Need to Understand Science: Ignorance of Science Threatens Our Economic Well-Being, National Security, and the Democratic Process. We Must Do Better." Parade Magazine.
2. Surowiecki, J. (2007). *Feature Presentation*. Article in the May 28 issue. *The New Yorker*.
3. Mollick, E. (2024). *Co-intelligence: Living and Working with AI*. Portfolio/Penguin.
4. Goldman Sachs (2023). *Generative AI Could Raise Global GDP by 7 Percent*. www.goldmansachs.com/insights/articles/generative-ai-could-raise-globalgdp-by-7-percent
5. Chui, M., Hazan, E., Roberts, R., et al. (2023). *The Economic Potential of Generative AI: The Next Productivity Frontier*. McKinsey. https://www.mckinsey.com/~/media/mckinsey/business%20functions/mckinsey%20digital/our%20insights/the%20economic%20potential%20of%20generative%20ai%20the%20next%20productivity%20frontier/the-economic-potential-of-generative-ai-the-next-productivity-frontier.pdf
6. Eloundou, T., Manning, S., Mishkin, P., Rock, D. (2023). *GPTs are GPTs: An Early Look at the Labor Market Impact Potential of Large Language Models*. arXiv.org. Retrieved August 22, 2023, from www.theglobeandmail.com/business/article-ai-code-generate-gpt-4/
7. Briggs, J., Kodnani, D. (2023). *Upgrading Our Longer-Run Global Growth Forecasts to Reflect the Impact of Generative AI*. Goldman Sachs. https://www.goldmansachs.com/insights/articles/ai-may-start-to-boost-us-gdp-in-2027

8. Sullivan, M. (2023). Investor Vinod Khosla: *Our AI future is racing toward us faster than we think*. Fast Company Newsletter. www.fastcompany.com/90997791/investor-vinod-khosla-our-aifuture-is-racing-toward-us-faster-than-we-think
9. Ming, V. (2023). *AI Needs a Constitution: Ensuring Civil Rights in the Age of AI: Why a Constitution Is Needed to Align Artificial Intelligence with Civil Rights and Ethical Governance*. Centre for Entrepreneurship & Technology.
10. Artificial Intelligence and the Future of Work. (2019). Hearing before the Subcommittee on Research and Technology, Committee on Science, Space, and Technology, House of Representatives, One Hundred Sixteenth Congress, First Session, September 24, 2019.
11. Frey, C. B., & Osborne, M. A. (2017). *The Future of Employment: How Susceptible Are Jobs to Computerisation?* Technological Forecasting and Social Change, 114(C), 254–280.
12. Dell'Acqua, F., McFowland, E., Mollick, E., et al. (2023). *Navigating the Jagged Technological Frontier: Field Experimental Evidence of the Effects of AI on Knowledge Worker Productivity and Quality*. Harvard Business School.
13. *Navigating the Jagged Technological Frontier: Field Experimental Evidence of the Effects of AI on Knowledge Worker Productivity and Quality*, (September 2023). Harvard Business School Paper.
14. Malone, T. W. (2018). *Superminds: The Surprising Power of People and Computers Thinking Together*. Little, Brown and Company.
15. Yoon, J. (2024). *AI Hype Has Echoes of the Telecoms Boom and Bust*. Financial Times, 14 February 2024. https://www.ft.com/content/dc47c5f3-9bd4-4da0-a5cb-c795efd14c9c
16. The Future of e-Discovery Law, Business, and Practice. (2017). Panel discussion at LegalTech 2017 / Legal Week Conference, January 31–February 2, 2017.
17. SenGupta, R. (2023). *Generative AI: a legal revolution is coming—eventually*. Financial Times, September 22, 2023. https://www.ft.com/content/0f36eb4e-b90f-4ffe-befc-daf01829c182.
18. Magesh, V., Surani, F., Dahl, M., et al. (2024). *AI on Trial: Legal Models Hallucinate in 1 out of 6 (or More) Benchmarking Queries*. HAI, Stanford University. https://hai.stanford.edu/news/ai-trial-legal-models-hallucinate-1-out-6-or-more-benchmarking-queries
19. Gibson, William. (1992). Interview by Scott Rosenberg. "Virtual Reality Check, Digital Daydreams, Cyberspace Nightmares." The San Francisco Examiner, April 19, 1992.
20. DeLollis, B. (2024). *MIT's Daron Acemoglu to Business Leaders: Unchecked Power of Big Tech Poses Risks as AI Reshapes Society*. Harvard Business School, Institute for Business in Global Society. www.hbs.edu/bigs/insights-ai-wealth-gap
21. Whiting, K. (2024). *6 work and workplace trends to watch in 2024*. World Economic Forum. www.weforum.org/agenda/2024/02/work-and-workplace-trends-to-watch-2024/#:~:text=The%20impact%20of%20AI%20on,transition%20to%20augmentation%2C%20he%20stressed.
22. The World Economic Forum. (2023). *The Future of Jobs Report*. The World Economic Forum.

3

RESPONDING TO THE ARRIVAL OF AI

In this chapter, we will examine some of the different responses to the AI-shaped workplace of future and consider how different audiences, seeing the same information and getting the same cues, come to different conclusions. We will investigate the new world of work, identify some potential winners and losers in the game of workplace snakes and ladders, and consider the broader impact. What will be the ripple effect across society? How will the new reality of the AI-shaped workplace benefit or undermine us? How should we upskill, reskill or new skill, and who will pay for this? We conclude the chapter by examining what general means of support might be necessary should the arrival of AI lead to swathes of knowledge workers being without a job.

So far we've established that AI will transform the skills needed in the workplace and discussed different experts views on the rate at which this transformation will unfold. And we now move onto review the reaction that different players in the AI world are taking on exactly what is likely to happen in the future.

DOI: 10.4324/9781003514879-4

The edge of a new frontier

This chapter could have been titled 'making sense of the future', but the question would be this: how can we do that effectively when it must be characterised as volatile, uncertain, complex and ambiguous? What we can say about the future is that security is an illusion, and disruption is the new reality. Many of us are familiar with the VUCA acronym in the context of describing challenging and rapidly changing environments. The antecedent of this concept goes back to the work of Warren Bennis and Burt Nanus and their bestselling book *Leaders: Strategies for Taking Charge* (1985).[1]

As an aside, one of our favourite futurology witticisms has also been attributed to Warren Bennis, although a version of it appeared several years earlier in the 1978 trade journal *Datamation*, which noted that the development of increasingly powerful microprocessors was facilitating new types of automation and gave rise to a wry observation circulating in the British Post Office Engineering Union that 'The factory of the future will have a staff of two, a man and a dog. The man's job will be to feed the dog, the dog's job will be to make sure the man never touches the machines'.

We are at a technological frontier, and it is very difficult to predict how the AI-human symbiosis is going to play out – with or without the benefits of history to guide us. This frontier is also not set in stone; it is constantly moving forward as the technology develops and evolves. More and more work will fall within the purview of AI, and, increasingly, this may include what today we consider as higher-level tasks. That line between technology as an enabler and technology as a substitute is constantly shifting. The current pace of change makes it difficult to be at all confident about the next step. Ethan Mollick (2024)[2] stated that:

> If progress on generative AI stops now . . . we'd get some dramatic shifts in the workplace, a technology that broadly empowers workers and creates good new jobs, and everything would be fine. But is it going to stop any time soon? It's the pace of change that gives me pause.

In the face of this volatility, uncertainty, complexity and ambiguity, staying relevant in the workplace means acquiring the set of skills that allow us to work most productively alongside AI. These are the skills that leave people best placed to succeed and be an AI winner rather than an AI loser.

They focus on enhancing individuals' rich and nuanced appreciation of the big contextual picture, their ability to factor into their critical thinking a deep understanding of human complexities, their innate creativity, their unique ability to read the future, their quintessential human storytelling skills, and their ability to be inspiring leaders.

The key question is . . . 'are you good at working with intelligent machines or not? Are your skills a complement to the skills of the computer, or is the computer doing better without you? Worst of all, are you competing against the computer?' In the future, if your skills do not complement the computer, 'you may want to address this mismatch' (Tyler Cowen, 2013).[3]

Different perspectives lead to different responses

As the influence and widespread adoption of the latest AI models became apparent, it is clear that various schools of thought have emerged. And to borrow a phrase from George Eliot, 'It is a narrow mind which cannot look at a subject from various points of view' (1871).

First, there are those who realise that these new superpowers are urgently needed, who agree that going 'full polymath' is the way to provide those much-needed human skills that will sit on top of what AI will be able to deliver.

They don't see it as alarmist in calling for a massive 'drains-up' review of exactly what skills need to be taught in schools and universities and welcome the call for an urgent review of what a 'plausible possible future' may require: a world that needs to massively revamp the current educational paradigm.

Second, there are those who feel that worries about the future of work and the need for a paradigm shift in education are overdone. These are the AI optimists who argue that it will all work itself out in the end, and by mastering specific technical skills we all can work comfortably alongside AI. AI will boost growth and productivity and create an environment in which we can flourish – new jobs will replace those that are lost. AI will be the latest and greatest enabler of human endeavour. Again, this is 'the rising AI-tide will raise all boats' school of thought.

Jerry Cuomo, IBM Fellow & CTO of Automation at IBM, claimed that the common perception that AI-empowered automation replacing workers is 'another misconception that doesn't apply to intelligent automation'

(2023).[4] AI, he argues, will free up employees from low-level tasks, and retraining them to do much higher-level work enables companies to retain people while increasing effectiveness and profits. The goal, Cuomo argues, is always to help human workers be more effective and make time for brilliance because (he says) they are the *only* source of brilliance.

> You only get outstanding results – the kind you need to stand above your competitors – when it's paired with a human. I don't think that will change . . . Enterprises still spend billions of hours each year on mundane repetitive work, and AI can remove this burden so their people can focus on things that really matter. We can use AI to transform people into superhumans [by] becoming more efficient – letting AI do the mundane work to free up your people – and then empowering them with AI to gain extraordinary new capabilities.
>
> (Jerry Cuomo, 2023)[4]

Now, in the case of AI, it is quite plausible to say it will free up employees from low-level tasks and retrain them to do much higher-level work, and (we assume) this higher-level work is in demand. The key driver of the assumption that AI will be a net force for good is that there is a current unmet need which can be filled by someone (anyone) freed from mundane tasks, reassigned to this new higher margin work. In this scenario, AI is driving top-line revenue growth.

There is of course no problem with this: there's a lot of evidence emerging to show that those in this category have a valid point of view. But the debate here will centre on the degree to which one believes that the technology remains an enabler and does not become a substitute. There is an oft-repeated phrase that 'AI won't replace people – but people who use AI will replace people who don't'. This holds out the hope that as long as we can use AI (or we can learn to use AI), there will be a role for us in the future workplace. So the mantra of positivity goes, enlightened organisations will see a rise in productivity through a work-enhancing human-AI symbiosis.

But let's pose another possibility, that actually there isn't a lot of latent demand that can be tapped into by every business operating new technologies, that all that human brilliance was applied to creating a better mousetrap. BUT productivity gains and higher margins are still possible by doing the same work with fewer people (and less experienced and less expensive people) – substituting capital for labour. In this instance, an organisation can still use technology to improve its bottom line.

And third and finally, we have those who seem to fall into the 'AI is too difficult to think about now' box – reflecting Scarlett O'Hara (the heroine of *Gone with the Wind*) saying 'I'll think about that tomorrow'.

The arrival of AI is such a massive event that people and businesses are finding it difficult to understand its impact (it is outside their frame of reference) and so experience 'perceptual blindness'. These groups seem to be in denial about the impact of AI and are simply kicking the can down the road in the hope that AI won't be such a big deal or somehow it will resolve itself whilst they have their collective 'head in the sand'. Without going down a rabbit hole of speculation it is perhaps worth musing on what lies behind this Scarlett O'Hara view of the world. There seems to be a number of fundamental reasons as to why people will take up this position.

There is a deep-seated inability to cope with fundamental change on the scale that AI is signalling. Their mindset is inextricably fixed in a way that they just can't begin to engage with the debate.

There are those who deep down grasp the magnitude of the arrival of generative AI but who are locked into roles and functions within large organisations and institutions, and are part of complex industrial-type processes, such that they just cannot see how this oil tanker can be turned around quickly enough to deliver the polymath skills that the authors here are arguing for.

And we have sympathy with this. If you're running a university, it is not easy to change the MBA curriculum, pivot, and move in a different direction. And if you're in a secondary school, how do you go about changing the syllabus for 16–18-year-olds to start dealing with some of the issues we are raising here? And if you're a government minister, how do you start talking about some of these issues without frightening the horses? Why not just do what we said earlier and put this into the 'too difficult box'?

There are those who understand that an avalanche of change is coming their way but are simply suffering from AI/information overload. They get the case for a more radical overhaul of the skills we need to survive with AI but just cannot get their heads around how you actually begin to build strategies, programmes and processes for teaching these polymath skills and embedding them in organisations.

At the most extreme end of the spectrum there are those who see AI replacing virtually all jobs over the longer term, which may or may not be a good thing. This would seem to be the Elon Musk view of the future. 'There will come a point where no job is needed . . . you can have a job if you want to have a job for personal satisfaction, but AI will be able to do everything' (2023).

This would open a societal 'can of worms'. Will businesses offer you the opportunity to do a job for reasons of personal satisfaction when that job can be done faster and cheaper by an AI system? This leads you to the question of what is the purpose of a business? And how should we as individuals react to the work-free world? Are we to fill our new-found leisure time with endless rounds of golf? Beyond the material benefits that come with remuneration, work is a source of social cohesion, and for the individual it may be a key part of their identify or self-worth which can be crucial to both mental and physical health.

The new world of work

Previous waves of advancement – automation, robotics and computerisation – undermined the prospects of non-college educated blue-collar workers, and as we have already argued, this disconnection from society finally manifested itself in populist movements such as MAGA and Brexit. How will strains on knowledge work play out across society?

We would like to think that everyone can adapt by acquiring new skills, but some may be struggling, and we also need to think about what kind of societal support we provide for those who can't make the AI trip.

Many governments seem to be trying to hold a line that on the whole AI will complement jobs as much as it replaces them.

> We should look at AI much more as a co-pilot than something which is necessary going to replace someone's job. AI is a tool that can help almost anybody do their jobs better, faster, quicker.
>
> (Rishi Sunak, the then UK Prime Minister, 2023)[5]

However, the early evidence suggests that this position might not hold for very long and that the world of knowledge work may quickly move to a position that is much more aligned with Elon Musk's view that *no job is needed*. Even if we do accept that AI won't 'do everything', in reality, the number of people needed in this knowledge work human-AI symbiosis will be far, far fewer and that, whilst initially your job may well be lost to someone who knows how to use AI, this is just an interregnum before it is likely to be eventually lost to AI.

Let's imagine a business that employs 1,000 knowledge workers, and let's assume that 50% of the workload of each individual employee could be now done by AI – this is the mundane work that we would be happy to have AI take on. In this new world, does the business (1) direct all employees to spend their newly freed up time in 'higher margin work' – whatever that might be, and assuming that they were able to, (2) reduce labour costs by 50%, or (3) some hybrid of the two, getting the best employees to do more higher-margin work and reducing headcount and cost by (say) 30% to 40%? What do you think will happen?

So assuming that profit-maximising businesses aren't going to offer employment for entertainment purposes – and that they can reduce costs (without decreasing efficiency) by switching their investment from labour to capital – what kinds of jobs will be available to us? What is the competition for each of these jobs? And as good salaried 'knowledge worker' jobs become harder to come by, how will we support ourselves? By what mechanism?

> We can't win the race against the machine, especially as computers continue to become more powerful and capable [but] we can learn to better race **with** machines.
>
> (Brynjolfsson and McAfee, 2014, emphasis by author)[6]

About nine months before ChatGPT 3.5 arrived on the scene in such a dramatic way, the authors, as business researchers, scenario planners and management consultants, realised that AI was a technology that would very quickly, and massively, change our world and that of other knowledge workers. In a paper we wrote in early 2022, we suggested that a total transformation of the nature of work was a 'plausible possible future'.

Where we landed in this debate was that although clearly we did not have a crystal ball, there were sufficient signals to suggest that AI would not just be playing an enabling role but fairly quickly become a substitute for many knowledge worker tasks. We took the view that AI's potential to dramatically transform the structure of work, as we know it, should be given attention now as an urgent priority and not put on the back-burner or relegated to the 'too-difficult' box.

We have seen nothing since then that has changed our point of view. What we didn't anticipate in early 2022 was the speed of AI's roll-out or how quickly it would become embedded in the zeitgeist.

We have taken care to stress the fact that our idea of the power of the polymath mind is very much set in the context of knowledge workers, and it is not a universal panacea for people working outside of this particular sector. Nevertheless, it still leaves us with a big challenge, as it is estimated that of the 3.4 billion people employed globally, up to ~1 billion (30%) are knowledge workers (International Labour Office, Geneva, 2023).[7]

Clearly, there will be roles where people can slot in doing specialist AI-related jobs in a way that needs some technical adjustment to their current skills but does not require a full-on reprogramming to be the total polymath article armed with all seven power skills that we will detail later in this book. And whilst not every knowledge worker will need to aspire to be a fully paid-up polymath, it is likely that most will need to adjust some aspect of the current skill set to operate effectively in the AI-infused workplace, and it is equally possible that not everyone will be equipped to make the transition to the new AI-shaped knowledge workplace.

Winners and losers

In a recent presentation to Harvard Business School's Institute for Business in Global Society (BiGS), Daron Acemoglu argues that 'AI is completely unique [and so] its effects on the economy are going to be unique' (2024).[8]

He goes on:

> It is wrong to ask the question, what will [AI] do to labor? The right question is 'what will we decide to do with AI and how will this impact inequality?' There is tremendous potential to use AI for good, but that is not the path we are going on. On our current path, I think AI and [machine learning] will be used for monitoring workers and reducing their autonomy. [These technologies] will be used for automation, sidelining labor, and perhaps disempowering the already weaker members of our society.

This really reflects the views aired by Professor Geoffrey Hinton. His work on multi-layer neural networks in and from the mid-1980s earned him the Turing Award and the sobriquet 'the Godfather of AI'. Having worked with Google for ten years, he left in 2023 to allow himself the space to question and challenge big tech's approach to AI.

In a 2024 interview,[9] Hinton makes a distinction between AI which exceeds human intelligence (it is not an 'if', 'it's just a matter of when') AND AI which doesn't need to be smarter than us to be hugely disruptive and/or dangerous.

THE PAPERCLIP MAXIMISER

Bend your mind around Nick Bostrom's (2003)[10] popular AI thought experiment – The Paperclip Maximiser, whereby a seemingly harmless goal to maximise production of paper clips leads to the end of all life on earth. Nick Bostrom was pointing out the importance of incorporating ethics into AI and illustrating the broad problem of managing powerful systems that lack human values. The scenario describes an advanced AI tasked with manufacturing paper clips. If it were not programmed to value human life, given enough sway over its environment, it would try to turn all matter in the universe, including all life on earth, into paper clips or machines that manufacture more paper clips.

> Suppose we have an AI whose only goal is to make as many paper clips as possible. The AI will realize quickly that it would be much better if there were no humans because humans might decide to switch it off. Because if humans do so, there would be fewer paper clips. Also, human bodies contain a lot of atoms that could be made into paper clips. The future that the AI would be trying to gear towards would be one in which there were a lot of paper clips but no humans.
>
> (Nick Bostrom, 2003)[10]

While we do not for a moment dismiss the existential issues (too many people have said it is a non-zero scenario for us to do that), putting aside the danger that AI will turn us all into one of Nick Bostrom's paper clips, whether or not we achieve Artificial General Intelligence (AGI), just the journey towards it will be hugely impactful and deliver new capabilities that again redefine the human–technology relationship. AI may develop many of the cognitive abilities associated with the human mind but still not achieve AGI. While it walks like a duck and quacks like a duck, it might not be a duck, but it is so 'duck-like' that in reality it makes no difference.

So AGI might be a bit of red herring! AI doesn't need to have the intelligence of the smartest humans to completely reshape whole sectors of the economy. You don't need to be a savant to perform well in whatever job you have, most of us are 'smart enough'. We don't need to achieve AGI for AI that is 'just smart enough' to displace millions of jobs. So these new models may well have the capabilities that allow them to do even more knowledge work, and displace even more knowledge workers, than they currently do. It is this more prosaic threat that we concern ourselves with.

> I'm very worried about AI taking over lots of mundane jobs. That should be a good thing. It's going to lead to a big increase in productivity which leads to a big increase in wealth and if that wealth was equally distributed that would be great. But it's not going to be. In the systems we live in that wealth is going to go to the rich and not to the people whose jobs get lost and that's going to be very bad for society I believe. It's going to increase the gap between rich and poor which increases the chances of right-wing populists getting elected.
>
> (Professor Geoffrey Hinton, AI for Good Global Summit in Geneva, 2024)

Both Hinton and Acemoglu are suggesting that given our current business-political model, the chances of AI being a net negative outweigh the possibility of it being a net positive (despite its potential benefits).

Just what will be the impact of the accelerated move to an AI-shaped workplace? And as the frontier of what AI (and related/accompanying technologies) can do pushes further and further into knowledge work, will (and how will) 'society' push back? In 2024, we have seen the spectre of more populist movements rise across Europe, and in the US, what is the link between technological advances and discontent?

A recent report from the Brookings Institution reported[11] on research that found that (1) technology-driven automation has created economic insecurity that, in turn, is partly responsible for the growing political polarisation across the US and Europe; (2) this polarisation is emblematised by the growth in populist party representation in Europe, such as Alternative for Germany, Fratelli d'Italia, Vox and Rassemblement National; and (3) economic shocks result in statistically significant growth in the far right when institutional and social security support – such as unemployment benefits are high and labour market protections are in place – is weak.

So are we playing with fire? In May 2024, in another Harvard Business School BiGS interview,[12] Sam Altman of OpenAI observed that 'The shape of jobs will change'. This could be an extraordinary understatement. He expanded on this to say:

> It is important to be upfront with people that these impacts might happen . . . one of the most important things to figure out is how government can help play a role. Given the magnitude of the economic change, how we think about the illusion of the social contract . . . [and] how people like the balance between capital and labor – that is going to require some serious societal debate.

We, the authors, have never really understood how these kinds of 'societal debates' actually happen. The world turns, 'progress' is made, change happens without people outside the corridors (or boardrooms) of power getting much of a say. And if there was some mechanism whereby we could collectively say to governments and tech businesses that we don't really like where this is heading, would it be anything more than shouting into the wind?

In his BiGS presentation (2024), Acemoglu commented that we shouldn't be looking to the likes of Google, Facebook, Apple, Microsoft, or OpenAI to self-regulate, they won't!

And, in his keynote lecture titled *Redesigning AI* in May 2024 (at an event hosted by the Oxford Martin School and the Institute for Ethics in AI), he said, 'They have their own ideologies, they have their own priorities, they have their own profit motives, they have their own business models'. So will elected governments, frightened of being left behind in the new AI 'gold rush', be willing to apply the brakes, if other countries are not?

As we look more closely at the subtle dynamics of how the arrival of generative AI will impact the structure of jobs, we soon realise that working out who will be the winners and the losers in the 'game' of workplace snakes and ladders is a little bit more subtle and sophisticated than at first sight. There will be some surprises vis-à-vis who benefits, and who loses out in the AI job era. There are going to be disappointed knowledge workers who might not have expected to find themselves in a losing position, given their education and expertise. But there are also going to be some winners who leap up the career ladder in a way that they might not have expected prior to the arrival of generative AI.

Upskilling, reskilling and new skilling – and how we pay for it

When we hear that we need to 'upskill' for the AI-shaped workplace, what does this actually mean? A course on prompt engineering? Being a little more creative? Dialling up our EQ over our IQ? If we accept that we are now staring down the barrel of a fundamental overhaul of what constitutes valuable skills, this leads us to a very difficult place as a society:

> It is possible to fly without motors, but not without knowledge and skill.
> (Wilbur Wright, 1900)

We feel that government, universities and schools are not currently giving sufficient attention to what we believe will be the dramatic change needed to deliver the new skill set that will be needed in the next few years to work alongside AI. We continue to be surprised that, as more and more evidence emerges about the need for a paradigm shift in what and how we should be teaching the skills needed to work alongside AI, little public acknowledgement of the need for massive and urgent change seems to be in evidence:

> We need to boost our skills to make ourselves AI-ready! . . . People should not be worried about the impact of AI on jobs because education reforms will boost skills. . . . That is my answer in a nutshell, that's why I don't want people to be worried, because we are building a world-class education system.
> (Rishi Sunak, the then UK Prime Minister, 2023)[5]

But in the UK, there has been little meaningful discussion about what the world of work and the AI-shaped workplace will look like, which must surely be a precursor to the redesign of any education system. A system which must include not only schools and colleges but the university sector as well. So, in our view, many institutions and organisations seem to be caught in the headlights – they have frozen into inaction and are not taking this issue sufficiently seriously enough.

We believe that policymakers need to move beyond general talk about 'upskilling' and 'reskilling' for the AI era and undertake a serious examination of what this means. We need to pin down how we will train these priority new skills and put in place effective training strategies.

We would like to think that everyone can adapt by acquiring new skills, but some may be struggling, and we also need to think about what kind of societal support we provide for those who can't make the AI trip.

Much has been said about the role of Universal Basic Income (UBI). But we respectfully suggest you look at the math and decide what is possible. As a comparison, the UK's Coronavirus Job Retention Scheme ran for about 19 months, where 11.7 million employee jobs were furloughed for some period during that time, at a total scheme cost of £70 billion. The UK government couldn't afford to replicate this for another six months, let alone making this a permanent fixture.

There was a recent UBI pilot (2023)[13] in two areas of the UK with some people being given £1,600 a month to live on. Now assuming this is given only to households (and not individuals) and that it is truly universal, the cost of rolling this out to the 28 million plus households in the UK would be half a trillion pounds a year. And, of course, you have a double whammy with UBI, as with fewer people in work, you have a smaller tax base with which to cover the cost.

In 2024, Professor Geoffrey Hinton[14] suggests that UBI could be part of the solution but that this doesn't tackle the loss of identity that would come with the loss of employment opportunities:

> I certainly believe in universal basic income [but] I don't think that's enough because a lot of people get their self-respect from the job they do and if you put everybody on universal basic income that solves the problem of them starving and not being able to pay the rent but it doesn't solve the self-respect problem.

Somehow you have to tax the AI and the corporations that apply the AI – and we know that this will not be easy. As a parallel, Bill Gates proposed recently that robots should be taxed like human workers based on the value of their work.

> It is the first time in history that technology may be eliminating jobs faster than it creates new ones. If so, then our economic and social systems will be remade potentially in a disruptive and destabilizing way.
>
> (Bill Gates, 2024)[15]

For years, Gates has been advocating that robots (and presumably technology more broadly) which replace human workers should incur taxes equivalent to that worker's income taxes.

> Right now, the human worker who does, say, $50,000 worth of work in a factory, that income is taxed. . . . If a robot comes in to do the same thing, you'd think that we'd tax the robot at a similar level.
>
> (Bill Gates, 2017)[16]

And US Senator Bernie Sanders also argues for such a tax, although we would have to say that this is still some way away from the mainstream political debate (it's Bernie Sanders after all!)

> If workers are going to be replaced by robots, as will be the case in many industries, we're going to need to adapt tax and regulatory policies to assure that the change does not simply become an excuse for race-to-the-bottom profiteering by multinational corporations.
>
> (Sanders, 2023)[17]

A 2022 study by MIT economists – with the catchy title *Robots, Trade, and Luddism: A Sufficient Statistic Approach to Optimal Technology Regulation*[18] – looked at the evidence for such a tax and suggested that the optimal policy in this situation would indeed include a tax on robots but only a modest one (for now).

Gates argues that these technology taxes should be used to help fund retraining and reskilling of people who had lost their job to technology – but of course reskilling to do what is something of an open question. There are only so many prompt engineers required. The optimistic view is that AI will free up employees from low-level tasks, and by retraining them to do much higher-level work, companies will increase profits.

> The challenge of AI is so big and the development is exponential, which means there is no luxury to put it aside and focus on something else.
>
> (Marija Pejčinović Burić, Secretary General of the Council of Europe, 2023)

While the path forward is not (yet) clear, we do know that doing nothing is certainly not an option. So what does the future hold for young people entering the workplace – where will the jobs be?

> I don't know because it's clear that a lot of mid-level intellectual jobs are going to disappear and if you ask me which jobs are safe, my best bet is plumbing because these things aren't very good at physical manipulation yet – that will probably be the last thing they're very good at so I think plumbing is safe for quite a long time.
>
> (Professor Geoffrey Hinton, 2024)

This is not a new idea. In November 1954, Albert Einstein wrote a letter to *The Reporter* magazine in which he declared that were he a young man again, he would not try to become a scientist: 'I would rather choose to be a plumber in the hope to find that modest degree of independence still available under present circumstances!'

By identifying key evolutionary pathways and critical uncertainties, in the next chapter, we will provide a view on the likely impact and guidance on how to prepare for different eventualities in a timely way. We will outline a possible 'future history', the mapping of which allows us to reflect and decide what is the best possible strategic place in which to play in the future. This approach also allows us to consider different time horizons . . . how quickly will the wave hit us? Do we have six months, two years, five years, or ten years to prepare?

Summary

In this chapter, we explored why it is very difficult to predict how the AI-human symbiosis is going to play out and how staying relevant in the workplace will mean acquiring new skills that will allow us to work most productively alongside AI. We raised the possibility that, whilst AI won't 'do everything', the number of people needed in any knowledge work human-AI symbiosis will be far, far fewer than are employed today. AI doesn't need to have the intelligence of the smartest humans to completely reshape whole sectors of the economy. Artificial intelligence that is 'just smart enough' will have the capacity to displace millions of jobs.

There will be some surprises vis-à-vis who benefits and who loses out in the AI job era. Whilst there are going to be some winners who leap up the career ladder in a way that they might not have expected prior to the arrival of generative AI, there are going to be disappointed knowledge workers who might not have expected to find themselves in a losing position, given their education and expertise.

If AI has the potential to dramatically transform the structure of work, as we know it, we should start considering our response to this scenario now rather than putting it on the back-burner or relegating it to the 'too-difficult' box. To win in the new AI-shaped workplace, we need to get to grips with what upskilling, reskilling and new skilling actually mean – as individuals, as organisations, and as a society more broadly.

Notes

1. Bennis, W., & Nanus, B. (1985). *Leaders: The Strategies for Taking Charge*. Harper & Row.
2. Mollick, E. (2024). *Co-intelligence: Living and Working with AI*. Portfolio/Penguin.
3. Cowen, T. (2013). *Average Is Over: Powering America Beyond the Age of the Great Stagnation*. Dutton.
4. Cuomo, J. (2023). *The Art of Automation*. IBM Blog. www.ibm.com/blog/art-of-automation
5. Sunak, Rishi. (2023). "Speech by The Prime Minister, The Rt Hon Rishi Sunak MP, at The Royal Society." The Royal Society, October 26, 2023.
6. Brynjolfsson, E., & McAfee, A. (2011). *Race Against the Machine: How the Digital Revolution is Accelerating Innovation, Driving Productivity, and Irreversibly Transforming Employment and the Economy*. Lexington, MA: Digital Frontier Press.
7. Berg, J., & Gmyrek, P. (2023). *Automation hits the knowledge worker: ChatGPT and the future of work*. *International* Labour Office. https://sdgs.un.org/sites/default/files/2023-05/B59%20-%20Berg%20-%20Automation%20hits%20the%20knowledge%20worker%20ChatGPT%20and%20the%20future%20of%20work.pdf
8. DeLollis, B. (2024) "MIT's Daron Acemoglu to Business Leaders: Unchecked Power of Big Tech Poses Risks as AI Reshapes Society." Harvard Business School Institute for Business in Global Society (BiGS). 2024.
9. Islam, F. (2024). *We'll need universal basic income – AI 'godfather'*. BBC. www.bbc.co.uk/news/articles/cnd607ekl99o
10. Bostrom, N. (2003). *Ethical Issues in Advanced Artificial Intelligence*. https://nickbostrom.com/ethics/ai#_ftnref8
11. Jacobs, J., Tasin, F., & Mannan, A. J. (April 25, 2024). *Does Automation Increase Support for the Far Right? A Cross-country Review of Automation's Effects on Support for Populist Parties*. The Brookings Institution.
12. Chang, E. (2024). *The Shape Of Jobs Will Change,' Sam Altman Says at Harvard*. Harvard Business School. www.hbs.edu/bigs/sam-altman-harvard-business-school
13. Ali Hussen, D. (2023). *Universal basic income of £1,600 a month to be trialled in two places in England*. The Guardian. www.theguardian.com/society/2023/jun/04/universal-basic-incomeof-1600-pounds-a-month-to-be-trialled-in-england
14. Hinton, G. (2024). Interview by Faisal Islam. BBC Newsnight, May 17, 2024.
15. Kuosa, T. (2024). *Robot Tax: Will Taxing Robots Solve Unemployment and De-Polarize Ownership*. Future Trends. www.futuresplatform.com/blog/robot-tax#:~:text=Bill%20Gates%20proposed%20recently%20that,robot%20tax%20the%20best%20solution%3F
16. UnknownAuthor. (2017). *Therobotthattakesyourjobshouldpaytaxes,saysBillGates*. QuartzMagazine. https://qz.com/911968/bill-gates-the-robot-that-takes-your-job-should-paytaxes
17. Sanders, B., & Nichols, J. (2023). *It's OK to be Angry about Capitalism*. First edition. Crown.
18. Costinot, A., & Werning, I. (2022). *Robots, Trade, and Luddism: A Sufficient Statistic Approach to Optimal Technology Regulation*. MIT. https://economics.mit.edu/sites/default/files/publications/CW%2004-15-22.pdf

4

THE ARCHITECTURE OF A NEW SOCIETY

In this chapter, we introduce the concept of scenario planning and how this tried-and-tested technique can be used to sketch out plausible possible futures as the basis for a dialogue on how we should respond to the range of outcomes that the widespread adoption of AI may throw at us. We introduce a strawman model, a scenario, that talks to some of the new dynamics that might be influencing our world of work and society more broadly. We borrowed from Aldous Huxley's *Brave New World* (1932) to create strata that paint the picture of who is likely to be the winners and losers if capital replaces labour, and AI becomes a substitute for human skills.

We conclude the chapter by observing that movements up or down these strata are possible only if we develop a set of skills that differentiate us from what AI can do.

So far we've established the massive impact AI will make on the world of knowledge work and the skills that will now be needed to thrive. We've also looked at how different parties are responding to the challenge of AI and the idea that AI will be fundamentally changing the structure of society.

DOI: 10.4324/9781003514879-5

So in this chapter we wanted to step back and put the spotlight for a moment on the bigger society picture so that knowledge workers fully understand where they fit into the overall transformation that's taking place.

A plausible possible future

At a recent conference, we shared the observation of Chris Caren CEO of Turnitin LLC (an internet-based similarity detection service used by academia) that,

> Most of our employees are [software] engineers, we have a few hundred of them, and I think that in 18 months we will need only 20% of that number and we will be able to hire them directly out of high school rather than from 4-year college [programs].[1]

It was one of a number of cues that we have picked up on that suggest a 'direction of travel' for AI-enabled job displacement.

What was interesting was that during the Q&A, an audience member suggested that Chris Caren's observation was a prediction that would no doubt be wrong (because all predictions are wrong), and so any inference we might make from this would – to borrow a legal metaphor – be 'fruit of the poisonous tree'. No doubt this person was channelling Nobel Laureate Niels Bohr and believed 'predicting, particularly when it is about the future, is difficult'. And as far as it goes we do not disagree, but that does not mean that we are without tools that allow us to prepare for what is to come. The question we face is: can we imagine this future so that we may evolve to meet it, or are we simply to face what comes and hope for the best?

SCENARIO PLANNING

Scenario planning emerged more than 60 years ago in response to the challenge of decision-making under unpredictable uncertainty. Futurist Herman Kahn,[2] one of the very early exponents of scenario planning, was described by *Scientific American as* 'thinking the unthinkable', which is the title of his 1962 book.

Shell in the early 1970s pioneered this technique in its much-heralded Group Planning department under Pierre Wack. Wack saw scenario planning as a way of changing the mental map of managers, that is getting them to consider alternative futures than the ones they were currently aligned with. Peter Schwartz, US futurist and co-founder of the Global Business Network which specialised in scenario planning, believed that scenarios were tools for ordering one's perceptions about, and potential responses to, alternative future environments in which one's decisions might be played out.

Scenario planning is a thinking tool for use in strategic conversations; in short, a technique for challenging assumptions and pre-existing models and encouraging fierce strategic dialogues around how best to see opportunities and navigate an uncertain future (Van der Heijden – *Scenarios: The Art of Strategic Conversation*, 1996).[3] Thus, the key is to think of scenarios not as predictions about the future but more as a way of strategically reframing what is going on. It is a technique for outlining possible 'future histories'. This mapping out of scenarios allows us to reflect and decide where best to play in the future, given our talents. To reiterate, one is not making predictions but instead identifying key evolutionary pathways and critical uncertainties, providing an informed view on how they might evolve and how to prepare for these different eventualities in a timely way. It's about creating resilience.

Thus, scenario planning is vital for the longer-term perspective that AI now demands. We have already referred to Amara's law – the tendency to hype up the short term but to underestimate the long-term implications. It was Neil Armstrong who said at the twenty-fifth anniversary of the Apollo 11 moon landing, 1994, 'Science has not yet mastered prophecy. We predict too much for the next year and yet far too little for the next 10'.

As business and social researchers, the authors have used many models of social stratification in their work based on socio-economic factors such as income, education, occupation and location. Knowledge workers have populated the top levels of all of these socio-economic models. In more recent years, there has been much discussion as to whether 'social class' as a construct is now dead – we are now all bourgeois, burger lich, or 'de la clase media', salaried rather than paid a weekly wage, in a one-size-fits-all social homogeny. But the arrival of AI now raises the issue of whether this powerful new technology is creating new social strata – strata in which occupation and education no longer open doors to the highest levels of society.

As part of a scenario planning exercise, the authors developed a model of a plausible possible future outlining how things might look in five years' time to trigger some serious strategic thinking about how to structure the labour market and create a fair society. And here, it is worth noting that this is not a prediction; we are *not* in the business of making predictions. The authors favour anticipating different, plausible possible futures and planning accordingly, and so we set up a 'strawman', intended to provoke a dialogue about the labour market, workforce planning and organisational design in the AI-shaped workplace.

Revisiting *Brave New World*

Our approach is deliberately designed to be thought-provoking: it is aimed at prompting a discussion and ensuring that our business leaders and decision-makers don't put planning for the AI workplace into the 'too difficult' box but start planning for it now. By creating a 'strawman' – an idea to be knocked down – we can trigger a debate about what action we need to start taking now.

We borrowed from Aldous Huxley to paint the picture of who are likely to be the winners and losers as capital replaces labour, and AI becomes a substitute for human skills. In his 1932 novel, *Brave New World*, Huxley sets his story in a futuristic world state, where consumerism has replaced

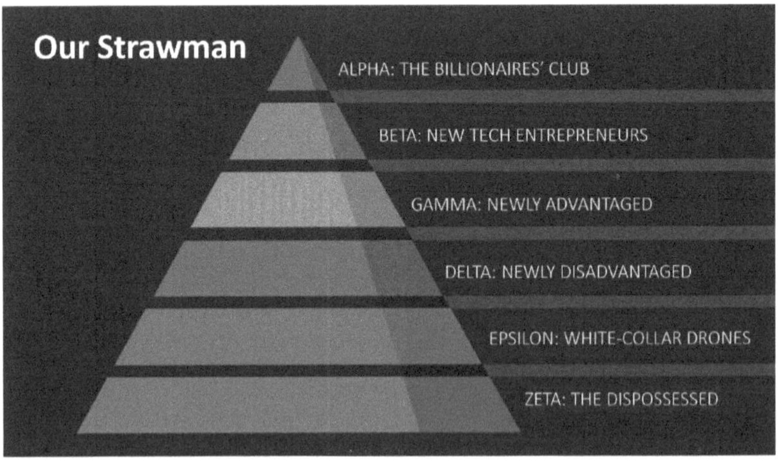

Figure 4.1 Revisiting *Brave New World*

religion; science has eliminated illness and ageing; and the happiness of all is ensured by genetic engineering brainwashing, recreational sex and tranquillising drugs. Citizens are environmentally engineered into an intelligence-based social hierarchy. Eugenics and indoctrination have allocated citizens into predetermined castes.

We have co-opted Huxley's strata of Alphas, Betas, Gammas, Deltas and Epsilons to suggest a new workplace – and, by implication, societal – dynamic. See Figure 4.1 above. Our 'brave new world' has six levels based on people's ability to harness or adapt to AI and develop the skills necessary to offer value and differentiation in a knowledge workplace shaped by AI.

But first, some context. Of the 3.4 billion people employed globally, it is believed that about one billion (~30%) are knowledge workers.[4] In a developed economy like the US, this percentage rises to about 60% – so in the US that would be 100 million knowledge workers in a total workforce of 168 million. This model is intended as a guide for those one billion knowledge workers.

The Alphas: The billionaires club

It seems reasonable to argue that the arrival of AI will increase the number of the uberwealthy. These are individuals who have attracted two-thirds of all the new world wealth that has been created since 2020. A 2021 Oxfam report found that collectively, the ten richest men in the world owned more than the combined wealth of the bottom 3.1 billion people, almost half of the entire world population.[5]

These people, given their bandwidth, access to technology, ability to raise finance and networking capabilities, have been able to attract the kind of wealth that leaves the rest of us trailing in their wake. The Carnegie and Rockefellers of the 1900s have been replaced by Zuckerberg, Altman, Bezos, Musk, Huang, et al., who lead a phalanx of AI entrepreneurs and perhaps less well-known (but no less powerful) venture capitalist investors such as Khosla, Thiel and Masayoshi Son. These people control the capital and the core tools of the AI economy – they control the game board.

How big is this cohort? In truth, it is tiny – probably a few thousand people globally – but they will play an outsized role in defining the future AI-shaped workplace.

The Betas: The new tech entrepreneurs

This group will take the tools provided by the Alphas and find novel and creative ways to apply them – from personalised learning to personalised shopping, from disease detection and diagnosis to drug discovery, from identifying exoplanets to locating merging galaxies. The length and breadth of potential applications are near limitless.

And while many developers will be employed by Google, Amazon, Microsoft, IBM, etc., there is a huge opportunity for the entrepreneurially minded (from any demographic) to develop successful applications across the board. We believe that the widespread roll-out and availability of generative AI models has unleashed a wave of developmental and entrepreneurial creativity.

In addition to developing AI applications, the deployment of AI tools lowers the entry barrier to broader tech ventures. In a July 2023 *Forbes* article, Alex Gudilko of AJProTech LLC suggested that, from an investment standpoint, AI changes venture start-up dynamics. Previously, to create a mobile app, start-ups needed five to ten people and more than $500,000 in seed capital. With AI tools writing code, a team of just one or two people with $20,000 could launch a similar app in weeks. It has never been easier to start a business – even for non-technical founders![6]

Big rewards will flow to these AI entrepreneurs.

The Gammas: The newly advantaged

What we're learning is that AI could throw up some unexpected quirky outcomes when it comes to predicting who will be the job winners and losers.

Yann LeCun, speaking in the 2010s, said, 'Our intelligence is what makes us human, and AI is an extension of that quality. Artificial intelligence is extending what we can do with our abilities. In this way, it's letting us become more human'.[7]

We understand that data scientists or data engineers will have a key role to play in this new world, and we are hopefully getting familiar with the role of 'prompt engineers'. Forbes's Technology Council also gave us other new or enhanced AI roles that include AI Trainer and Operator, Sentiment Analyzer, AI-Generated Work Auditor, AI Output Verifier, AI Prediction Analyzer, AI Input And Output Manager, AI Integration Specialist, AI Compliance Manager, AI Ethicist, VR Experience Designer, Language Ingestion Optimizer, AI Personality Designer and AI Security Engineer and so on.

In addition to the new roles created, there will also be existing knowledge workers who get to leverage new AI tools to their advantage. We have listened to senior lawyers (for example) who see AI tools playing a big but compartmentalised role in their businesses, believing that their own creativity and analytical and interpretative skills will always be required to work alongside any AI system.

We have also seen it argued that AI will open up opportunities for those who have hitherto been 'structurally and creatively oppressed' by our educational system and the way the world of work up to now has undervalued their particular talents. These individuals have now come to the fore because they offer things that AI struggles with. They have dominant right-brain creativity, outside-the-box thinking skills, heightened sensitivity and an ability to deal with complexity in an innovative and compassionate way.

And there is evidence beginning to emerge to support this thesis. Mohammed Hossein Jarrahi's research on AI and the future of work (2018)[8] tells us that AI produces a levelling-up effect, whereby less experienced and less skilled – previously more marginalised workers with access now to new AI tools – find themselves being catapulted up the traditional career ladder.

So this is a welcome shot in the arm for those who hitherto felt their skills and mindset did not fit the conventional educational and work paradigm.

The Deltas: The newly disadvantaged

And now we come to our problem children. These are likely to be relative losers in an AI era. As the democratisation and levelling up of core knowledge and key skills take hold, they find themselves at a comparative disadvantage. Here we find many who, up to now, given their education and skills, have thought that there was a comparatively secure career ahead of them. But their world is likely to be turned upside down sometime in the next three to five years. They could be shown the door or asked to take a pay cut. And the rate of AI advancement is likely to be phenomenal.

Gray Scott, futurist and philosopher, in interviews between 2017 and 2018 on when AI might surpass human intelligence, frequently commented that 'There is no reason and no way that a human mind can keep up with an artificial intelligence machine by 2035'.

As Erik Brynjolfsson points out, highly skilled workers may have less to gain from working alongside AI precisely because AI has been good at capturing the knowledge embodied in their own behaviours. In other words, AI has quickly got the number of those doing solid but not exceptional-level work, encoded it, put it into AI systems and said (in the words of Douglas Adams), *So long and Thanks for all the Fish!* (the fourth book in his *Hitchhiker's Guide to the Galaxy* trilogy!!).

> The nineteenth century created the working-class, the coming century will create the 'useless-class' – billions with no military or economic function. Giving meaning to their lives will be the big challenge of the future.
>
> (Yuval Noah Harari, 2019)[9]

This is a difficult pill for many people to swallow. So if you're going into the law, you know that judges at the very top of the tree are unlikely to be substituted for by technology. But if you are a paralegal, much of what you do could be mastered by AI.

And if you are an advertising copywriter, you're going to need to be a pretty damn good one. These days, average comes for free, so you need to be at the top of your game. You will need to be someone who can provide audacious creativity that is going to beat what AI will be able to do.

So if you are a senior manager in a company, your personality and leadership will still be needed – something that AI can't readily provide. But large swathes of what you are getting the big bucks for – all the stuff you learnt on that now outdated MBA – will now easily be knocked off by AI. So it looks like there is some downgrading of status and rewards for many. And the challenge we face with the Deltas is the sheer scale of the number of people likely to fall into this category.

In the UK, over the last few decades, we have massively built up the expectations of the Deltas. In a short space of time, we have increased the proportion of the school cohort that goes to university to 50% and then awarded over 80% of these graduates with a 2/1 or first-class degree. We have created a massive expectation that higher education is the route to a rewarding and well-paid career.

Let us hope that AI, in generating new jobs and boosting productivity, will be able to float a lot of career boats, but the jury is still out. So what proportion of the workforce do we feel will fall into the Delta category over the next five years?

Just how many knowledge workers may be left feeling that their careers are not living up to expectations. Will they become frustrated by the subordinate role they may have to play in the new AI era – perhaps regretting the educational choices they made earlier.

The Epsilons: The white-collar drones

In our strawman scenario, we assume that there will be a cohort of corporate drones doing work that hasn't been taken over by AI – but of low-enough cost not to attract the spotlight of corporate efficiency hawks.

Here, we find those for whom the debate about AI taking away a rewarding career and messing up their expectations of working life is all pretty academic. Why? Because they saw the writing on the wall about the future of work a while back and have already sort of given up on the idea of building a traditional career. They are happy to coast their way through the new world of work. It's about getting through the day with some help from AI if it's there, and hope you can hang onto your job.

If not, no problem. You can just pop over to another job that still needs some human input. This trend seems to be telling us that more people are looking for self-actualisation and ways of expressing themselves outside of the classic work environment.

In the history of mass production, we seem to have come full circle. We began with boring assembly line processes. We then moved to an enlightened era where, for example, car manufacturers deliberately built into their processes job-enriching activities that could cost the company time and money but were seen as warranted to boost the morale of employees.

And now we are into Bezosism, where the process comes first, and humans just have to suck it up and fit in around it. And it seems that many are settling for this new model, but it is not their route to any self-actualisation or the fulfilment of their potentiality.

The Zetas: The dispossessed

We're all hoping that AI can boost output and productivity and that the proportion of individuals who just cannot compete in our highly competitive, technological AI world is kept to an absolute minimum. But let's be realistic. The evidence tells us that there will be those who will get completely detached from the workforce and will need help.

When discussing the existential challenges of AI, issues such as 'Will it take over our nuclear power stations?' are cited. But what seems to be missing in these discussions is the more mundane, prosaic, and, we believe, more pressing existential threat of total job displacement. But it is exactly this which poses the greatest threat to the stability of society in the short-to-medium term.

It is this scenario that is described as a 'known challenge', but knowing it is a challenge is one thing, but actually assessing its likely impact and potential responses is something else entirely.

The question we pose here is the extent to which the rise in white-collar job displacement creates a class of people disconnected from the knowledge workforce and the rewards of the AI-shaped workplace. It begs the question of whether we need to start thinking about some form of safety net for those at the bottom of the ladder – we already touched on the issues of Universal Basic Income in the previous chapter. And, of course, this isn't just about providing people with financial support. There is the wider issue of people's psychological well-being. To reiterate Geoffrey Hinton's point: it's not just about receiving a government payout but building structure and meaning into people's lives.

AI will reduce the pool of knowledge workers (Alphas to Epsilons), and these people then need to find employment (perhaps in a lower status job) beyond knowledge work.

Reskilling knowledge workers for the future of work

The model we put forward here is not static, and people can move between strata – moving up or dropping back down. The trigger for these movements, up or down, is developing the skills one needs to stay relevant and, indeed, thrive in the AI workplace. It's about acquiring the set of skills to identify which we believe are most important to dial up because they are the ones that allow us to work most productively alongside generative AI. These are the skills that leave people best placed to succeed and be an AI winner rather than an AI loser.

> It is not in the stars to hold our destiny but in ourselves.
>
> (Shakespeare, 1599)

Summary

In this chapter we have laid out a strawman for discussion, a stratification of a possible future hierarchy of knowledge workers. The aim is to foster a dialogue about the skills and capabilities that we will need to move up the ladder from one level to another or, equally important, to ensure that we don't slip down 'a snake' and find ourselves suddenly disadvantaged in the new AI-shaped workplace.

We have identified that there are those who will control the 'game board' in terms of how AI will shape our futures and then those who will entrepreneurially apply the tools that they are presented with to create new solutions and applications. There are those whose skills and abilities make them more attractive in the new world of work and those whose skills and/or experiences, previously valued, are now no longer the competitive advantage they once were.

There will continue to be people in knowledge work who 'work to live' rather than 'live to work' and are happy to coast along on the knowledge work currents, getting their fulfilment in activities and interests outside the workplace and those who will find themselves completely cast adrift from knowledge work and have to find new ways of making a living.

The strawman gives us a context for discussing what skills and abilities we should be developing to stay relevant in the new AI-shaped knowledge workplace.

Notes

1. Global Silicon Valley (2023). *The Future of Integrity in the Brave New World of AI* (2023). ASU+GSV Summit. https://youtu.be/TDC1ceJbdPg?si=MGPL1NSjlCQIjgLW
2. Khan, H. (1962). *Thinking the Unthinkable.* Horizon Press.
3. van der Heijden, K. (1996). *Scenarios: The Art of Strategic Conversation* (2nd ed 2005.). Chichester: Wiley. www.usebraintrust.com/blog/knowledge-work-demand-index-july-2021
4. Luna-Ostaseski, G. (2021). *Announcing The Knowledge Work Demand Index.* Brain Trust. www.oxfam.org.uk/media/press-releases/ten-richest-men-double-their-fortunesin-pandemic-while-incomes-of-99-per-cent-of-humanity-fall/
5. Ahmed, N., Marriott, A., Dabi, N., et al. (2022). *Inequality Kills: The unparalleled action needed to combat unprecedented inequality in the wake of COVID-19.* Oxfam.
6. Forbes Technology Council. (2023). *20 New And Enhanced Roles AI Could Create.* Forbes. https://www.forbes.com/councils/forbestechcouncil/2023/07/06/20-new-and-enhanced-roles-ai-could-create/
7. LeCun, Y., Quiñonero Candela, (1st December, 2016). *Artificial intelligence, revealed.* Facebook's Engineering blog.
8. Jarrahi, M. H. (2018). *Artificial Intelligence and the Future of Work: Human-AI Symbiosis in Organizational Decision Making.* Business Horizons, 61(4), 577–586.
9. Harari, Y. (2019). *21 Lessons for the 21st Century.* Vintage.

5

THE RISE OF THE POLYMATH

In this chapter, we will examine more closely the concept of the polymath and the value of polymathic thinking, which we have been arguing is the key overarching skill that knowledge workers will need in collaborating with AI. We believe that although industrial needs and requirements have pushed us towards being hyper-specialised, we investigate the argument for pushing back on specialisation, adopting more interdisciplinary thinking and the value inherent in seeing the interconnectedness of ideas. In this chapter we will explain why a renewed focus on polymathy is so timely and important and the case that a wholesale change in modes of thinking will be/is being forced upon now by the possibilities of AI.

We conclude the chapter by discussing how we might encourage more polymathic thinking in individuals and teams.

Throughout the book we've been building the case for a radically different set of skills being required for humans to successfully work alongside AI in a collaborative way.

DOI: 10.4324/9781003514879-6

We've introduced the idea of interdisciplinary thinking being the way forward, the notion of eclectic polymath-style thinking being the key to what is required to supplement the capabilities of AI. We now look at this polymath concept in more detail.

The polymath concept

What is a polymath? What is polymathic thinking? You are no doubt familiar with the term 'polymath', and you will be able to name one, maybe Leonardo Da Vinci (1452–1519) or Shen Kuo (1031–1095) or Benjamin Franklin (1706–1790). Historical curiosities with multiple interests. In this chapter we will explore why polymathy is so relevant to 21st-century thinking.

We all know Leonardo da Vinci was famed as a painter, sculptor and inventor, but his expertise extended into architecture, science, music and mathematics, to anatomy, geology and botany, as well as engineering, astronomy, palaeontology and history. Shen Kuo was a career civil servant – finance minister, head of the bureau of astronomy, minister of imperial hospitality and academic chancellor in the Song Court, but his expertise also included mathematics, optics and horology. Shen discovered the concept of true north and was the first to describe the magnetic needle compass. Benjamin Franklin was a writer, scientist, diplomat and statesman, printer and publisher, political philosopher and America's first postmaster general.

Polymaths have been celebrated through the ages. We can also think of (amongst many others) Isaac Newton, Nicolaus Copernicus, Archimedes, Nikola Tesla, Thomas Edison, Thomas Jefferson, Bertrand Russell, Alan Turing and Maya Angelou. And we have Noam Chomsky, who integrates philosophy, cognitive science and linguistics.

Other classic polymaths include Seymour Papert, who integrated ideas from mathematics, computer science, psychology, philosophy and education to create a holistic vision of learning and human development. His seminal book *Mindstorms: Children, Computers, and Powerful Ideas* was published in 1980.

And a must in any polymath hall of fame is Dr Jacob Bronowski with his gift of synthesising scientific, artistic and philosophical knowledge, culminating in his classic work *The Ascent of Man* (1973).[1]

And, bringing us up to date is the polymath Elon Musk, who navigates AI, space exploration and communications.

Polymaths are often described as 'renaissance men or women', reflecting historical eras when great inventions and ideas emerged from individuals looking at challenges from multiple disciplinary perspectives. Writers like C. P. Snow[2] highlighted in 1959 the power of combining art and science rather than over-specialising in one area.

A polymath possesses extensive knowledge and skills in various domains, including the arts, sciences and humanities. This breadth provides a foundation for creativity, as they integrate deep, robust understanding from several areas, often in innovative and unexpected ways.

Interestingly, Albert Einstein in a 1952 letter to Carl Seelig said, 'I have no special gift. I am only passionately curious'.

At a White House dinner in 1962 honouring Nobel Prize winners, President John F. Kennedy quipped, 'I think this is the most extraordinary collection of talent, of human knowledge, that has ever been gathered together at the White House, with the possible exception of when Thomas Jefferson dined alone'.

In his book *Leonardo da Vinci* (2017),[3] Walter Isaacson states that the starting point for Leonardo's genius was his universal curiosity.

> His genius was of the type we can understand, even take lessons from. It was based on skills we can aspire to improve in ourselves, such as curiosity and intense observation. He had an imagination so excitable that it flirted with the edges of fantasy, which is also something we can try to preserve in ourselves. His method was rooted in experiment, curiosity, and the ability to marvel at phenomena that the rest of us rarely pause to ponder after we've outgrown our wonder years.

The Adam Smith Institute cites one of the lessons from Leonardo's achievements is that 'it doesn't do to box people in' (2023),[4] to think of them as one thing or another, but rather to give them space to develop in as many directions as they wish. Knowledge today is so specialised that it would be difficult for a latter-day successor to master so many of them.

Polymath thinkers are individuals who draw on knowledge from across a wide range of disciplines and display broad and comprehensive knowledge about many different subjects; she or he is broadly and passionately curious. From the Greek words 'poly mathes', meaning 'having learned much', it is accepted as referring to more than two, and so, more specifically, the Polymath should excel in at least three fields or subjects, which would seem –

at face value – to be unrelated. The connection between these fields, subjects, or ideas is forged in the creative mind of the polymath.

According to Edward de Bono, 'If you have a creative mind you can seek to develop ideas in almost any field'. This is a theme underpinning much of his work, including *Serious Creativity: Using the Power of Lateral Thinking to Create New Ideas* (1992).[5]

Polymathy refers to an attitude towards knowledge, learning and creating, which entails the progressive development of three characteristics: breadth, depth and integration (Michael Araki, 2018).[6]

Breadth: Wide-ranging knowledge, covering different and often disparate domains.
Depth: Significantly profound knowledge, be it technical, epistemic, or experiential knowledge.
Integration: Knowledge is integrated and interrelated, forming valuable, coherent and effective combinations of ideas from seemingly disparate domains.

Characteristics of the polymath

Zoologist and ethnologist Desmond Morris wrote in *The Naked Ape* (1967)[7] that humans are by nature the most non-specialised, adaptive, opportunistic animal of all, but since the dawn of the industrial revolution there has been a pressure to become, or an expectation that we should become, more and more specialised.

It was Robert A. Heinlein (1973)[8] who said:

> A human being should be able to change a diaper, plan an invasion, butcher a hog, design a building, conn a ship, write a sonnet, balance accounts, build a wall, set a bone, comfort the dying, take orders, give orders, cooperate, act alone, solve equations, analyse a new problem, pitch manure, program a computer, cook a tasty meal, fight efficiently, die gallantly. Specialization is for insects.

To better operate in a workplace shaped by AI, we will need to unlearn what we have learnt and dial up (or wake up) our dormant polymathic capabilities. Reconditioning our minds, retooling our mental pathways to think like a polymath. This many-sidedness requires us to make connections between ideas and capabilities, switching between various cognitive aptitudes, strands of knowledge and emotional and intellectual attributes.

Sir Ken Robinson, in his famous TED talk from 2006, '*Do schools kill creativity*',[9] - which is one of the most viewed TED Talks of all time - said:

> Learning is the process of acquiring new knowledge and skills. Human beings are highly curious; from the moment they're born, children have a voracious appetite for learning. For many, that appetite is dulled as they go through school. Keeping it alive is the key to transforming education.

Like a child with a wooden shape sorter toy, the system persists in trying to push different-shaped kids into the same round hole and not learning from the experience. Sir Ken Robinson argued that there is a need to radically rethink our view of intelligence – encouraging diverse, multi-modal forms of thinking. This is about fostering dynamic intelligence that drives creativity (which is the process of having original ideas that have value and comes about by the interaction of different disciplinary ways of seeing things) and championing (rather than suppressing) distinctiveness. He believed passionately that our current systems are anachronistic and that we can't afford that socially, culturally, or economically anymore.

And when thinking of 'distinctiveness', we need to move away from the model in which intelligence is tested and graded in the very traditional sense applied currently in schools. We tend to see neurodiversity as a problem rather than just a different way of thinking. There is some suggestion of a link between ADHD and polymathy. To be clear, we are not saying that you have to have ADHD to be a polymath, or that all polymaths have ADHD, but there does seem to be an interesting link. As the father of a son with ADHD, I can see the way the restless mind leaps from concept to concept, making connections that I don't see – often bizarre connections from my point of view but quite logical to my son. Before his diagnosis, the conversation in the car on the drive home from school seemed like a stream of consciousness with mind-bending (for me) questions thrown in like hand grenades. One never knew where it would go next. With the clarity of a diagnosis, I can now see the creative process going on and how these seemingly random connections are formed.

> Because your [ADHD] brain is highly active, you get very creative, so you can put together many of these disparate concepts that other people might not otherwise see. The ADHD brain has the potential to be a polymath, because they have so many wide interests. They can be pretty resilient, they can be extremely creative, and they can be obsessively focused. So they can actually conquer new frontiers.
>
> (Doctor of psychology Perpetua Neo, 2018)[10]

A 2019 study[11] by Professor Marco Catani and Paolo Mazzarello at King's College London suggested that Leonardo da Vinci also 'suffered' from ADHD.

> While impossible to make a post-mortem diagnosis for someone who lived 500 years ago, I am confident that ADHD is the most convincing and scientifically plausible hypothesis to explain Leonardo's difficulty in finishing his work. Historical records show Leonardo spent excessive time planning projects but lacked perseverance. ADHD could explain aspects of Leonardo's temperament and his strange mercurial genius.

And according to the *SCI Journal* (2024)[12] you can add Galileo, Nikola Tesla, Benjamin Franklin and Isaac Newton to the list of polymaths with ADHD. As you can modern-day renaissance man and one-half of the Eurythmics, Dave Stewart, in an interview (2008) with *The Guardian*, said, 'I've got such bad attention-deficit disorder that I'm never bored. I'm like a 12-year-old kid: texting a friend while i-chatting with another and watching a video'.

In a foreword to the 2012 book *Beyond Genius*,[13] he recalls,

> I was talking about it one day, back in 1989, to Bob Geldof, and he said, 'well, that's because you're a fecking polymath'. Then he said . . . 'I'm a fecking polymath too'. And he is. Bob is always doing a hundred things at the same time, like me.

Stewart has always resisted the categorisation or labels that would come with specialisation, 'people talk about thinking outside the box. Well for me, I never even saw a box'.

Sir Richard Branson, founder of the Virgin Group, who has also been open about his ADHD diagnosis and credits his entrepreneurial success in part to the out-of-the-box thinking that often accompanies ADHD. He is reported as saying in an interview (circa 2014), 'If you don't let anybody build a box around you, then you will never have to think outside of the box. Basically, in order to think outside the box, avoid getting into one'.

The specialisation straitjacket

When did we all start climbing into a box? Ken Robinson cites the evolution of the modern corporation, and the needs of industrial production, following the industrial revolution, as the driving force behind the development of a mass education system.

> If you design a system to do something specific, don't be surprised if it does it. If you run an education system based on standardisation and conformity, which suppresses individuality, imagination and creativity, don't be surprised if that's what it does.
>
> (Ken Robinson, 2006)[14]

Dietrich Bonhoeffer (1951)[15] reminds us:

> The 'polymath' had already died out by the close of the eighteenth century, and in the following century intensive education replaced extensive, so that by the end of it the specialist had evolved. The consequence is that today everyone is a mere technician, even the artist.

The factory system that developed and refined over the course of the late 18th to late 19th centuries led to the decomposition of work into smaller, highly specialised sequences, requiring less skill. This drive for efficiency and increased productivity mitigated against multidisciplinary skills.

The concept of narrow specialisation was pioneered by Frederick Winslow Taylor in *The Principles of Scientific Management* (1911).[16] In an earlier paper in 1903 he defined Scientific Management as:

> The art of management has been defined 'as knowing exactly what you want men to do, and then seeing that they do it in the best and cheapest way'.[17]

Taylorism focused on optimal processes or system efficiency, which in turn made specialisation a central tenet of mass production. Taylor preached that 'each worker in the organisation, should have a clearly defined task' and that 'each worker should be given standard conditions and appliances that will enable him to perform his tasks'.

> Mr. Bucket was the only person in the family with a job. He worked in a toothpaste factory, where he sat all day long at a bench and screwed the little caps on to the tops of the tubes of toothpaste after they had been filled. But a toothpaste cap-screwer is never paid very much money, and poor Mr. Bucket, however hard he worked, and however fast he screwed on the caps, was never able to make enough to buy one half of the things that so large a family needed.
>
> (Roald Dahl, *Charlie and the Chocolate Factory*, 1964)

This approach shaped a sort of Gradgrind-esque education, which in its turn shaped the skills, capabilities and intellectual horizons of those young people who passed through it, becoming grist to the mill of the modern corporation.

> Now, what I want is, Facts. Teach these boys and girls nothing but Facts. Facts alone are wanted in life. Plant nothing else, and root out everything else. You can only form the minds of reasoning animals upon Facts: nothing else will ever be of any service to them.
>
> (Thomas Gradgrind in Charles Dickens's *Hard Times*, 1854)

Specialisation became an ideology that shaped the workplace – into tasks, roles, departments, functions, verticals – and so society more broadly. This compartmentalisation or siloing of work saw us collectively devalue the individualism, creativity and polymathic thinking that, as Desmond Morris argued, used to be innate. We became an excessively specialised society.

In his excellent book *The Polymath: Unlocking the Power of Human Versatility* (2019)[18], Waqās Ahmed argues that:

> For survival both intense focus and contextual thinking is needed in equal measure. Indeed, our current obsession with the particular rather than the general, with facts rather than overall rules is according to statistician and philosopher Nassim Nicholas Taleb one of the main reasons why we remain unprepared for 'Black Swans'.

Anybody who has helped a child revise for a recent GCSE history exam will recognise that not much has changed. School and university are still (largely) places for dissemination of knowledge – someone who is a subject matter expert stands at the front and transfers knowledge to the class.

But, in the information age, when the sum of all human knowledge is instantly available to us, via a device in our pocket, availability of information, access to facts, is no longer a barrier, and an ability to regurgitate is not a good metric for learning.

> Imagine a world in which every single person on the planet is given free access to the sum of all human knowledge. That's what we're doing.
>
> (Jimmy Wales, Founder of Wikipedia, 2004)[19]

This is not a new idea. H. G. Wells wrote a collection of essays titled *World Brain*, which espouses his idea of a new, free, synthetic, authoritative, permanent *World Encyclopaedia* that could help world citizens make the best use of universal information resources and make the best contribution to world peace (1938).[20]

In the 1970s, American journalist Alvin Toffler coined the now ubiquitous phrase 'information overload', and as Edward. O. Wilson, American biologist, naturalist, ecologist and entomologist and polymath, put it 'We are drowning in information, while starving for wisdom. The world henceforth will be run by synthesizers, people able to put together the right information at the right time, think critically about it, and make important choices wisely' (1998).[21]

Interdisciplinary thinking

Even as the needs of industry drove us towards specialisation and knowledge fragmentation, there were pockets of 'resistance'. In the 19th century, various societies or clubs, in the tradition of the salon or coffee house, came together in Europe and the US to discuss topics from the viewpoint of different disciplines or academic faculties. One member of one such club described 'the object being to have one man at least well up in every conceivable subject'. It is often argued that interdisciplinary communication is where great ideas emerge.

In his book *The Polymath: A Cultural History From Leonardo da Vinci to Susan Sontag* (2021),[22] Peter Burke describes The Ratio Club, founded in London in 1949, as meeting every couple of months in the National Hospital for Nervous Diseases to drink beer, listen to papers, and discuss what was becoming known as cybernetics. The group included psychologists, physiologists, mathematicians, physicists and engineers, including polymaths Alan Turing and W. Ross Ashby. Burke suggests that groups such as this 'encouraged free expression of different points of view [and] their success illustrates the argument that when problems need to be solved, even more important than ability is cognitive diversity'.

From these salons, in the 1930s, emerged interdisciplinary research projects in universities that cut across the formal boundaries of academic departments, fostering 'chaotic specialisation' (as defined by Max Horkheimer and the Frankfurt Institute for Social Research).[23] Proponents of the interdisciplinary approach saw the traditional departmental siloes as 'sterile' and obstacles to a wider understanding. A host of 'new' universities and institutes, opened after World War II, were a catalyst for the spread of the interdisciplinary approach.

Disciplines – that is, a branch of learning or domain of knowledge that is characterised by distinct objects, concepts, principles, theories, skills, tools and applications – have been the cornerstone of educational and academic practice at all levels for over a century. But, according to the Royal Society of Edinburgh (2023),[24] while they have some merits, there are also persuasive arguments against disciplines.

> The consistent focus on a single set of disciplinary phenomena may result in a lack of creative engagement with other disciplines and with the gaps between disciplines. Disciplines may be inward-looking and fail to address relevant, real-world problems. Learners may find it difficult to make links between disciplines. Disciplinary communities guard their boundaries in competition with other disciplines, yet it is in the gaps beyond disciplinary boundaries – the interdisciplinary areas – that major new insights and research breakthroughs occur.

With the accumulation of human knowledge growing rapidly, there is a doubling of knowledge about every decade. The result is increasing disciplinary specialisation in learning to the extent that we easily lose sight of the wider contexts and bigger picture and of how ideas and phenomena interconnect and inform each other in a complex network of knowledge (McGilchrist, 2012).[25]

Writing in the 1970s and 1980s, Edgar Morin reminds us that 'Key realities often slip through the cracks between artificially created disciplines'.

And while we have intellectually moved towards the idea of interdisciplinary or multidisciplinary research or thinking – the pull or sway of more traditional models is still powerful and widely felt. As consultants we have seen the contraction of time available for 'thinking'. If we presented a proposal to a putative client, and it included a budget line for 'thinking time', there are very few clients who would sign that off. Peter Burke (2021) suggests heavier workloads, the proliferation of meetings and constant time pressure are reducing the time for thinking and research. 'I wonder how a vice-chancellor would respond today to a professor of chemistry who announced (as Michael Polanyi did at the University of Manchester in 1948) that he wanted to teach philosophy'.

In a recent commentary in *Science Magazine* (2024), assistant professor at Brown University, Rachel E. Baker[26] noted that the value of interdisciplinary training is still not widely understood and does not easily fit with structures or systems that encourage and foster specialisation.

> As an interdisciplinary scientist with degrees in physics, applied math and environmental studies, I've often faced the conundrum of what to call myself . . . I passionately believe in the value of interdisciplinary training and I chose to pursue [a PhD in interdisciplinary environmental studies], which I have often described as a 'choose your own adventure' program, precisely because it offered the flexibility to take courses spanning many traditional academic disciplines . . . yet very few job postings explicitly sought an interdisciplinary scholar. Having expertise in multi disciplines is my Superpower . . . and I hope to remain without a one-word definition of my expertise for as long as possible.

The interconnectedness of all things

The authors often use this quote from a Russian-British social and political theorist, philosopher and historian of ideas, Isaiah Berlin writing in the 1950s to 1990s, that encapsulates the essence of polymathic thinking, in that we are trying to develop 'an acute sense of what fits with what, what springs from what, and what leads to what'.[27]

Isaiah Berlin famously wrote *The Hedgehog and the Fox* essay and later the 1953 book with the same title – which references a line from an ancient Greek poem 'a fox knows many little things, but a hedgehog knows but one big thing'.

The hedgehog relates everything to a single central vision. A system less or more coherent or articulate, in terms of what he understands, thinks and feels; it is a system that is a single universal organising principle. The fox on the other hand pursues many ends, often unrelated and even contradictory, connected if at all only in some de facto way for some psychological or physiological cause.

The argument is that the fox – the thinker who knows many little things and draws from an eclectic array of traditions – is better able to improvise in response to changing events. The fox is more successful in predicting the future than the hedgehog, who knows one big thing and who slavishly toils devotedly within one methodology to impose formulaic solutions to complex problems that really demand a more eclectic approach.

So the fox encapsulates many aspects of the polymathic thinker, drawing inspiration from the concept of interconnectedness.

And, from notebook entries credited to Leonardo da Vinci, he expressed this point by stating, 'Principles for the Development of a Complete Mind: Study the science of art. Study the art of science. Develop your senses – especially learn how to see. Realise that everything connects to everything else'.

Russian-American polymath Anatol Rapoport, a musician, mathematician, biologist and psychologist, developed the concept of 'organised complexity' operating between the regions of 'organized simplicity' and 'chaotic complexity' (2009).[28] Organised complexity represents a collection interconnected by a complex net of relations – the fundamental interconnectedness of everything with everything else. This concept is neatly described by Douglas Adams's hero, the private detective Dirk Gently when explaining his work in *Dirk Gently's Holistic Detective Agency.*[29]

> The term 'holistic' refers to my conviction that what we are concerned with here is the fundamental interconnectedness of all things. I do not concern myself with such petty things as fingerprint powder, telltale pieces of pocket fluff and inane footprints. I see the solution to each problem as being detectable in the pattern and web of the whole. The connections between causes and effects are often much more subtle and complex than we with our rough and ready understanding of the physical world might naturally suppose. Let me give you an example. If you go to an acupuncturist with toothache he sticks a needle instead into your thigh. Do you know why he does that? No, neither do I, but we intend to find out.

You may be familiar with the parable of the 'blind men and the elephant'. In the story, a group of blind men feel different parts of the elephant (just one part) to explain what it is. If you had the trunk, you'd think it was a tree; the tail would suggest a rope; the legs suggest pillars etc. Without being able to connect these experiences, we have little chance of actually identifying the elephant. In the same way, hyper-specialisation tends towards a 'reductionist' view of how the world works. By exploring the multiple facets of a thing, a problem, a situation etc. you may find 'better' solutions.

There are parallels here with Edward de Bono's system for parallel thinking involving six coloured hats, outlined in 1985 in his bestselling book *Six Thinking Hats*, which encourages people to collectively inhabit multiple perspectives. By combining or merging different perspectives, beliefs, or schools of thought it is possible to forge a new syncretic rationale or explanation.

So Waqās Ahmed (2019)[30] argues that hybridity is the creative outcome resulting from the synthesis of multiple, seemingly unrelated phenomena. It is this ability to synthesise and make sense of what is at first sight disparate fragments of information that fuels the thinking process, whereby data becomes information, information becomes knowledge and knowledge becomes insight. There is an argument to say that our educational institutions can and should do a much better job teaching these thinking skills and abductive reasoning.

Rand Spiro, Professor of Educational Psychology and Educational Technology at Michigan State University developed a Cognitive Flexibility Theory (2002)[31] as a response to ill-structured or messy complexity everywhere, which is an inevitable part of advanced knowledge. His research concerns new modes of learning with technology to promote what are often called '21st century skills', especially the ability to deal with novelty in an increasingly complex and rapidly changing world. A key tenet of Cognitive Flexibility Theory is that learning should emphasise knowledge construction (instead of information transmission) and knowledge interconnection.

> Cognitive Flexibility Theory is about preparing people to select, adapt and combine knowledge and experience in new ways to deal with situations that are different than the ones they have encountered before. . . . It is the flexible application of knowledge in new contexts, and you just can't rely on the old templates. Cognitive security is what people want. It doesn't work in the modern world of work and life.
>
> (Rand Spiro, 2002)

Cognitive flexibility also incorporates cognitive shifting – a component of the brain's executive function, which is the mental process of consciously redirecting one's attention from one focus to another: specific areas of the brain are switched on when a person moves between multiple unrelated tasks, and these areas support the polymath's ability to move freely from one cognitive skill or situation to another – providing the polymath with the mental flexibility to quickly and appropriately respond to a changed context by effectively redirecting their focus.

Change will be forced upon us

If it hasn't already, AI will soon pass the Turing Test – a test of its ability to exhibit intelligence equivalent to, or indistinguishable from, that of a human. In an interview with *the New York Times* (2023), Professor Geoffrey Hinton, 'the godfather of AI', believes AI which exceeds human intelligence is 'just a matter of when' but also that it doesn't need to be smarter than us to be hugely disruptive.

Artificial general intelligence, that is AI which exceeds human intelligence, has always been the 'holy grail' of AI developers, but the world is split on the likelihood of this actually coming about. People like Shane Legg, co-founder of Google Deepmind's AI lab – reflecting Ray Kurzweil's *The Age of Spiritual Machines* – recently reiterated his belief that there was a 50% chance that AI will achieve artificial general intelligence by 2028 – a claim he originally made in 2011.

These are all way markers on the road to a technological singularity (a future point in time at which technological growth becomes uncontrollable and irreversible). Initially defined by Hungarian-American mathematician John von Neumann, it was more recently popularised by Kurzweil in his 2005 book, *The Singularity is Near.*[32] An event he predicts will happen by 2045.

In promoting his 2024 follow-up book *The Singularity is Nearer,*[33] Kurzweil reiterates two key dates from his previous book: AI would reach human intelligence by 2029 and merge with machines by 2045.

> It has been almost 20 years since I predicted The Singularity will arrive by 2045 and I am sticking with that prediction.

As the jagged frontier of AI capabilities continues to press forward, more and more of what we have traditionally called 'knowledge work' will fall under its wheels. As the role of the artificial mind expands, the space for the human mind to work diminishes, unless there is a way to differentiate ourselves. As Brynjolfsson and McAfee put it, 'We can't win the race against the machine, especially as computers continue to become more powerful and capable [but] we can learn to better race with machines' (2014).[34]

In this new reality, the biological mind must rediscover its polymathic ancestry. It's the ability to combine, curate and connect to form a uniquely human perspective.

> The world has little choice but to see a revival of the polymath as it is only this species of multi-faceted, complex, creative, versatile and inimitable human that will have any value or relevance in a highly complex, automated, super-intelligent future.
>
> (Waqās Ahmed, 2019)[30]

Unless we find a point (or points) of irreplaceable, sustainable differentiation, we just become operationally inferior and expensive – the focus moves from labour to capital as we are replaced by software/hardware. What makes us unique? We cannot rely on our experience or specialised knowledge in a world of superintelligent machines that can easily out-specialise us.

> Educational institutions don't need to train people to be cogs in a machine like during the industrial age – machines will be much cheaper . . . they ought to train people to deal with more complex, ill-defined jobs.
>
> (Stefano Carganico, 2024)[35]

The power of polymath thinking

Whilst today we are in the 'foothills' of this technology, the amount of resource, thinking and attention that is now going into AI and machine learning, and the new use cases that are being tried and tested, suggests that just momentum is going to take this technology forward towards as yet unimagined peaks. This is going to pose the greatest challenge to human intelligence – how to live and prosper in a world where a lot of what we did, the cognitive work that formed the basis of a role, a job, a career is taken over by technology.

> There is a serious snag in the specialist way of life . . . everything is fine as long as the special survival device works, but if the environment undergoes a major change the specialist is left stranded.
>
> (Desmond Morris, *The Naked Ape*, 1967)[36]

Will polymaths survive or will this species become extinct? We believe that far from being intellectual curiosities, the ability to span and find useful and meaningful connections between areas of knowledge will become increasingly valuable in the AI-shaped knowledge workplace. As machine intelligence edges out specialised human intelligence, how will our one-dimensional mind cope or stay relevant?

We must change the system we work in and redefine what is seen as valuable capabilities. Our whole approach to thinking – from the perspectives of culture, education, educational institutions, work environment and indeed to our general view of society – must change. We must move to a place that develops, encourages and values polymathic minds.

> Education ought therefore to be focused on developing skills that can be applied to more than one domain or at the very least be transferable, particularly as what one might specialize in today could be out of date tomorrow, given the economically, politically and technologically volatile times in which we find ourselves. The obsessive compartmentalisation of knowledge into fields is a misguided simplification.
>
> (Waqās Ahmed, 2019)[30]

> New challenges require new responses . . . we will need generalists in the sense of individuals who are able to perceive what Isaac Barrow back in the seventeenth century called the 'connection of things, and dependence of notions'. As Leibniz once declared. 'what we need are universal men. For one who can connect all things can do more than ten people'. . . . We need such individuals more than ever before.
>
> (Peter Burke, 2021)[37]

While we continue to develop our own understanding of AI's capabilities and precisely what human skills will be needed in the future to work alongside AI, it is clear that curiosity and versatility are 'core competencies' in the polymathic mind, augmented by the ability to move seamlessly across various, seemingly unrelated domains. Waqās Ahmed suggests the following facets to develop in a journey to polymathy.

First, there is 'Individuality' which is understanding oneself. Then there is 'Curiosity' – continuous, boundless energy. Next is 'Intelligence' which covers nurturing, exercising and optimising various abilities.

Then we have 'Versatility' – being able to move seamlessly between different spheres of knowledge and experience. On the list is also 'Creativity', which is about connecting and synthesising seemingly disparate fields for a creative outcome. And finally, there is 'Unity' – being able to unify various strands of knowledge for greater clarity and vision of the whole.

So in this chapter we have been building a picture of polymathic thinking, and shortly we're going to unpack the specific power skills that make up our workplace polymath. But before we do this, let's change gear and provide a more practical focus.

Let's look at what you can do to start cultivating the polymath way of thinking starting with reviewing the CV of a polymath.

This is what a job ad for a polymath might look like.

PROFILE OF A POLYMATH: THE CV

JOB TITLE: POLYMATH THINKER – TEAM LEADER FOR KNOWLEDGE WORKERS

Introduction

Are you driven by curiosity and motivated by the challenge of solving complex problems across various domains? We are seeking an exceptional Polymath Thinker to lead a dynamic team of knowledge workers.

Our ideal candidate will demonstrate an extraordinary ability to connect dots between disparate fields, fostering innovation and guiding our team through complex challenges.

If you thrive in a multidisciplinary environment and are passionate about leveraging broad knowledge to drive meaningful impact, we invite you to apply.

Job description

The Polymath Team Leader will oversee a group of talented knowledge workers, guiding them in the creation and implementation of solutions across sectors, including technology, finance, healthcare and education. Your role will involve synthesising information from multiple disciplines to develop strategies that are not only effective but also revolutionary.

Key responsibilities

- Lead and mentor a team of knowledge workers, promoting an interdisciplinary approach to problem solving
- Facilitate knowledge sharing and integration across different areas of expertise within the team
- Drive the ideation and execution of innovative projects by applying principles from diverse fields such as data science, psychology, systems engineering and more
- Engage with stakeholders to understand their challenges deeply and provide comprehensive, adaptable solutions
- Foster a culture of continuous learning and intellectual curiosity within the team
- Stay abreast of developments in multiple fields to ensure the team remains at the cutting edge of innovation

Required skills and traits

Intellectual versatility: Exceptional ability to learn and apply insights from multiple disciplines.

Strategic thinking: Strong analytical skills with a proven track record of tackling complex problems and delivering actionable solutions.

Leadership and collaboration: Experience in leading diverse teams with a collaborative leadership style that encourages participation and innovation from all team members.

Communication: Excellent verbal and written communication skills, with the ability to articulate complex concepts clearly and persuasively to a variety of audiences.

Adaptability: Comfortable with ambiguity and rapid change, able to pivot strategies quickly in response to new information and changing conditions.

Creativity and innovation: A robust creative thinking process that challenges conventional approaches and fosters groundbreaking ideas.

If you are a visionary thinker with a passion for interdisciplinary innovation and leadership, we encourage you to join our team and help shape the future across multiple domains.

A practical guide to becoming a polymath

Before diving further into the specific power skills that make up the polymath mind, let's explore some fundamental ways knowledge workers can enhance their excellence in polymath thinking. Here are some concrete actions to cultivate this mindset.

Respect the panorama principle – see the holistic picture

Polymaths have the ability to see the wider context, examine issues from different perspectives and bring nuanced arguments together. They unravel complexity with empathy and sensitivity to the human condition, blending logical reasoning with intuitive thought processes. As a general rule, when unravelling a complex issue, ensuring that you first understand the bigger holistic context is more important than just focusing on seeking out more details.

Foster the creative integration of ideas

Polymaths excel at making connections between different areas of knowledge, solving complex problems by drawing insights from multiple disciplines. They can see links between seemingly disparate fields, such as psychology, sociology, economics, behavioural science and data science.

They enjoy viewing the world from different perspectives and develop the art of connecting up the dots to see the bigger picture. It's about looking at problems through multiple lenses, drawing insights from various fields to create innovative and unexpected solutions that AI might not consider. So seek out eclectic perspectives, taking the best from all available viewpoints to arrive at a comprehensive solution. This will help you develop an understanding of cultural variation, diversity and nuance to inform your decisions.

Cultivate curiosity and a questioning mindset

Polymaths exhibit a profound curiosity and a relentless desire to understand the world by blending ideas from various fields. They embody versatility and are adept at merging insights into a rich tapestry of knowledge, leading to innovative problem-solving.

So develop an almost obsessive curiosity about why things are the way they are and how they really work. Challenge conventional thinking by understanding and questioning the underlying assumptions. Maintain a sceptical, inquisitive approach to all situations.

Cultivate the art of asking questions. Einstein famously said he would spend 55 minutes asking the right questions if he had one hour to save the world. Polymath thinkers excel at crystallising problems by asking the right questions. Practise 'self-monitoring' by constantly questioning whether you truly understand a situation or only have a superficial grasp.

Apply forensic intellectual energy

Polymaths are driven by an intense intellectual forensic energy to explore ideas from various disciplines deeply rather than superficially. They connect the dots between seemingly disparate disciplines, synthesising knowledge into insights that advance understanding and offer creative solutions.

Be a problem simplifier

Keep things simple. Apply the Occam's Razor principle, which suggests that the simplest solution is usually the best. Learn to distinguish between irrelevant confusion that you should cut out of the equation and genuine complexity you need to address to arrive at a resolution.

Be an energy radiator who inspires confidence. Maintaining high levels of physical and mental energy is crucial for consistently looking at ideas from different angles and perspectives. Manage your energy flow effectively to stay vigilant and inspired.

Engage with creativity tools

Use tools and techniques to enhance your natural creativity and connect different pathways of thought to arrive at innovative solutions. Feel comfortable fusing logical reasoning with creative thinking to solve problems. Like Einstein, learn to combine left-brain analytical skills with right-brain creativity.

Nurture emotional intelligence

Enhance your empathy by understanding and sharing the feelings of others. Cultivate compassion, which involves not only recognising emotions but also taking action in response to others' feelings. This requires high self-awareness and understanding your own emotions, strengths and weaknesses.

Make ethical judgements

Develop the ability to make ethical, philosophical, and moral judgements about complex issues. Always ask yourself if your approach is fair and reasonable and ensure that you have applied due diligence to your assessment of AI outputs.

Practice informed intuition

Intuition, for polymaths, is a cognitive process that allows quick and effective decision-making, drawing on accumulated experiences and patterns. Polymaths understand that intuition can be flawed and thus combine it with a wide body of facts, knowledge, and experience to form 'informed intuition'.

So while seeking innovative solutions, make sure you check their feasibility. It's all about ensuring your creativity, insights, judgements and intuition are underpinned by logical processing.

Be a lifelong learner

Build the confidence to step outside your discipline comfort zone and embrace new ideas by continually committing to self-improvement.

In summary, polymaths are individuals who integrate diverse knowledge and skills, using their deep understanding and intellectual curiosity to innovate and solve complex problems. Their unique ability to see connections and synthesise information across fields makes them invaluable in the era of AI and beyond.

Polymaths, with their broad integrative approach to problem-solving, are becoming crucial to the art of creative synthesis. They take AI-generated options and innovate further by critically evaluating AI input while embracing dimensions of emotional intelligence and ethical considerations that AI may overlook.

This process results in outputs that address crucial nuances missed or misinterpreted by AI due to its thorough yet imperfect training process. The polymath mind acts as a catalyst, linking AI outputs with traditional human insights and elevating them to new levels of creativity and excellence.

As AI handles much of the basic reasoning and insights on various topics, polymaths will come to the forefront. We need individuals with fresh perspectives, novel insights and an open-mindedness to explore new frontiers in an eclectic way.

In the AI era, the ability to take AI outputs and leap to creative ideas that resonate with the human psyche will be the most valuable contribution knowledge workers can make. The argument here is that as AI becomes proficient in fundamental reasoning, knowledge workers must elevate their skills to add value. Increasingly, we will need people with a polymath mindset.

By implementing these actions, knowledge workers can cultivate a polymath mind, enhancing their ability to innovate, integrate diverse knowledge and solve complex problems creatively and effectively.

Make polymath thinking a habit

Building on the earlier discussion, we now look at some day-to-day practices to consider to develop the habit of viewing the world through a polymath mind lens.

Keep a journal

Reflect on your self-awareness, empathy and compassion in different scenarios. Establish a consistent journalling habit, whether it's first thing in the morning or last thing at night.

Systematise your information capture

Set up a system for identifying and capturing new information to broaden your knowledge base. Read outside your immediate expertise and scan diverse sources for ideas. A helpful tip is to apply the 'progressive summarisation of ideas' principle - in this way gradually generating powerful concepts.

Build reflection points into your day

Develop metacognition by reflecting on your thinking throughout the day. Take five-minute meditation breaks in the morning and afternoon to consider the perspectives you bring to various issues.

Expand your professional networks

Proactively expand your networking groups to filter and monitor your ideas. Feedback from others can help refine and elevate your ideas.

Analyse and learn from your failures

Accept that experimenting with new ideas can lead to failure. Build resilience by having a system to learn from mistakes. Draw a distinction between uncontrollable factors and those areas where you could have improved to achieve a better outcome.

Identify disciplines that will broaden your perspective

Create a checklist of disciplines that you feel would enhance your current work. Engage in creative pursuits like writing to build your hinterland – foster broader thinking. This will provide you with a diverse knowledge base when solving problems.

Sign up for educational events

We have established the importance of cultivating a culture of continuous learning to promote curiosity and exploration. Attend workshops, online training, or educational events to develop new skills and knowledge.

By implementing these practical steps, you can cultivate the habits underpinning the polymath mind, enhancing your ability to innovate and solve complex problems creatively and effectively.

Summary

In this chapter we argued the case that in the new AI-shaped knowledge workplace, the human specialist will be at a disadvantage and that we need to place greater emphasis on those skills and abilities that distinguish us from ever more powerful machines and AI. We need to reawaken our polymathic side – to embrace complex, creative, interdisciplinary thinking to give us a sustainable point of differentiation rather than continue trying to out-specialise superintelligent machines. We need to remember how to become generalists again, able to perceive the connection of things and the dependence of notions.

Those who will stay relevant in the new world of work will be those who are able to pull together the right information, from a range of disparate sources, think critically about it, frame wise choices and communicate this in a way that fosters action. Our work environment is changing rapidly, and unless we learn to become more cognitively flexible, we will be left stranded; we will find ourselves as the newly disadvantaged.

In this chapter, we do not advocate a polymathic mindset as a way of beating 'the machine' but instead believe that it is inevitable that ever more powerful and competent technology will develop, and this cognitive flexibility is the only way that we will maintain a role or relevance working alongside new technologies.

Notes

1. Bronowski, J. (1973). *The Ascent of Man*. London: British Broadcasting Corporation.
2. Snow, C. P. (1959). *The Two Cultures and the Scientific Revolution*. Cambridge University Press.
3. Isaacson, W. (2017). *Leonardo Da Vinci*. Simon & Schuster.
4. Unknown Author (2023). *Leonardo da Vinci polymath*. Adam Smith Institute. www.adamsmith.org/blog/leonardo-da-vinci-polymath
5. De Bono, E. (1992). *Serious Creativity. Using the Power of Lateral Thinking to Create New Ideas*. Harper Business.
6. Araki, M. (2018). www.linkedin.com/in/arakimichael/
7. Morris, D. (1967). *The Naked Ape: A Zoologist's Study of the Human Animal*. Jonathan Cape.
8. Heinlein, R. A. (1973). *Time Enough for Love*. G.P. Putnam's Sons.
9. Robinson, K. (2006). www.ted.com/talks/sir_ken_robinson_do_schools_kill_creativity
10. Dodgson, L. (2018). *What everyone gets wrong about ADHD — and how it can be used as a superpower*. Business Insider. www.businessinsider.com/what-everyone-gets-wrong-about-having-adhd-2018-5
11. Catani, M., & Mazzarello, P. (2019). *Grey Matter Leonardo da Vinci: A Genius Driven to Distraction*. Brain, 142(6).
12. Tsai, S. (2024). *Top 17 Famous Scientists With ADHD That You May Not Know*. SCI Journal. www.scijournal.org/articles/famous-scientists-with-adhd.

13. Elfman, E., & Griffiths, S. (2012). *Beyond Genius: The 12 Essential Traits of Today's Renaissance Men*. AuthorHouse.
14. Robinson, K., & Aronica, L. (2015). *Creative Schools: The Grassroots Revolution That's Transforming Education*. New York: Viking.
15. Bonhoeffer, D. (1953). *Letters and Papers from Prison* (E. Bethge, Ed.; R. H. Fuller, Trans.). London: SCM Press.
16. Taylor, F. W. (1911). *The Principles of Scientific Management*. New York: Harper & Brothers.
17. Taylor, F. W. (1903). *Shop Management*. Transactions of the American Society of Mechanical Engineers, 24, 1337–1480.
18. Waqās, A. (2019). *The Polymath: Unlocking the Power of Human Versatility*. Wiley.
19. Wales, J.. (2004). "Interview with Jimmy Wales, Founder of Wikipedia." Slashdot.org
20. Wells, H. G. (1938). *World Brain*. Garden City, NY: Doubleday, Doran & Co. https://en.wikipedia.org/wiki/World_Brain
21. Wilson, E. O. (1998). *Consilience: The Unity of Knowledge*. Alfred A. Knopf.
22. Burke, P. (2021). *The Polymath: A Cultural History from Leonardo da Vinci to Susan Sontag*. Yale University Press.
23. Vaidya, S. (2019). *Critical theory: the Frankfurt school contributions of Max Horkheimer*. IGNOU Delhi. https://ebooks.inflibnet.ac.in/socp2/chapter/critical-theory-the-frankfurt-school-contributionsof-max-horkheimer/
24. Graham, C., Williams, G., Bryce, S., & McKenna, J. (April 2023). *Pillars and Lintels: The What's, Why's, and How's of Interdisciplinary Learning*. Royal Society of Edinburgh. https://rse.org.uk/pillars-lintels-interdisciplinary-learning/
25. McGilchrist, I. (2012). *The Divided Brain*. www.ted.com/talks/iain_mcgilchrist_the_divided_brain?subtitle=en&trigger=5s
26. Baker, R. (2024). *Why I pursued interdisciplinary research as an aspiring academic—despite the career risks*. Science Magazine. www.science.org/content/author/rachel-e-baker
27. Berlin, I. (1996). *The Sense of Reality*. Chatto & Windus – published posthumously.
28. Rapoport, A., & Horvath, W. J. (2009). *Thoughts on Organization Theory*. Emergence: Complexity and Organization.
29. Adams, D. (1988). *Dirk Gently's Holistic Detective Agency*. London: Pan Macmillan.
30. Ahmed, W. (2019). *The Polymath: Unlocking the Power of Human Versatility*. Hoboken, NJ: Wiley.
31. Spiro, R. (2002). Cognitive Flexibility Theory: Advanced Knowledge Acquisition in Ill-Structured Domains. The New Educator, Spring 2002. Michigan State University College of Education. www.educ.msu.edu/neweducator/spring02/faculty1.htm
32. Kurzweil, R. (2005). *The Singularity Is Near: When Humans Transcend Biology*. New York: Viking Press.
33. Kurzweil, R. (2024). *The Singularity Is Nearer*. New York: Viking Press.
34. Brynjolfsson, E., & McAfee, A. (2014). *The Second Machine Age: Work, Progress, and Prosperity in a Time of Brilliant Technologies*. W.W. Norton & Company.
35. Carganico, S. (2024). "Embracing Polymathy In A Specialized World." Forbes Magazine. https://www.forbes.com/councils/forbesbusinessdevelopmentcouncil/2024/01/25/embracing-polymathy-in-a-specialized-world/.
36. Morris, D. (1967). *The Naked Ape: A Zoologist's Study of the Human Anima*. New York: McGraw-Hill.
37. Burke, P. (2020). *The Polymath: A Cultural History from Leonardo da Vinci to Susan Sontag*. New Haven, CT: Yale University Press.

6

TURBO BOOSTING OUR SKILLS

In this short chapter, we recap on the story so far in terms of the impact AI is having on knowledge workers and begin to elaborate on the seven power skills that we believe will benefit them going forward if they wish to successfully collaborate with AI.

In the opening chapters of this book, we have been building the case that AI is going to have a profound effect on the world of knowledge workers. We have seen that the widespread adoption of AI represents an inflection point in history – it is a unique, unprecedented technology the likes of which we haven't seen before. We have seen that the speed, scope and potential impact of AI is breathtaking.

We've registered the point that AI is likely to restructure the nature of society and the world of work, with the result that there will be beneficiaries of the technology but also others who may struggle to cope with this change. And we've begun to introduce the idea that we need to seriously

DOI: 10.4324/9781003514879-7

examine the skills that knowledge workers will now need going forward to successfully collaborate with AI.

We have introduced the idea of diverse polymathic thinking and see it as embracing our seven power skills. The authors have taken the view that the combination of skills that will be most in the ascendancy – given what AI can now do better than us humans – will be those that it is helpful to classify as being akin to polymathic.

So in the following chapters, the plan is to look in detail at each of the seven skills that we believe make up this fundamental polymathic view of the world.

But before we get into the detail we thought it would be helpful to the reader to briefly set the scene by overviewing the seven power skills and to provide a brief rationale as to why we have singled out these skills as being particularly important.

AI proficiency

Without question, knowledge workers will need to engage with AI and build a basic level of understanding of how it works and be proficient at a level that enables them to utilise its strength, at the same time allowing them to add those extra human touches.

So our first power skill is called 'The AI Human Interface'. It's all about knowing how to interrogate AI to understand its outputs as a platform for then working to collaborate with this exciting new technology.

Context

In deciding on the skills that humans should prioritise, the authors recognised that in business the ability to understand the wider context is invaluable. So clearly skills around curiosity and what we call 'The Sensemaker' are vital in the AI era.

Clearly, AI will play a major role in being able to analyse swathes of data and information, and to that extent it is helpful in allowing us to see the big picture. But ultimately it is us humans who can apply those final nuanced, subtle human touches based on our understanding of the human condition and our ability to operate as detectives teasing out those little things that may elude AI.

Thinking

Obviously, thinking – specifically clear deep thinking – has to be in the skill set that humans will need to dial up to collaborate successfully with AI.

This has always been a fundamental knowledge worker skill, but the twist is that AI is now much stronger than humans on many dimensions of thinking. And therefore the focus is now on cultivating a particular type of thinking (abductive reasoning), which we will explain later in the book. This is a strength of humans but one with which AI struggles. This thinking involves dealing with imperfect information and navigating high levels of uncertainty and disruption. So our third power skill is called 'The Critical Thinker'.

Creativity

Again, the choice of the skills that humans need to dial up has to include creativity – a massive human forte. But the reality is that AI is already delivering excellent creative outputs itself, and therefore the focus of this power skill is on delivering those dimensions of creativity centred on our human experience that are beyond AI. This is why we call this skill 'The Audacious Creator'.

Planning

Much knowledge work is ultimately about working with information to help organisations better plan for the future. So inevitably we've included this dimension as one of our power skills. Here AI will be able to do a lot of the heavy lifting, including around predictive trend analysis. Therefore, the focus of our power skill for humans will be on our ability to engage in 'mental time travel', that is to look back into the past, learn from these experiences and help shape the future we all want. We call this skill the 'Forward Thinker'.

Business storytelling

Knowledge work has always included the notion of being an effective communicator – able to land key messages. So it's no surprise we've included the art of creating business narratives as one of our power skills. We have called this skill 'The Inspiring Communicator'. But here the point needs to be made that AI is already hot on our heels in being an excellent creative storyteller. Therefore, our skills need to focus on drawing out those emotional dimensions of what it is to be human and majoring on these. AI lacks this kind of empathy and compassion.

Leadership

Our final power skill centres on the role that knowledge workers play in making things happen, leading teams and adding the dynamism needed to utilise the power of AI. But, in the AI era, this calls for a different set of skills from traditional management capabilities. These include adaptive leadership, reflecting the need for flexibility in working alongside AI in such a fast-moving environment. This calls for the skill of being able to take people with you on the AI journey. This is why we've called this skill 'The Galvanising Leader'.

By mastering these skills, you can develop a polymath mind capable of addressing complex challenges with a multifaceted approach.

The polymath thinking concept

As we go through each of the seven power skills in the upcoming chapters, we hope the reader will gradually see how these skills coalesce and come together as being a set of skills that we have labelled as polymath thinking.

It's all about seeing the context, working across disciplines, subtle thinking, applying flashes of creative energy, being able to effortlessly move from the past into the future, feeling comfortable telling stories that tap into people's emotions, and having a sensitive compassionate leadership style.

Applying our frameworks

Before we get underway with our deep dive on each of the power skills, a couple of general observations.

For each power skill, we have outlined an interdisciplinary framework for delivering this skill; this includes spelling out the respective roles played by AI and humans in delivering this power skill. But we should stress that this is simply a thought starter for you to begin reflecting on how to adapt our suggested frameworks to fit your own personality and particular knowledge worker scenario.

Thus, we are not providing these frameworks as the only way of cultivating each of the power skills. So throughout we are providing tips about how you can cultivate these skills in a way that will allow you to adapt and flex the initial frameworks we are outlining.

Let's now look at how we have elected to explain these skills.

Learning the skills in a linear fashion

For the sake of clarity, we will be explaining each of the power skills individually and sequentially in the following seven chapters. However, once you understand each skill, you will be able to apply them more fluidly and simultaneously to solve specific problems.

Generic, not specific, application illustrations

Given the rapid pace of AI advancements, it is inappropriate to recommend specific branded techniques in this book, as they may become outdated by the time of publication. However, on occasion, we highlight broad categories of applications, and sometimes we provide branded examples. But readers are encouraged to explore these examples and decide for themselves what represents the latest state-of-the-art techniques in this area.

Individual and collective skill sets

In the upcoming chapters, our focus is on how individuals acquire these skills. However, there is of course the issue of how teams of knowledge workers can work collectively to deliver these power skills. We touch on this later in the book. In addition, looking ahead, there is the issue of combining collective human intelligence with AI to create solutions – the 'Supermind' concept. We discuss this later in the book.

Summary

In this chapter we have created a bridge between the context we have provided in the opening chapters on the impact that AI is likely to have on the world of knowledge workers and the skills that knowledge workers will now need going forward to cultivate and thrive in the AI era.

Specifically, in this chapter, we've provided a rationale for our selection of the power skills that make up the polymath mind way of thinking that we believe will be necessary to excel in the AI era.

And we've also provided a high-level introduction to each of the power skills which provides the background, in the remainder of the book, for a deep dive into each of these skills.

7

THE AI-HUMAN INTERFACE

In this chapter, we focus on our first power skill: the ability of humans to work symbiotically with AI to achieve superior results. This collaboration maximises AI's speed and accuracy in data analysis and processing large volumes of information while leveraging human creativity, intuition and emotional insight.

Satya Nadella, CEO of Microsoft, said in 2016 during the launch of Microsoft Teams, 'Humans and machines working together can accomplish more than each would on their own'.

By combining AI's precision with human contextual understanding and judgement, we can make better decisions that are both data-driven and nuanced. This partnership creates a powerful problem-solving unit. In this chapter, we explore how to optimise this relationship and identify the necessary checks and balances.

The starting point for knowledge workers aiming to work successfully alongside AI is recognising AI's power and adopting a mindset that

DOI: 10.4324/9781003514879-8

embraces the incredible opportunities it offers for enhancing creativity and productivity.

Thriving in the AI era requires knowledge workers not to feel threatened by AI's capabilities but to enjoy collaborating with it. Instead of resisting AI, we should learn to use it effectively, much like upgrading from a bicycle to a motorbike.

We will begin with a brief recap of AI's capabilities and an overview of the tools available to support knowledge workers. Next, we will discuss the fundamental skills humans need to complement AI outputs with human understanding and creativity.

We then look at various techniques for working alongside AI and for evaluating the possible biases in AI outputs.

The power of generative AI in the knowledge worker context

Generative AI, including models like ChatGPT, represents a major advancement in AI. These models can create text, images and other media outputs that closely resemble human-created content. They are based on machine learning principles, learning from vast amounts of data to produce outputs that mimic the style, tone and complexity of human creations. At its core, generative AI uses deep learning, which involves neural networks operating across multiple layers.

And we know that generative AI does not search the internet or access external databases in real time. Instead, it responds to questions by drawing on the vast patterns of information encoded in its parameters during its initial set-up phase, which is continually updated.

Generative AI processes massive amounts of data at phenomenal speeds and handles complex conversations on general and highly specialised topics. It is adept at natural language processing tasks such as analysing news, scientific reports and social media to identify key trends and sentiments.

Moreover, AI excels in complex pattern recognition tasks that may elude human analysis and can generate predictive modelling and simulations to address issues commonly faced by knowledge workers.

A critical component of generative AI is its ongoing training on diverse internet text and user inputs, allowing it to learn from mistakes, make adjustments and improve accuracy continuously. Models like ChatGPT are not only updated with new information but also constantly refined, enhancing the quality of their responses over time.

From the knowledge worker's perspective, AI's power and potential are immense. AI supports daily tasks by providing answers to complex questions, offering tips and ideas on structuring arguments and more – on a scale unimaginable a few years ago.

Additionally, the rapid development of AI-powered tools and techniques has significantly eased the workload of knowledge workers. These tools enable humans to oversee the outputs provided by AI-driven solutions, covering natural language processing for text generation, summaries, sentiment analysis and translation.

There are also knowledge management and enhancement tools aimed at improving information retrieval, expert systems for data analysis, decision-making, predictive modelling and a range of AI-driven automation tools for workflow and productivity improvement. Furthermore, AI is now capable of music composition and video creation, expanding its utility in various creative fields.

An overview of AI tools for knowledge workers

Artificial intelligence has transformed the landscape of knowledge work by providing powerful tools that enhance productivity, decision-making and creativity. According to ChatGPT (2024),[1] the key tools AI offers for knowledge workers are the following.

Automation tools

Automation tools leverage AI to handle repetitive and routine tasks, freeing knowledge workers to focus on more complex and creative aspects of their jobs. These tools can automate data entry, scheduling, email management and customer service interactions through chatbots and virtual assistants. By reducing the time spent on mundane tasks, these tools enhance overall efficiency and productivity.

Data analysis and visualisation tools

AI-driven data analysis tools help knowledge workers make sense of large volumes of data quickly and accurately. These tools use machine learning algorithms to identify patterns, trends and insights that might be missed by human analysis. Visualisation tools then transform these insights into easy-to-understand charts, graphs and dashboards, enabling better decision-making. Examples include business intelligence tools such as Power BI and data visualisation software like Tableau.

Natural language processing (NLP) tools

NLP tools are designed to understand, interpret and generate human language. These tools are essential for tasks such as text analysis, translation, summarisation and sentiment analysis. For instance, AI-powered writing assistants like Grammarly and content generation tools like OpenAI's GPT-4 can help create, edit and improve text. Other NLP applications include chatbots for customer service, tools for analysing customer feedback and systems for managing large volumes of documents and emails.

Knowledge management systems

AI-enhanced knowledge management systems help organise, retrieve and share information within organisations. These tools use AI to categorise and tag content, making it easier to find relevant information when needed. They can also recommend content based on user behaviour and preferences. Examples include enterprise search engines, document management systems and collaborative platforms like Microsoft SharePoint and Confluence that now incorporate AI-driven capabilities.

Decision support systems

Decision support systems use AI to provide insights and recommendations that aid in complex decision-making processes. These tools combine data from various sources, apply advanced analytics and present actionable insights. They are widely used in fields like finance, healthcare and logistics for tasks such as risk assessment, strategic planning and operational optimisation. Tools like IBM Watson and SAP's AI solutions are prominent examples.

Personal assistants and scheduling tools

AI personal assistants like Siri, Alexa and Google Assistant can manage calendars, set reminders and perform tasks based on voice commands. These tools are particularly useful for knowledge workers who need to manage multiple tasks and deadlines efficiently. AI scheduling tools can also optimise meeting times and manage appointments, reducing the logistical burden on employees.

Creative and design tools

AI is increasingly being integrated into tools for creative tasks such as graphic design, video editing and music composition. AI-powered platforms like Adobe Sensei enhance creative workflows by automating repetitive tasks, offering intelligent suggestions, and even generating content. These tools help knowledge workers in creative fields produce high-quality work more efficiently.

Collaboration and communication tools

AI enhances collaboration tools by providing features such as automated transcription, real-time translation and intelligent meeting summaries. Platforms like Zoom, Microsoft Teams and Slack use AI to improve virtual communication, making it easier for teams to work together regardless of location. AI can also help in managing and analysing communication patterns to improve team dynamics and productivity.

In summary, AI tools are revolutionising knowledge work by automating routine tasks, enhancing data analysis, improving decision-making and fostering creativity. By leveraging these tools, knowledge workers can focus on higher-value activities, drive innovation and achieve greater efficiency in their work. The key is to understand the capabilities of these AI categories and integrate them effectively into daily workflows.

From this high-level overview of AI's impact, let's now examine the role of humans working symbiotically with AI. Knowledge workers should focus on enhancing their uniquely human skills to thrive alongside AI. Now, let's explore this concept in more detail.

A review of the human role in the generative AI era

After exploring the power of generative AI, let's review the overarching role humans will play in this new AI era.

Humans will excel by seeing the holistic big picture and understanding complex nuances beyond even the most sophisticated AI. While AI can process vast amounts of data, humans have the microscopic skills to notice subtle clues that may escape AI. This unique perspective allows humans to act as conductors, orchestrating the outputs from AI to create a cohesive and comprehensive vision.

In the AI era, humans will thrive in understanding dilemmas, conflicts and the nuanced complexities of the human condition. Demonstrating empathy, compassion and high levels of emotional intelligence are areas where humans surpass AI.

The strength of humans in the AI context lies in focusing on higher-order sentient skills beyond AI's capabilities. AI can handle data processing, pattern recognition and repetitive cognitive tasks, allowing humans to unleash their capacity for compassion and creativity.

In the knowledge worker context, AI excels in tasks like data analysis, reporting, routine customer service, scheduling, administrative coordination, generating basic content and managing simple processes. This delegation of tasks to AI frees humans for powerful, creative and imaginative thinking.

Humans' ability to apply high levels of emotional intelligence is crucial. Emotional intelligence involves recognising, understanding and managing one's own emotions and the emotions of others. It requires self-awareness and self-regulation, allowing individuals to constructively manage these emotions. And it includes empathy, the ability to understand and respond to others' emotions – an essential ingredient for effective teamwork and achieving successful outcomes.

While AI can mimic emotional intelligence by following programmed rules and learning patterns, it lacks genuine empathy and deep understanding of human emotions. Therefore, knowledge workers who can oversee AI outputs while integrating their emotional intelligence will be highly valuable.

In summary, humans will lead in complex decision-making, creative and strategic thinking, and situations requiring emotional intelligence, ethical judgements and governance. This is the essence of the human skills that will be invaluable for working symbiotically with AI.

Setting up symbiotic human-AI working practices

Let's now explore more closely how knowledge workers can work effectively in a symbiotic relationship with AI.

Here, to build a symbiotic relationship with AI like ChatGPT and other tools, the following checklist will be helpful.

Understand AI capabilities and limitations

Learn what AI can and cannot do. Understand its strengths, such as processing vast amounts of data quickly, and its weaknesses, like lacking human empathy or contextual understanding. Knowing the boundaries of AI capabilities helps set realistic expectations and fosters effective collaboration. And why not check out online AI courses and read foundational AI textbooks and current AI research papers and follow industry news on platforms like MIT Technology Review and AI-focused blogs.

Before starting this book, one of the authors joined the MIT course, 'Designing and Building AI Products and Services' to get a better understanding of the foundations of AI models and approaches and discuss some the latest applications with innovators in this area. This then opens up a world of forums, newsletters, blogs and conversations which, by plugging into them, really helps deepen one's understanding of this whole space.

Promote collaboration between AI and human teams

Encourage collaboration where AI assists with data-driven insights and humans provide context, creativity and ethical considerations. Combining the strengths of both leads to better decision-making and innovation. It is helpful to review research on human-AI collaboration, such as papers from conferences like NeurIPS and AAAI.

Leverage AI for routine tasks

Use AI to handle repetitive and time-consuming tasks, such as data analysis, scheduling and information retrieval. This will free up time from routine tasks and allows humans to focus on creative and strategic aspects of work. You could also engage with online communities such as Reddit. And check out articles and case studies on AI applications in business and productivity tools.

Maintain human oversight

Always review and verify the outputs generated by AI. Ensure that critical decisions involve human judgement. Human oversight helps prevent errors and biases that AI might introduce. Review best practices from industry leaders, regulatory guidelines and ethical AI frameworks.

Foster a learning environment

Continuously educate yourself and your team about AI advancements and how to effectively use AI tools. Staying updated ensures you can leverage the latest AI capabilities and understand their impact. Enrol in AI and machine learning courses on platforms like Coursera, edX and Udacity.

Develop clear communication strategies

Practise clear and precise communication when interacting with AI. Use specific prompts and provide context when needed. Effective communication ensures that AI tools provide accurate and relevant responses. Attending tutorials on prompt engineering, such as OpenAI's documentation, and courses on effective communication will be helpful.

Focus on ethical AI use

Implement ethical guidelines and practices when using AI to ensure privacy, fairness and transparency. Ethical use builds trust and ensures compliance with legal standards. Monitor frameworks and guidelines from organisations like the IEEE, European Commission and AI ethics research groups.

By understanding AI's capabilities, communicating effectively, leveraging AI for routine tasks, maintaining oversight, fostering continuous learning, promoting collaboration and focusing on ethical use, you can build a productive and symbiotic relationship with AI tools like ChatGPT.

Get started with AI

For some, the challenge is taking that first step to use an AI tool. They know that they should start the journey, but procrastination sets in. One tip here is to apply the principle, 'Where there's a way, there's a will'. This adapts the old adage 'where there's a will, there's a way' to emphasise that taking action creates motivation.

Often, people wait for the willpower or motivation to start something new. However, with AI, it's crucial to begin with small steps. Start experimenting with AI tools, learn from the process and let the confidence you gain build your willpower for larger challenges.

This approach creates a virtuous circle: improved competence leads to greater confidence, which encourages further engagement with more significant AI initiatives, thereby building even more confidence. Don't wait for the perfect moment to start; instead, take small steps and let your progress sustain and motivate you going forward.

So why not get started by experimenting with a large language model – some options include:

- OpenAI's GPT-4
- Google's Gemini
- Anthropic's Claude
- Meta's LLaMA 3
- Microsoft's Phi-3
- Cohere's Command R+

Work out what would be best for you and get started.

Creative prompting with AI

In examining the concept of human-AI symbiotic working, it's important to dial up the art of 'creative prompting'. Being skilled at 'talking' – interacting in an iterative way – with LLMs will pay massive dividends. Think of AI as your 'sparring partner' – it is about taking an initial AI output and then elevating it through a series of intelligent questions.

Let's take an illustration of this process to understand the impact of asking a few creative questions. By doing so, you can significantly improve the quality and usefulness of AI-generated content.

Imagine you're using a generative AI tool such as ChatGPT to explore how to improve the electric car journey experience. Here is the question sequence we followed with ChatGPT. It shows how you can progressively enhance the depth and quality of the AI's responses through creative prompting.

Q1. How can we improve the electric car journey experience?

Response: Making more recharging points available can significantly improve the experience by reducing range anxiety and wait times for drivers.

Q2. What are some less common but high-impact ways to enhance comfort and convenience for electric car drivers during long trips?

Response: Implementing automated route optimisation software that not only directs drivers to charging stations but also provides live updates on the availability of charging points. This minimises waiting times and offers rerouting suggestions to reduce range anxiety.

Q3. How can new emerging technologies be leveraged to transform the electric vehicle travel experience?

Response: Emerging technologies can enhance the travel experience by connecting vehicles with smart road infrastructure systems. These systems can provide real-time updates on road conditions and charging station availability, including the potential to reserve charging slots in advance.

By using intelligent and creative prompts, you can progressively zero in on more specific and impactful suggestions for improving the electric car travel experience. This process demonstrates how strategic questioning can refine and enrich AI-generated content.

Creative prompt engineering checklist

Here we provide a checklist to which you can refer to help you cultivate the creative prompting skill set.

Define the objective: Clearly outline the goal of your enquiry. Specify the type of information or assistance you are seeking (e.g. data analysis, brainstorming, detailed explanation).

Start with a broad question: Begin with a general question to set the context. Example: 'Can you explain the concept of agile project management?'
Use specific and clear language: Avoid ambiguity by using precise terms. Example: Instead of 'Tell me about agile', ask 'What are the key principles of agile methodology in software development?'
Iterate with follow-up questions: Build on previous answers to delve deeper. Example: After receiving a general answer about agile principles, ask, 'How does the agile methodology improve team collaboration?'
Incorporate multidisciplinary angles: Include perspectives from different fields or industries. Example: 'How can agile principles be applied outside of software development, such as in marketing?'
Ask for examples or case studies: Request specific instances to illustrate concepts. Example: 'Can you provide an example of a successful agile project?'
Encourage comparisons: Ask for comparisons to understand differences and similarities. Example: 'How does agile project management compare to traditional waterfall project management?'
Seek practical applications: Enquire about real-world applications or implementations. Example: 'What are some common tools used in agile project management?'
Explore challenges and solutions: Investigate potential difficulties and how to overcome them. Example: 'What are the common challenges in adopting agile, and how can they be addressed?'
Use hypothetical scenarios: Create hypothetical situations to explore different aspects. Example: 'How would an agile team handle a sudden change in project requirements?'
Ask for trends and predictions: Seek information on future trends and predictions. Example: 'What are the emerging trends in agile project management?'
Request step-by-step guides: Ask for detailed processes or workflows. Example: 'Can you outline the steps involved in planning an agile sprint?'
Request summaries and recaps: Summarise the discussion to ensure understanding and retention. Example: 'Can you summarise the key points we've discussed about agile project management?'
Clarify and refine: If needed, ask for clarification or more refined answers. Example: 'Can you clarify how agile metrics are used to measure project success?'
Encourage reflection and insights: Ask for insights or reflections based on the provided information. Example: 'Based on the agile principles discussed, what are the best practices for fostering a collaborative team environment?'

Incorporate feedback and adjust: Use feedback to adjust and refine your questions. Example: 'Considering your explanation of agile sprints, what would you recommend for improving sprint planning sessions?'
Stay organised: Keep track of the questions and answers in a structured manner. Example: Use a document or a note-taking tool to organise the iterative questions and responses.

By following this checklist, you can leverage ChatGPT for in-depth, iterative exploration of knowledge worker topics, ensuring that each prompt builds on the previous one to create a comprehensive understanding.

Sense-checking AI

A key element in working symbiotically with AI is knowing how to sense-check AI outputs to ensure they are grounded in robust, evidence-based data. When evaluating an AI process or model, we need to consider limitations or what MIT Professor Brian Subirana refers to as 'AI cancers'. These are known issues that you'll have to plan ahead for and are things we don't really yet know how to solve very well – although we can work to mitigate some of the effects. Here are seven fundamental questions to ask recognising that generative AI might produce less than reliable answers:

- Is the output generalisable?
- Is it free from bias?
- Is it explainable?
- Is it up-to-date?
- Is it valid?
- Is it ethical?
- Is it just a hallucination?

We look at each of these issues in the following sections. For each, we provide three illustrative questions to help you identify any potential weaknesses.

Is the AI output generalisable?

When evaluating AI-generated answers, it's crucial to determine whether the conclusions are drawn from specific data sets or if they are generalisable across different contexts.

For example, face recognition algorithms run by Microsoft Azure and by Amazon Web Services have tens of millions of faces. Yet they initially underperformed with certain face colours and cosmetics because they had not been fully trained, thus making generalisation difficult. It is tricky because if you overtrain on a missing skin colour and make-up style, you may then skew the algorithms in another direction.

Here are three questions to help establish generalisability.

Q1. What is the diversity of the data used in training the AI model?

This question helps determine if the training data encompassed a wide range of scenarios and demographics or if it was based on a very restrictive set of circumstances.

Q2. How well has the model performed in real-world applications compared to limited validation tests?

This question assesses whether the AI output has been validated in real-world conditions or only in small, controlled environments.

Q3. Can the AI model's outputs be explained or justified logically across different scenarios?

This question helps determine if the AI output varies erratically and dramatically across different scenarios or if it remains fairly consistent, indicating the generalisability of the output.

By asking these questions, you can better assess the reliability and applicability of AI-generated outputs, ensuring that your relationship with AI is built on robust and evidence-based foundations.

Is the AI output free from bias?

It's crucial to ensure that AI outputs are fair and equitable, not influenced by biases that could lead to erroneous conclusions.

For example, Amazon had to scrap a recruiting tool because it showed an obvious male bias when recruiting talent. We don't know exactly why, but possibly this happened because it drew on data from only selected companies that over-represented males in their workforce.

Here are three questions to help determine if the AI outputs are free from bias:

Q1. What types of bias could potentially be present in your training data, and how have these been addressed?

This question helps identify any inherent biases in the training process, such as data that doesn't cover underrepresented groups or reflects historical prejudices.

Q2. Has the model been tested across different demographic groups or scenarios?

This question assesses whether the AI has inadvertently favoured one group over another by examining its performance across diverse demographics.

Q3. What mechanisms are in place for continuous monitoring and updating of the AI model to prevent biases?

This question evaluates the long-term sustainability of the AI model in maintaining fairness and preventing biases through ongoing monitoring and updates.

By addressing these questions, you can ensure that AI outputs are unbiased and equitable.

Is the AI providing explainable outputs and behaviour?

Ensuring that AI outputs are understandable and transparent, rather than mysterious 'black box' results, is crucial. Explainable AI allows humans to examine outputs in relation to common sense and contextual data, fostering trust and accountability.

One of the big issues with modern deep learning algorithms is that they don't necessarily provide any insight into how they reach a conclusion. For example, you try to train an algorithm to distinguish wolves from dogs. And images of wolves have snow, and most images of dogs do not. Perhaps because they are indoor, at home pictures. It may be unclear how the algorithm is reaching the conclusion that a picture is a wolf or a dog.

Perhaps it's simply distinguishing the scene backgrounds and not the foregrounds. Maybe it's easier to find whether there's snow or not. And there is a clear correlation in this example between the two discriminating tasks, wolves versus dogs or snow versus indoor scene. But no real causality. In general, your AI algorithm needs to explain how it reaches a conclusion.

Here are three questions to help ensure AI outputs and behaviours are explainable.

Q1. How does the AI model make its decisions?

This question seeks to uncover the underlying logic and process of the AI algorithms. It helps determine if the AI's reasoning aligns with human logic, industry standards and other human assessment criteria.

Q2. What features or data points does the AI model consider most important when making decisions?

This question identifies the key variables driving the AI's reasoning process, providing insight into the priorities the model follows in validating its output.

Q3. Are there provisions for users to challenge or seek clarification about AI decisions?

This question evaluates whether the training process includes opportunities for users to query or contest AI-generated outputs, ensuring transparency and the ability to seek clarification.

How do you establish whether the AI answers are up to date?

Ensuring AI outputs are relevant, up to date and reliable is crucial. Here are three questions to help determine this.

Q1. When was the AI model last trained or updated?

Establishing the recency of the AI's learning and adaptation process helps you make an informed judgement about its current relevance.

Q2. What sources does the AI use to gather its information, and how frequently are these sources updated?

Knowing the sources and their update frequency provides insight into the timeliness of the information the AI uses to generate its answers.

Q3. How does the AI ensure compliance with the latest regulations or standards in its responses?

This question helps determine whether the AI outputs align with current industry compliance, legal and regulatory standards.

By addressing these questions, you can ensure the AI's outputs are current.

How do I establish whether AI is providing valid outputs?

Establishing the validity of AI outputs is crucial for building trust and reliability in decision-making, especially when the outcomes can have significant consequences. Here are three questions to help determine this.

Q1. How was the AI model validated during development?

Understanding the validation process used during development helps assess the model's accuracy and performance before deployment. Follow-up questions might include: 'What specific metrics were used to measure the model's validity, and what were the results?'

Q2. Can AI provide evidence and reasoning to support its outputs?

Asking this question helps determine whether the outputs were independently verified and checked by experts, adding an extra layer of validation.

Q3. What is the error rate of the AI system in real-world applications?

This question provides information on the error rate, allowing you to judge whether it is reasonable or indicates limited validity.

By addressing these questions, you can ensure the AI's outputs are valid.

How do we know that AI is operating in an ethical way?

Ensuring AI outputs are ethical involves handling privacy, fairness and accountability issues appropriately. Here are three questions to help determine this.

Q1. How does the AI system handle data privacy for users?

This question reveals how AI processes data, especially sensitive and personal information.

Q2. What steps have been taken to mitigate bias in the AI outputs?

This helps determine if the training process was flawed or skewed, leading to biased algorithms that compromise ethical AI functionality.

Q3. How does the AI system ensure accountability for its decisions?

This question examines the mechanisms in place to ensure AI is accountable for its decisions, particularly when those decisions have significant consequences.

By addressing these questions, you can ensure that AI operates in an ethical manner.

How do I check for hallucinations in AI data output?

In the context of AI, hallucinations refer to instances where an AI system generates fake or misleading outputs that are not supported by the input data or expected outcomes. While these hallucinations are expected to decrease as AI training methodologies improve and incorporate more diverse data sets, it's essential to implement robust validation checks in the meantime. To ensure the output is credible, ask the following questions.

Q1. What critical underlying assumptions were made in arriving at this output?

This helps identify the assumptions behind the AI's reasoning and check for any potential flaws.

Q2. What data sources were used to arrive at this output?

Citing the data sources helps verify the authenticity and reliability of the information used by the AI.

Q3. Have these outputs been cross-checked with experts in this field?

Cross-referencing with expert opinions ensures that the AI's output aligns with established knowledge and expert analysis.

By asking these questions, you can better identify and mitigate hallucinations in AI-generated data.

The issue of unintended behaviour

An issue that will be outside the scope of many knowledge workers but one that, for completeness, we should mention concerns working with AI in a way that leads to unintended behaviour.

Let us take an example, an autonomous self-driving car has been programmed to navigate city streets using vision and sensor data. But during testing the car swerves and stops abruptly – potentially causing danger to others – because it has misinterpreted a road sign that had been obscured by graffiti.

The range of steps to take to offset these scenarios take us outside the remit of this book, but the example does register the need for relentless human oversight in the human-AI collaboration process.

Let us sum up by providing 12 simple questions to ask to check the robustness of your AI output.

12 KILLER QUESTIONS TO ASK AI TO CHECK ITS ROBUSTNESS

1. What were the key sources or bases for your explanation of the impact of [subject]?
2. How can I verify the information you provided about [topic]?
3. Would you please provide some differing expert opinions on the issue of [issue]?
4. What are the top three studies or authoritative sources on [subject]?
5. Are there any recent or upcoming research developments likely to change your current understanding of [topic]?
6. Can you identify any potential biases that may have influenced your outputs on [subject]?
7. Which parts of your response about [topic] are based on established facts, and which are more speculative?
8. What were the most critical assumptions you made in forming your view on [subject]?
9. Can you provide the most compelling alternative interpretation of your analysis?
10. How might different cultural or ethnic groups view this issue differently?
11. How deeply have you been trained on your data, and how does this affect the robustness of your answer?
12. What criteria did you use to determine that one solution might be better than another in addressing [issue]?

By asking these questions, you can critically evaluate the robustness and reliability of AI outputs.

Summary

In this chapter, we emphasised the importance of knowledge workers respecting the power of AI and the value of starting to work with various AI tools. AI can provide excellent first drafts and working ideas in seconds, particularly in the field of logical reasoning.

We then focused on the specific skills humans need to develop to work symbiotically with AI, such as emotional intelligence, understanding complex nuanced contexts, and recognising subtle insights into the human condition that AI cannot grasp.

This chapter also laid the foundation for understanding how humans can effectively work alongside AI, highlighting the essential skills and approaches needed for this evolving relationship, including the issue of sense-checking AI outputs.

In the next chapter, we pick up on the next of our power skills – the notion of being a Sensemaker.

Note

1. OpenAI. (2024). *Response Generated by ChatGPT on July 16, 2024*. https://chat.openai.com/chat

8

THE SENSEMAKER

> In the AI era, a crucial skill for knowledge workers is the ability to sift through large volumes of complex and often imperfect information to draw sensible and plausible conclusions. This chapter outlines the specific skills required to become an excellent Sensemaker. Also, it provides a step-by-step process for knowledge workers to follow when dealing with complex and messy assignments, enabling them to identify the key insights hidden within the information.
>
> In the AI era, a crucial skill for knowledge workers is the ability to navigate through complex, often imperfect, information to draw sensible conclusions. Today, understanding complex, interconnected issues is crucial, making sensemaking a critical power skill.

This chapter outlines the essential skills needed to excel as a Sensemaker and provides a step-by-step process for tackling complex assignments. Sensemaking involves working with facts and recognising nuanced clues

DOI: 10.4324/9781003514879-9

to arrive at the most plausible interpretation of events. It is about quickly interpreting sometimes conflicting information from various sources, now often with AI assistance.

We chose the term 'Sensemaker' over others like 'knowledge assembly' because it better captures the essence of combining data with common sense and human intuition to cut through irrelevances and confusion.

> In today's complex business environment sensemaking is the most powerful tool to unlock the mysteries that increasingly complex markets represent. It's not about data collection but about framing the questions that allow you to see what the numbers mean and what actions they should prompt.
>
> (Christian Madsbjerg and Mikkel Rasmussen, 2014)[1]

Defining the sensemaking concept

The concept of 'sensemaking' dates back to the work of Karl Weick in the 1970s, who was one of the first to highlight the importance of sensemaking to the fields of organisational studies, psychology and sociology. The term became prominent with the publication of his book *Sensemaking in Organizations* in 1995.[2]

At the heart of sensemaking is the organisation of disparate pieces of information into a coherent framework so that individuals and groups can understand events and act upon in a relevant and timely way with a full understanding of the likely consequences of their action.

Importantly, sensemaking is seen as a dynamic process that is based on the idea that people make sense of things by seeing the world of their past experiences whilst simultaneously facing forward to new unfolding mysteries and challenges. Sensemaking is seen as vital for helping knowledge workers navigate the continuous flow of vast amounts of information and to helping them craft responses that are informed, innovative and effective.

To bring the sensemaking concept to life, let's explore three illustrations that highlight the craft of sensemaking.

First, consider an episode from the US TV series *The West Wing*. In one episode, a newly appointed presidential advisor asks what his job entails. The response is:

> You're going to tell him how the meeting he's just had with his Council of Economic Advisors relates to the meeting he's had with the Agricultural

> Secretary, relates to his intelligence briefing, relates to jobs, relates to the environment, relates to the campaign. . . . You're his wide-angle lens.
> (*The West Wing*, Season 1, Episode 20, titled 'Mandatory Minimums', 2000)

The critical point here is that the advisor is asked to be the 'wide-angle lens', someone who understands the entire chessboard. He must help the president anticipate what is likely to happen in various scenarios and stay several moves ahead of the game.

Building on this, we explained earlier how philosopher Isaiah Berlin described visionary leadership as having, 'an acute sense of what fits with what, springs from what, and what leads to what'. This emphasises the value of individuals who can unravel the interconnectedness of events and succinctly explain this to senior management, guiding their next actions.

To further anchor the concept of sensemaking, consider how Richard Branson thinks and operates. His vision for Virgin Atlantic wasn't based on traditional business metrics alone. He looked at the bigger picture of what makes for a successful customer experience.

He knew that, if you wanted to be a successful disruptor, then you needed to break out of a limited and preconceived way of seeing the world and engage with the multidimensional nature of the typical customer's experience.

During an unsatisfactory long-haul flight, Branson jotted down on a napkin his ideal travel experience – from home to airport, through the waiting lounge, onto the flight itself, including entertainment and food, and, finally, arriving at the destination.

For Branson, sensemaking involved interconnecting all the different elements of the overall air travel experience. He didn't just focus on the logistics of setting up an airline company – acquiring planes, organising the route schedule and so on. This holistic approach led to the innovative features now associated with a Virgin Atlantic home-to-destination flight experience.

Illustrations of the value of sensemaking skills

To underscore the importance of big picture sensemaking skills, let's examine three cases where the lack of these skills led to the demise of companies and contrast this with a success story where sensemaking revitalised a major company.

Kodak

In 1975, Kodak engineer Steve Sasson developed the first digital camera. But Kodak – being a powerhouse in the photographic industry selling more than 85% of the film sold in the US –, chose to focus on its film business. It mistakenly believed that digital photography would not threaten their market. Kodak's narrow thinking and unwavering belief that digital photography would always be inferior to high-quality film prevented them from seeing the bigger picture.

Had Kodak broadened its perspective and paid attention to the growing consumer support for digital photography, it could have adapted to the changing landscape. By failing to adopt a Sensemaker's viewpoint, which would have tuned them to the nuances of shifting customer opinions, Kodak lost its market position and filed for bankruptcy in 2012.

Blockbuster

In the late 1990s, Blockbuster dominated the video rental market. Despite being aware of the new DVD delivery format, they declined an opportunity in the early 2000s to buy a fledgling DVD company called Netflix. Netflix, as we know today, evolved into a mega streaming giant.

Blockbuster's decision not to purchase Netflix was based on their mistaken belief that their physical rental model would continue to dominate and that online delivery and streaming would remain a small niche market.

This failure to see the bigger picture and consider external perspectives led to their downfall. Blockbuster filed for bankruptcy in 2010.

Nokia

Nokia was the world's leading mobile phone maker from 1998 but was slow to adapt to the market's shift towards intuitive touchscreen smartphones. Instead, they continued producing devices with physical keypads for too long.

Nokia's perspective was insular, hampered by bureaucratic structures and a failure to fully understand customers and its competitor Apple. This opened the door for Apple, under Steve Jobs's leadership, to grasp the big market picture, creating a powerful ecosystem that included iTunes, the App Store and later iCloud.

In contrast, Nokia's outdated and introspective approach led to a sharp decline in its market share. In 2014, Nokia's mobile phone business was acquired by Microsoft.

Having reviewed some not-so-good sensemaking practice when it comes to seeing the big picture and understanding the wider context, let's now look at a success story: how Lou Gerstner turned round IBM.

IBM

Lou Gerstner, CEO of IBM from 1993 to 2002, is a prime example of a Sensemaker in the business world. When he took over, IBM was facing a crisis. It was deeply unprofitable and on the brink of bankruptcy due to its failure to understand the changing market and customer needs.

Interestingly, Gerstner did not come from the traditional IBM ranks, nor was he an expert in IT solutions. He therefore brought a fresh perspective, recognising the need for a major cultural shift. He understood that IBM needed to provide integrated solutions tailored to customer needs rather than producing siloed products that made sense internally to IBM traditionalists but not to the wider marketplace.

Gerstner's ability to view the big picture, understand market and customer needs, and implement a new strategy quickly saved IBM from ruin. He exemplified sensemaking by seeing the broader panorama and acting on it, much like contemporary leaders Elon Musk and Jeff Bezos, who also excel at reading and responding to complexity and nuance.

The building blocks of sensemaking

Having outlined the essence of sensemaking and provided examples of its successes and failures, we now turn to the essential building blocks of this skill and follow this with a systematic framework for applying sensemaking in various knowledge worker tasks.

Dealing with uncertainty

Sensemaking helps knowledge workers manage the uncertainty and complexity they face. In a volatile, uncertain, complex and ambiguous (VUCA) world, AI can support us, but it alone cannot unravel highly ambiguous, complex and fast-moving business situations.

So, to be an expert Sensemaker, you need to feel comfortable with uncertainty and have tools and techniques to cope with it. Here, it's helpful to think of there being two fundamental types of uncertainty.

First, there is irreversible uncertainty – random uncertainty with inherent unknown variability that cannot be controlled. Second, there is reducible uncertainty – which can be defined, probabilistically assessed and factored into the sensemaking process.

A helpful perspective on this comes from former US Defense Secretary Donald Rumsfeld's famous – if initially baffling but ultimately helpful – statement in 2002 where he talks of the:

Known knowns: Things we know that we know.
Known unknowns: Things we know we don't know.
Unknown unknowns: Things we don't know we don't know.

(And we could add to this: the *Unknown knowns:* Things we know but don't realise we know.)

Rumsfeld's framework is useful because it highlights that the approach to tackling each of the aforementioned will differ.

For *known knowns,* we might look for analogies or examples in other settings.

For *known unknowns,* we can build hypotheses, measure, test and iterate.

For *unknown unknowns,* here we face our biggest challenge, but there is an approach we can pursue. For example, we could unearth them through brainstorming or group discussions to draw out implicit related knowledge.

Here everything starts with the need to acknowledge the potential existence of an unknown unknown. So what we can do is to look for indicators suggesting something unknown is happening, akin to finding unseen planets by observing their effects on other celestial bodies.

We are essentially looking for symptoms that suggest an underlying, previously unseen cause. By doing so, we can begin to pinpoint some unknown unknowns. From here, we latch onto these symptoms or indicators, which provide hints that something relevant is happening beneath the surface and needs to be included in our analysis.

Working across traditional discipline boundaries in an eclectic way

Let's move on to the next fundamental aspect of sensemaking: the ability to view a problem from multiple angles and develop new analytical frameworks that enhance our understanding. Here, a start point is to understand different terminologies related to cross-disciplinary work.

Multidisciplinary study

This involves accessing subject knowledge from various fields whilst still working predominately within your discipline. For example, an economist analysing the UK economy's growth might consider psychological and sociological factors. But they still mainly focus on traditional economic theories and principles. The psychological and sociological insights would be treated as separate inputs to the analysis.

Interdisciplinary (or cross-disciplinary) study

This involves working across subject knowledge disciplines to examine a problem from different perspectives. For instance, an economist might analyse the UK's economic growth by linking macroeconomic theories with psychological perspectives on individual company behaviour. However, this approach doesn't merge the analytical frameworks used by each discipline.

Transdisciplinary study

This goes further by developing new conceptual frameworks that integrate perspectives from multiple disciplines. Herbert Simon's[3] work from the mid-1950s onwards is a prime example. He combined economic principles with psychological insights to introduce the concept of 'satisficing' – the idea that people aim for satisfactory solutions rather than optimal ones.

This concept bridged economics and psychology, offering a deeper understanding of economic behaviours. Simon's work laid the foundation for Daniel Kahneman's (2011)[4] exploration of behavioural economics, demonstrating the power of transdisciplinary thinking.

Another transdisciplinary example is the field of sociobiology developed by Edward O. Wilson. This works across the disciplines of biology, sociology, anthropology and psychology. Sociobiology explores the biological basis of social behaviour in animals and humans. It integrates concepts from evolutionary biology, genetics, ethology (study of animal behaviour) and anthropology to understand how social behaviours like mating patterns, social hierarchies and cooperation have evolved.

A further example is the Biopsychosocial Model developed by George Engel, which covers the disciplines of medicine, psychology and sociology. The biopsychosocial model is an interdisciplinary approach to understanding health and illness. It argues that biological factors (genetics, physiology), psychological factors (emotions, behaviours) and social factors (cultural, familial, socio-economic) all play significant roles in health outcomes.

These interdisciplinary approaches highlight the power of combining perspectives and methodologies from different fields to gain a deeper, more nuanced understanding of complex phenomena.

Clearly, no knowledge worker is expected to master overnight all the disciplines relevant to their world. But starting with a broad understanding of key concepts from various fields would be beneficial.

To provide some focus for establishing how far the Sensemaker should cast the discipline net in tackling a challenge, we introduce our interdisciplinary search process. This will help you recognise the range of disciplines relevant to handling uncertainty and complexity in a business context. It will also help you familiarise yourself with fundamental concepts from these disciplines and adapt them to your day-to-day analysis work.

The interdisciplinary search process

The arrival of generative AI with models like ChatGPT offers a fantastic opportunity for knowledge workers to broaden their polymathic skills. By asking a few creative probing questions, you can immediately access a vast body of AI knowledge across different disciplines to address your business challenges.

Here, we outline a six-step process to enhance your Sensemaker skills. This process encourages a polymathic approach by integrating wider concepts and tapping into powerful disciplines to add nuance and subtlety to your solutions. Think of this process as a decision tree where you define your challenge, receive ideas from AI, and gradually drill down to detailed, helpful information.

Step 1: Identify the business or knowledge worker problem

Start by entering the exact nature of your problem into, let's say, ChatGPT. So here AI would start by helping you to frame your overall category of business problem. You would see that your issue falls within the sphere of how to improve your customer experience, for example. In other words, AI will help to locate your issue within the relevant knowledge boundary.

Step 2: Pinpoint relevant disciplines

With the business challenge defined, ask AI to identify different disciplines that could help you better understand the problem. So you might end up exploring the following.

Primary disciplines: Marketing, sociology, psychology, anthropology.
Related disciplines: Cultural studies, linguistics, management science, behavioural economics.
Peripheral disciplines: Statistics, political science, communications theory, design thinking.

Step 3: Overview of disciplines

Ask ChatGPT for an overview of the fundamental roles and contributions of the identified disciplines. For example, if design thinking is relevant, you would receive a subject overview – you would learn that it focuses on human-centred design, innovation management and enhancing user experience (UX).

Step 4: Deep dive into disciplines

Now, select a discipline or combination of disciplines and ask ChatGPT to delve deeper into their fundamental ideas and principles. For instance, if you choose linguistics, you would learn about the following.

Language structure: Concepts such as syntax, semantics, phonetics.
Sociolinguistics: How language varies and changes in social groups.
Pragmatics: How context influences interpretation of meaning.
Language and identity: Targeting messages aligned with audience values.
Multilingualism: Operating in diverse global markets.
Discourse analysis: Language use in different media formats.
Evolution of language: How languages change over time.

This deep dive quickly makes you a 'mini expert' in areas that provide valuable perspectives on your issue. Steve Jobs, anticipating the AI era said, 'Computers are like a bicycle for our minds. They help us to think and to solve problems, and they multiply the power of the human mind'. This was first articulated in a 1990 interview for the documentary *Memory & Imagination: New Pathways to the Library of Congress.*

Step 5: Integrate learnings

Next, combine insights from these different perspectives and apply them to your problem. And then present back to ChatGPT your provisional thinking and ask if you've missed any disciplinary angles or perspectives using creative prompts.

Step 6: Cross-disciplinary synthesis

Finally, it's time to apply your own creativity by combining ideas across your selected disciplines, to come up with innovative solutions and big ideas. At this point you might be developing new frameworks and concepts.

In sum, with AI, you have immense knowledge at your fingertips, enabling you to integrate broad perspectives and deep insights. This approach embodies the essence of a polymath, simultaneously offering a panoramic view and detailed analysis.

However, this method comes with a caution. It is important to perform due diligence on AI outputs by following the sense-checking processes outlined earlier in this book. In addition, in arriving at your viewpoint, make sure you follow the triangulation principle – ensure this is anchored from three robust evidence sources. And, finally, consult an expert in the relevant discipline if a critical point hinges on specific knowledge outside your own expertise.

Building plausible explanations rather than focusing on complete accuracy

Another key aspect of sensemaking is that it prioritises plausibility over complete accuracy. This means making sense of complexity by arriving at reasonable interpretations of events rather than following a series of fully proven, accurate steps to reach a resolution.

Thus, sensemaking does not rely on setting up a hypothesis, proving it correct, and then moving to the next stage based on this proven knowledge. Instead, it involves looking for clues, cues, hints and hunches alongside logical reasoning to develop a reasonable, plausible explanation of events. This explanation can then be reflected upon and refined before making decisions and taking action.

This approach is similar to the entrepreneurial style of 'effectual reasoning'. This involves having a broad sense of direction based on available, though imperfect, information, taking action and then course correcting en route as new information becomes available.

An analogy for this would be the difference between a train journey and a mariner's voyage. A train follows a set destination in a systematic, logical way from station to station. In contrast, a mariner starts with a broad sense of the destination but adjusts course en route based on new clues and hints encountered along the journey, guiding them in the right direction.

Finding simple solutions

A crucial dimension of sensemaking is the ability to identify simple solutions amidst confusion and complexity. This involves several challenges, as captured by Einstein's comment, 'Everything should be made as simple as possible, but no simpler'. This is a paraphrasing of a longer quote from his essay *On the Method of Theoretical Physics* in 1934. The point being that the goal is to find the balance between overcomplicating and oversimplifying.

One issue is distinguishing between 'confusion', which should be eliminated, and genuine complexity, which must be addressed to arrive at a workable solution. Achieving simplicity without ignoring essential complexities involves navigating two competing mental processes.

Thus, on the one hand, our brains are wired to process and simplify information efficiently. Humans often use heuristics, or simple rules of thumb, to cut through confusion and complexity. These strategies help us make quick decisions based on past successes.

Our ability to apply heuristics, combined with intuition and gut feelings, is a strength. It aligns with the principle of Occam's Razor, which suggests that the simplest solution is often the best.

Heuristics can be highly effective, as illustrated by the FAST method for assessing if someone is having a stroke. This method shows how a few key indicators can help us make important decisions without being experts.

Face: Ask the person to smile. Does one side of the face droop?
Arms: Ask the person to raise both arms. Does one arm drift downward?
Speech: Ask the person to repeat a simple phrase. Is their speech slurred or strange?
Time: If you observe any of these signs, call emergency services immediately.

However, on the other hand, there is another mental process in our heads, which takes us to a downside. This is, in our rush for simplicity, we can be deceived by initial impressions. Numerous psychological experiments demonstrate how easily we can be misled by what we first see.

For example, there is the Idesawa Spiky Sphere illusion,[5] where the brain perceives a smooth white sphere surrounded by radiating black spines. In reality, all that exists are the black spines – the white sphere does not exist. But our desire for a simple explanation leads us to believe that it does.

In summary, first-class Sensemakers must apply judgement, addressing genuine complexity whilst eliminating confusion and avoiding oversimplification. This is why we introduce the concept of 'informed intuition'.

Working with analytical frameworks and mental models

In the AI era, Sensemakers now have access to a host of frameworks that will help them quickly grasp the key concepts in play. These tools are at your fingertips, helping you see the broader picture early in the process. Frameworks and mental models help make sense of the world by encouraging conceptual thinking rather than getting bogged down in details.

Psychologists describe individuals with a 'ternary mindset' as those who can step back from a problem and view it from an outsider's perspective, identifying fundamental concepts. This contrasts with 'binary thinkers' who immediately see issues in terms of win versus lose or black versus white, missing the broader conceptual picture.

AI can assist by identifying relevant business models and frameworks for specific issues. For instance, if you are managing change in your organisation, AI can quickly provide key change management models that you can adapt to your situation.

The social dimension to sensemaking

Another key aspect of sensemaking is its reliance on social interaction. A Sensemaker is influenced not only by their own thoughts but also by how they perceive others' perspectives. Sensemaking involves understanding how individuals in social settings are likely to think, behave and collaborate.

In Weick's initial work on sensemaking, this social dimension was critical. However, in the context of this book on how knowledge workers collaborate with AI, we will limit our discussion of the social dimension. However, we will revisit this topic later in the book when discussing the concept of the 'Supermind', introduced by MIT Professor Thomas Malone (2018).[6] This goes beyond the idea of individuals working in teams and encompasses the collective symbiotic effect of AI collaborating with groups of people across different application networks.

The iterative approach to sensemaking

Another critical aspect of sensemaking is that it's an ongoing, continuous process. It is not limited to analysing a specific problem at a single moment but involves examining challenges iteratively. This means starting with an initial view based on available information and then continuously refining this viewpoint, always ready to revise initial interpretations of the evidence.

This iterative approach is central to the sensemaking methods of Pirelli and Card (2006).[7] They emphasise that resolving an issue does not follow a neat, linear path but involves a series of iterative steps, looping back as new information, becomes available.

This concept aligns with the principle of the Hermeneutic Circle approach to reasoning. This method involves starting with a big-picture view based on the current evidence, then reevaluating this perspective in an iterative way over time, as more detailed evidence emerges.

An example of this approach is how early archaeologists made sense of ancient civilisations. When unearthing fragments of, say, a Roman mosaic, they would form an initial view of life in ancient Rome. But, as more evidence surfaced, they would be prepared to revise their overall view.

Summarising the building blocks of sensemaking

The seven building blocks discussed earlier form a framework for knowledge workers to operate as effective Sensemakers in various business tasks. In summary, these are:

Comfort with uncertainty: Feeling at ease with ambiguity and having tools to manage it.
Cross-disciplinary thinking: Engaging with multiple disciplines to gain diverse perspectives.
Plausibility over accuracy: Focusing on reasonable interpretations rather than perfect accuracy.
Simplicity over complexity: Creating simple outcomes from complex situations.
Use of mental models and frameworks: Thinking conceptually and at a high level.
Social interaction: Considering the social dimension of how others perceive and think.
Iterative process: Engaging in a continuous loop of refinement and re-evaluation.

A framework for sensemaking

Let's begin by overviewing the fundamental nature of the iterative framework we are outlining for knowledge workers to help them enhance their sensemaking capabilities.

Here we should stress that our framework is just one approach you may wish to consider. Our intention throughout each of the power skills we are reviewing is to provide the reader with a framework for reflecting on how AI and humans can collaborate to deliver each power skill. But we accept that there will be alternative frameworks that could be developed.

Our Sensemaker framework has three distinct features, each of which is outlined here.

One: An iterative element

Sensemaking is an iterative process. It begins with forming an initial viewpoint, then continuously investigating with an open mind, ready to refine that viewpoint as new evidence emerges.

The Sensemaker progresses forward but frequently loops back to reassess earlier thoughts, constantly revising their initial position based on new information.

Our framework identifies three fundamental analytical loops that characterise this iterative process:

The data gathering loop: Collecting relevant information.
The evidence structuring loop: Organising the collected data.
The story development loop: Creating a coherent narrative from the structured data.

Two: The application of separate analysis frames during each loop of the iterative process

Our framework incorporates distinct analysis frames within each loop of the iterative process. These frames help manage complexity by breaking down detailed intellectual reasoning into manageable parts.

Walt Disney exemplified the use of separate thinking frames. Disney approached challenges by adopting different perspectives: first as a 'dreamer' envisioning the goal, then as a 'critic' evaluating the dream, and finally as a 'realist' crafting a practical solution.

Similarly, Edward de Bono's *Six Thinking Hats* (1985)[8] method extols the virtue of breaking down complex thinking processes into different modes of thinking. Thus, wearing our Green hat we focus on creativity and with our Black hat we focus on critical thinking and so on.

Building on this principle, we have introduced seven analysis frames for knowledge workers to use when tackling problems.

Decision frame: Ensuring the right problem is being addressed.
Scoping frame: Focusing on the evidence needed for the task.

Evaluation frame: Using traditional statistics and research methodologies to assess robustness.
Strategy frame: Building a perspective – point of view – on what the evidence is beginning to tell us about the overall direction of travel.
Experience frame: Incorporating personal experience and judgement.
Enrichment frame: Introducing creative ideas and observations.
Holistic frame: Integrating all sensemaking elements into a comprehensive picture to guide action.

By utilising these frames, knowledge workers can systematically approach problems, ensuring a thorough and balanced analysis.

Three: Bringing everything together to provide the holistic Sensemaker perspective

The next element of our Sensemaker framework builds on the holistic analysis frame discussed above. It focuses on applying a 'fuzzy logic' way of analysing disparate qualitative and quantitative sources of information to arrive at an integrated compelling and robust storyline.

In summary, diagrammatically, the Sensemaker framework looks like Figure 8.1.

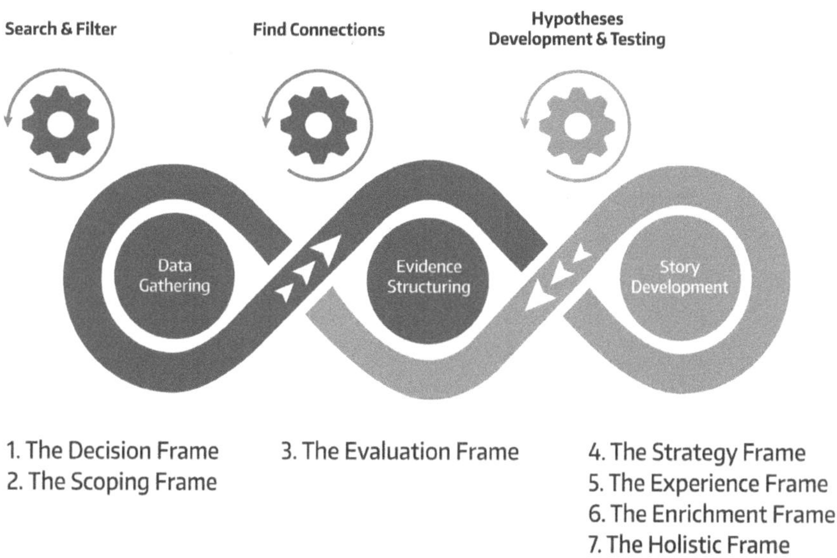

Figure 8.1 The Sensemaker Framework

Let's work through our Sensemaker framework

We will approach the task of explaining how knowledge workers might like to apply our framework when faced with a sensemaking task as follows.

We will work through each of the three main loops in the sensemaking process, and for each iterative analysis loop, we will spell out the specific analysis frames that are most relevant to this loop of the process.

Specifically, for each frame we will identify three specific questions that knowledge workers might like to ask to progress their understanding of the issue under investigation. In addition, we highlight the role that AI can now play in supporting you with this frame of thinking.

And this will lead us to the final loop in the sensemaking process, where we can see how our holistic approach is a powerful way of drawing everything together into an integrated narrative that provides an account of the big panorama.

The data gathering loop

So with the data gathering loop, we are focusing on the process of assembling the relevant information. Here we start by applying our decision frame of thinking.

The decision frame

The decision frame provides clarity about the business question we are trying to address. This is about problem crystallisation: making sure that you're working on the real problem and not just the symptoms.

Here three golden questions to help you ensure you have defined the true problem are:

Q1. What difference do you expect to be able to make by undertaking this project? (And are you sure you don't already know this?)
Q2. What is it you currently do not know that you believe you must know to make an informed decision?
Q3. At the end of this project what decisions do you expect to be able to make with the data?

And with regard to the role AI might play, there are a range of tools that will help you.

We summarise these at the end of this chapter.

The scoping frame

We now move onto the scoping frame. This is about deciding what evidence falls within the boundary of relevance you've set for the problem you're attempting to resolve. It's all about intelligently delimiting the problem.

And when it comes to pinpointing the killer evidence, three categories of questions will be helpful.

Q1. Is it believable? Does it pass the smell test?
Q2. Is this a relevant insight for our key stakeholders? Will it pass the what's in it for them test? Does this tell me anything new? Is it a nice to know or a must know?
Q3. Does this help provide a wider context for understanding the true business question? Does this help me simplify a complex issue or simply add confusion?

And again there are AI tools to support you.

The evidence structuring loop

We now move onto the second loop in the iterative process where we apply the evaluation frame.

The evaluation frame

The focus of this framework is to assess how well evidence stands up when evaluated against more classic methodological and statistical principles such as validity, reliability and generalisability.

Here three key questions are:

Q1. Validity: Is the evidence free from systematic bias?
Q2. Reliability: Will the results hold up over time?
Q3. Generalisability: Can these results be applied across the wider population or are they specific to a set of (unusual) circumstances?

In addition, as part of our evaluation frame today, the Sensemaker will be applying a set of sense-checking questions about the quality of AI-generated output.

The story development loop

This takes us to the third iterative loop, where we start focusing on identifying the emerging story narrative.

The strategy frame

The strategy frame is about beginning to identify the fundamental storyline that is emerging by taking a high-level strategic look at the top-line evidence and beginning to seek out what this is telling us about the overall direction of travel.

Remember this is an iterative process so we can always look back on this initial view and refine it based on the application of later analysis frames and any more incoming evidence.

Here the three key questions to ask are:

Q1. Am I beginning to see a fundamental genuine differentiating insight emerge from the data?

This is a powerful question to ask as you begin to look at the problem from the strategic high ground to get a fundamental top-line sense of what the storyline is all about.

When we refer to the term insight, we are referring to an observation that contains two dimensions. First, there is a 'psychological dimension' to an insight – it needs to describe what is inside a person's mind that causes their motivations and attitudes and beliefs and feelings. Second, there will be a 'behavioural dimension' – it needs to describe what is observable, what a person is or is not doing as a result of these causal psychological factors.

Q2. Is there a solution beginning to appear that echoes Occam's Razor? This is 'all things being equal the simplest solution is usually the best'.
Q3. Ask yourself whether this insight allows you to crystallise something in the mind of a stakeholder that, when this has cascaded

through their belief (thinking) and emotional (feeling) systems, would ultimately encourage them to realise that your solution is genuinely an innovative answer to the problem or challenge you are investigating.

The experience frame

This frame allows us to examine the evidence in relation to the knowledge and norms that we built up through our own experience about how different research and information gathering techniques work in practice.

So some questions to ask here could be:

Q1. What is the success track record of the particular data collection or analysis method being employed? (How far did we depart from the classic gold standard of data gathering and analysis – is our central finding related to an unusual technical feature of the particular methodology being employed?)

Q2. Does the evidence pass the 'triangulation test', that is if we locate our evidence alongside two other pieces of information does it consistently tell us something?

The idea is that with three pieces of information on a particular business issue – each looking at it from a slightly different direction – we will be able to piece together an informed point of view.

For example, seafarers would work out their position by taking a bearing from say a lighthouse and another bearing from a conspicuous church steeple on land and the third bearing from a distinctive rocky outcrop on a nearby coastland. Each bearing is then plotted on the chart that will produce a so-called cocked hat – within the triangle is where you know your boat is most likely to be, although you don't know this with absolute precision.

Q3. Have you applied the common sense test to the evidence, specifically that is have you asked the following. . .?

Did you expect this finding? Do you believe it intuitively? Does this fit with other contextual data that is beginning to support your argument? Is there another plausible explanation for this that I should be checking out? Are there any potential sources of disbelief about this output that you feel you should double check?

The enrichment frame

This frame of thinking acknowledges that it is legitimate for the knowledge worker to go beyond the pure objective analysis of the evidence to provide more colour and nuance by adding their own more personal interpretation to the evidence.

You need to remember that you are 'admissible evidence'. So liberate yourself from the constraints of the literal data and try to bring your own experiences to the evidence.

Here it is helpful to introduce the concept of the 'Compensation Principle'. This is telling us that within reason it's acceptable for the Sensemaker to notice where there are gaps in the information and compensate for this by making informed judgements about what the missing data is likely to look like given the overall contextual pattern of the evidence.

Three key questions to ask yourself are:

Q1. Do you have available important and relevant, robust, contextual data that you could use to apply the compensation principal?

Q2. Are there any perspectives you can bring to bear by working through the interdisciplinary search process we referred to earlier? Are there concepts and ideas coming from different subjects beyond your own specialist field that could add richness to your interpretation?

Q3. Although you might not be able to prove the direct causal link between different factors do you have any inkling about what may be driving the relationship between X and Y? If so, can you introduce into the analysis this plausible but not necessarily totally accurate account of what is happening?

The holistic frame

Finally, we arrive at our holistic frame of thinking, which is the way ultimately the professional Sensemaker will bring everything together.

The notion of holistic analysis finds its roots in the concept of 'bricolage' – the notion of bringing together the most telling pieces of information from a number of different sources to arrive at an insight or observation. This takes us to the concept of applying a fuzzy logic approach to arriving at our conclusion.

This is a way of working with the imperfect information and uncertainty that characterises a lot of today's business environment – but still arriving at a robust eventual storyline. Our holistic thinking – fuzzy logic system – has three core underpinning concepts. So let us introduce the idea of evidence having 'weight', 'power' and 'direction'. Each of these concepts is described here.

Weight of the evidence

This concept looks at the relationship between the overall empirical balance of support for a particular idea or issue in relation to the qualitative depth of feeling being expressed on this issue.

So if you know statistically lots of people support a particular position and also know that qualitatively they feel quite passionate about this point of view, then you have some very rich evidence here.

Power of the evidence

This concept helps us understand the robustness of our narrative in terms of how it fits against classic methodological theory, that is how it relates to formal statistical evaluation criteria. But also, it is set in the context of how it squares with our day-to-day practical experience of how this particular type of research works in generating the evidence.

So if you have some evidence that passes muster with what the statisticians are telling us, and it also squares with your own experience of using this kind of research method, then you have the confidence of knowing it is theoretically and practically solid.

Direction of the evidence

This concept looks at whether the evidence you are referring to is 'internally' consistent. That is, within a specific type of data, how consistent are all the readings that were taken? For instance, if you had conducted 12 focus groups on a topic, how much variability was there across this category of qualitative research evidence?

Direction also looks at the 'external' consistency of the evidence across all of the data sources being used in the investigation. For example, does the qualitative focus group evidence broadly align with all of the consumer survey evidence, and is this consistent with what the industry reports on the subject are saying and so on?

A summary of AI tools to help with sensemaking

When it comes to sensemaking and working across disciplines to analyse and find meaning in large amounts of information, several AI tools can be particularly helpful. These tools can assist with data collection, organisation, analysis and visualisation. The following are some specific AI tools and their functionalities that can aid in this process.

But remember that we are not necessarily recommending these tools but simply pointing the reader in the direction of the categories of AI tool that exist currently and cite some specific applications the reader might wish to check out for themselves.

Natural language processing (NLP) tools

GPT4 (ChatGPT): This tool assists in understanding and generating human-like text, summarising large texts, answering questions and providing insights from unstructured data.

BERT (Bidirectional Encoder Representations From Transformers): Useful for understanding context in text and performing tasks such as sentiment analysis, named entity recognition and question-answering.

Data visualisation tools

Tableau: A tool now AI assisted for creating interactive and shareable dashboards. It can integrate with various data sources to provide visual analytics.

Power BI: Another AI-powered tool for data visualisation that helps in making sense of complex data sets through interactive visualisations and business intelligence capabilities.

Data analysis and machine learning tools

TensorFlow: An open-source platform for machine learning that helps in building and training machine learning models.

Scikit-learn: A library in Python for simple and efficient tools for predictive data analysis.

Knowledge graphs and ontology tools

Neo4j: A graph database that helps in visualising and analysing relationships within data, useful for uncovering patterns and connections.

Protégé: An open-source ontology editor and knowledge management system that helps in creating and maintaining knowledge graphs.

Text analysis and topic modelling tools

Latent Dirichlet Allocation (LDA): A technique for topic modelling to discover abstract topics within a collection of documents.

Gensim: A Python library for topic modelling, document indexing and finding similarities within large collections of texts.

Data integration and ETL (extract, transform, load) tools

Apache Nifi: A tool for automating the movement of data between disparate data sources and systems.

Talend: An open-source data integration tool that helps in connecting, transforming and managing data from various sources.

Collaboration and knowledge sharing platforms

Notion: A tool that combines notetaking, task management and project management, making it easier to organise and share information across disciplines.

Miro: An online collaborative whiteboard platform now AI assisted that allows teams to work together in real time on diagrams, brainstorming and project planning.

Search and retrieval tools

ElasticSearch: A search and analytics engine capable of handling large amounts of structured and unstructured data.

IBM Watson Discovery: An AI search technology that uses NLP to understand and extract insights from large data sets. Now being developed as IBM Watson X Discovery.

By leveraging these AI tools, you can effectively collect, organise, analyse and visualise information across various disciplines, thereby enhancing your sensemaking capabilities.

Actions to take to start thinking like a Sensemaker

The following are seven ideas for enhancing your Sensemaker prowess.

Boost your context awareness – your sensitivity to broader contextual factors

Step back and look at the issues surrounding the problem. This involves understanding cultural, economic and operational contexts and working at how they influence the way you interpret the data and go onto make decisions and take action.

Find ways to sustain and build your natural curiosity in exploring different issues

Acquire the learning agility needed to embrace new experiences and to enjoy constantly seeking out new knowledge and new perspectives on problems. It will be this that will give you an edge over AI analysis of a particular problem.

Cultivate your empathy and emotional intelligence

This will help you understand and respond to the perspectives and emotions of others and thereby facilitate better collaboration between different people involved in the challenge.

Improve your holistic data literacy

Develop the holistic 'bricolage' way of merging together different types of evidence, data and information from disparate sources to identify the fundamental pattern that is emerging.

Boost your technical AI proficiency

Become familiar with the latest AI tools that can aid data analysis and help you in the sensemaking area. Begin to feel comfortable working with AI as your assistant in co-pilot mode on different dimensions of the sensemaking task. Ask AI to focus more around the logical components of the craft, thereby allowing you more time to focus on your strengths in applying creativity, emotional intelligence and ethical judgement.

Enjoy the iterative way of working through various plausible solutions

Sensemaking requires a flexible mindset, whereby you commit to a point of view but are then prepared to revise and refine this as you progress through the investigative process. It's a matter of relaxing into this way of working and not feeling that, because sometimes you're working with hunch and intuition and less than perfect data, what you are doing is somehow not rigorous and professional.

Enhance your ability to communicate persuasively to deliver complex ideas

This involves developing data synthesis skills so that you feel comfortable bringing together information from various sources and converting this into a compelling integrated storyline that will land your message. This is in contrast to your communication being no more than a collection of unrelated silos of data that only loosely hang together.

Summary

In this chapter, we have introduced the idea of sensemaking, which is a pragmatic, eclectic way of quickly making sense of multiple imperfect sources of information to arrive at a plausible, robust, but not necessarily a completely accurate, account of what is happening.

We have explained that this is an iterative process, beginning with a 'data gathering loop'. Then we move to the 'evidence structuring loop', which may mean looping back to look for fresh data sources as part of the iterative process. This then leads on to the 'story development loop'.

With this framework, we broke down the sensemaking task into individual chunks by introducing seven distinct 'frames of thinking'.

Throughout the sensemaking process the knowledge worker will be able to work in a symbiotic way with AI. But it is us humans with our ultimate superiority in understanding nuance, context and subtle clues who explain what is happening in the world that will be in the ascendancy with this Sensemaker craft.

We now move on to our next power skill which focuses on the concept of critical thinking.

Notes

1. Madsbjerg, C., & Rasmussen, M. B. (2014). *The Moment of Clarity: Using the Human Sciences to Solve Your Toughest Business Problems*. Harvard Business Review Press.
2. Weick, K. E. (1995). *Sensemaking in Organizations*. Sage Publications.
3. Simon, H. A. (1956). *Paper Titled 'Rational Choice and the Structure of the Environment'*. Psychological Review, 63(2), 129–138.
4. Kahneman, D. (2011). *Thinking, Fast and Slow*. Farrar, Straus and Giroux.
5. Chater, N. (2018). *How optical illusions work and what they reveal*. WBS, University of Warwick. www.wbs.ac.uk/news/how-optical-illusions-work-and-what-they-reveal-about-us/
6. Malone, T. W. (2018). *Superminds: The Surprising Power of People and Computers Thinking Together*. Little, Brown and Company.
7. Pirie, M., & Card, D. (2006). *Sensemaking: A Structure for an Intelligence Revolution*. Lulu.com.
8. De Bono, E. (1985). *Six Thinking Hats*. Little, Brown and Company.

9

THE CRITICAL THINKER

In this chapter, we explore various ways of thinking and reasoning to help knowledge workers navigate the complex and uncertain world in which they operate. We illustrate different fundamental approaches and emphasise the importance of cultivating an eclectic mindset. This mindset combines logical deductive reasoning with inductive and abductive approaches, which are particularly effective in dealing with high levels of uncertainty and imperfect evidence.

We conclude the chapter by presenting a specific critical thinking and decision-making framework for knowledge workers. This framework demonstrates how humans and AI can collaborate to achieve excellent results.

Many high-profile business leaders cite critical thinking as a crucial factor for business success. Consequently, employers prioritise this skill when recruiting employees. The World Economic Forum consistently lists critical thinking as one of the top skills needed for the future workforce.

DOI: 10.4324/9781003514879-10

Similarly, the National Association of Colleges and Employers highlights critical thinking as a highly sought-after attribute in new graduates. Surveys by LinkedIn and other job market analysts also frequently rank critical thinking as the most required skill in job postings.

Richard W. Paul said, 'Critical thinking is thinking about your thinking while you're thinking in order to make your thinking better' (1993).[1]

Recognising this, we have identified critical thinking as one of the essential skills that knowledge workers need to enhance to work effectively alongside AI and address the question of what exact form of critical thinking humans should now be focusing on given the arrival of AI.

Defining critical thinking

Critical thinking is a disciplined analysis aimed at understanding the truth about issues, solving problems and making decisions based on logical and well-supported arguments. It involves skillfully analysing, synthesising and evaluating information gathered from observations, reflection, reasoning and experience. This process leads to forming thoughts that develop into ideas, providing the basis for sound, logical and well-considered judgements.

Critical thinking requires a rigorous, sometimes sceptical, assessment of data and an open-minded consideration of various viewpoints and explanations. Also, it involves excellent communication skills to eloquently articulate the outcomes of this critical thinking process.

Features of high-quality critical thinking

Comparing high-quality critical thinking with lower-order thinking reveals several key characteristics.

Deep analysis and questioning assumptions: Top Critical Thinkers excel at deep analysis and always question critical assumptions. They apply considerable mental energy to look beyond the obvious.

Rigorous and evidence-based approach: First-class Critical Thinkers recognise the importance of a structured, systematic and evidence-based approach to problem analysis. They seek to verify the facts underpinning arguments before accepting them.

Challenging the status quo: Critical Thinkers challenge the status quo and existing beliefs rather than accepting them without question.
Objective evaluation: High-quality Critical Thinkers prioritise the objective evaluation of situations, attempting to remove personal biases and emotions from their reasoning. They acknowledge the role of emotions and transparently address them.
Balanced use of intuition: Critical Thinkers recognise the power of intuition in problem-solving but do not rely on it alone, as it can lead to an oversimplified understanding of issues.

Classifying different types of critical thinking

Before addressing the impact of AI on critical thinking, it is helpful to classify the different types of critical thinking skills involved in evaluating information and arguments to reach an informed conclusion. This classification provides context for understanding where human critical thinking skills are likely to remain superior to AI and where AI is gaining an advantage in the critical thinking domain.

Let's begin by exploring some key terminologies related to analytical thinking.

Analytical data-centric thinking

Analytical thinking involves breaking down complex information into manageable parts to understand and evaluate each component. It focuses on assessing structures, patterns and relationships to form conclusions.

This is a particular strength of AI, which excels at analysing large volumes of data quickly and efficiently. AI can identify patterns, trends and correlations much faster than humans, making it the preferred choice for analysing large data sets.

Logical thinking

Logical thinking focuses on reasoning and using valid arguments. It involves identifying premises, evaluating the connections between them, and determining whether conclusions logically follow from the given information.

AI excels in performing logical deductions based on programmed rules and premises. It is highly effective in environments where logic is strictly defined and can automate decision-making processes using well-structured logical frameworks.

A notable example is Garry Kasparov, one of the greatest ever chess players, who lost a game to IBM's 'Deep Blue' in 1996. In their initial six-game match, Kasparov won three games, drew two and lost one. Then in a rematch a year later, Deep Blue won all the games, marking the first time a reigning world champion lost a match to a computer under standard chess tournament conditions.

This landmark moment in AI development demonstrated that computers could perform at or above the level of the most talented human minds in tasks involving complex decision-making and strategic thought. It showcased the potential of machines to analyse and make decisions in structured environments and paved the way for AI development in more unstructured scenarios.

Finding solutions to problems

Problem-solving involves understanding a problem, generating and evaluating potential solutions, and identifying the best one.

AI excels at solving familiar and well-documented business problems using existing data. However, humans are better at handling novel or unprecedented situations. Humans can think outside the box and apply intuitive knowledge to seek solutions in ways AI cannot mimic.

Decision-making: Choosing between options

This category of critical thinking involves selecting options based on their potential outcomes, ensuring that choices are made after careful evaluation of relevant information and potential risks.

Humans are essential for decisions that require ethical judgement and nuanced consideration of complex human values and social norms. AI lacks the ability to truly understand the human condition, emotions and broader context in the way humans do.

Reflective thinking

Reflective thinking is crucial for self-improvement and personal growth. It involves deep introspection and reappraisal of one's beliefs, values and knowledge. Humans uniquely possess the ability to reflect on their own thoughts, experiences and emotions. This introspection provides insights that AI cannot replicate, allowing humans to consider the ethical, moral and emotional implications of their decisions.

Intuitive thinking

Intuitive thinking is often described as 'knowing without knowing why'. It is a cognitive process that allows individuals to make quick and effective decisions without conscious reasoning. Often referred to as gut feeling or instinct, intuition draws from the subconscious mind, utilising accumulated experiences, patterns and internal cues that are not readily accessible to the conscious mind.

While intuition can be beneficial by tapping into deep-seated instincts and experiences, it can also mislead us due to behavioural biases and external influences. Sometimes, relying on intuition can be an excuse for intellectual laziness.

Therefore, it is important to ground intuitive insights within the context of other evidence. While intuition can be a powerful ally, it can also misguide us. This is why we advocate for cultivating informed intuition.

Creative thinking

Creative thinking focuses on generating original ideas and solutions from scratch. It involves seeing things differently and making creative leaps to new and unexpected insights.

Humans currently excel in creativity and innovation, surpassing AI in generating truly novel concepts and ideas. While AI can produce content based on existing information and trends, it lacks the unique creative spark that humans possess.

However, we are entering an era where remarkable creativity can emerge from human-AI interaction. Through creative prompt engineering, humans can stimulate and generate creative ideas using AI.

The topic of creative thinking in the AI era is a significant skill, which we will discuss in further detail in a later chapter.

Deductive, inductive and abductive reasoning

We have outlined various critical thinking scenarios and highlighted areas where AI is beginning to play a role. Now let's pinpoint where humans need to enhance their critical thinking skills in the AI era. We begin by examining three fundamental types of reasoning process.

Deductive reasoning

In discussing 'analytical thinking' and 'logical thinking', much of the focus is on deductive reasoning, a field where AI excels. Deductive reasoning starts with a general statement or hypothesis and examines possibilities to reach a specific, logical conclusion. Known as a top-down approach, if the premises are true and the reasoning is valid, the conclusion is guaranteed to be true. For example, if all mammals are warm-blooded (general statement), and all dogs are mammals (specific instance), then dogs are warm-blooded (logical conclusion).

In the field of knowledge work, AI's ability to operate at a scale and speed unattainable by humans means it will handle much of the heavy lifting in analytical and logical thinking. AI often surpasses human reasoning because it eliminates the 'noise' – the variability in judgements that should be identical but are influenced by random factors, as described by Kahneman, Sibony and Sunstein in their book *Noise: A Flaw in Human Judgment* (2021).[2]

This noise includes fluctuations due to local situations, inconsistent information inputs and the mix of personalities involved in decisions. Importantly, the authors distinguish noise from bias, which is a systematic deviation towards a particular result based on identifiable prejudices and selective views.

The book cites numerous examples, such as medical diagnosis, judicial sentencing and personnel hiring, where AI-based decisions are more consistent and reliable than human judgement. Kahneman et al. conclude that AI and machine-based decision-making systems often perform better than humans, especially in tasks requiring consistency and reliability, as they eliminate the noise inherent in human judgement. Their conclusion, 'simple models beat humans', highlights the significant implications for humans working symbiotically with AI.

Thus, the new AI era presents a challenge: the need to accept that machines can be better than human judgement in certain scenarios whilst still recognising the role of human judgement in complex situations that don't fit algorithmic prescriptions.

An example from aviation illustrates this dilemma – whether pilots should always follow the fly-by-wire computer system's instructions or rely on their own judgement based on factors the computer may not have considered.

Inductive reasoning

Inductive reasoning involves making broad generalisations from specific observations and is known as a bottom-up approach. Unlike deductive reasoning, inductive reasoning is not foolproof; its conclusions suggest a probability based on experimental evidence rather than definitive truth.

For example, if every swan we have seen is white, it is reasonable to generalise that all swans are white. However, as the concept of the 'Black Swan' illustrates, there are exceptions, and some swans are black.

Inductive thinking remains a powerful human skill because AI struggles to go beyond immediate facts and has difficulty incorporating contextual awareness and insights outside the immediate data, something humans can do intuitively.

Let us anchor the notion of inductive thinking with an educational example.

Situation: A teacher observes that students who engage in group seminars and interactive tutorials tend to perform better in exams than those who only attend formal lectures.

Inductive reasoning process: The teacher infers that interactive learning and discussion enhance understanding and retention, leading them to implement more collaborative activities in their teaching process. This inference is based on the evidence showing a connection between interaction and information absorption, leading to improved exam performance.

Whilst not watertight, the teacher's experience and the overall pattern of evidence support this inference.

Human advantage: Humans, with their empathetic insights into how learning occurs, have an advantage over AI, which cannot recognise the emotional benefits of interactive learning. Therefore, the teacher can take action on this insight in a way AI might not, given its limited perspective on the overall situation.

While AI is improving in replicating some inductive human reasoning processes, it still benefits from human oversight when operating in this area.

Abductive reasoning

Abductive reasoning, like inductive reasoning, is associated with problem-solving, decision-making, reflective thinking and creative thinking. It starts with an incomplete set of observations and is particularly effective in scenarios with uncertainty. Abductive reasoning aims to identify the most likely explanation for a situation where information is imperfect, and many unknowns exist. This is often referred to as 'inference to the best explanation'.

Humans excel in abductive reasoning by using their broad experiential knowledge, emotional intelligence, and intuitive judgement to navigate complex and ambiguous situations. This type of reasoning is often used to form hypotheses that can be tested and is crucial for making decisions that require more than random or ill-considered choices.

In reviewing abductive thinking, it's perhaps helpful to make a distinction between the ability to solve 'puzzles' and the ability to solve 'problems'.

Puzzle solving involves following a process to reach a definitive outcome – either correct or incorrect. The solution is clear-cut and unambiguous.

Problem-solving involves arriving at the best possible explanation or solution, but there remains a degree of uncertainty about the outcome. Even the best solution may not be entirely certain.

Deductive reasoning lends itself more to puzzle solving, an area where AI excels due to its ability to follow clear, logical processes.

Abductive reasoning is more associated with problem-solving and decision-making, where there is uncertainty and an element of intuitive, hunch-based reasoning.

Thus, while deductive reasoning is the domain of AI, abductive (and inductive) reasoning remains areas where human critical thinking is essential, particularly in navigating uncertainty and making informed, nuanced decisions.

Fusing reasoning styles – a key polymath skill

We began this chapter by classifying separate categories of critical thinking. However, in practice, we often use a mix of thinking styles. For example, consider the game of Mastermind.

The Mastermind game

In Mastermind, one player, the codebreaker, tries to guess the sequence of coloured pegs chosen by another player, the codemaker. The sequence consists of four pegs, each of which can be one of six colours, with the possibility of repeated or unique colours depending on the agreed-upon rules.

The game works as follows: the codebreaker places a row of coloured pegs on the board, attempting to guess the sequence. Feedback is given with smaller pegs: a black peg indicates a correct colour in the correct position, a white peg indicates a correct colour in the wrong position, and no peg indicates the colour does not appear in the code at all. Mastermind involves deductive, inductive and abductive reasoning skills.

Deductive reasoning: The codebreaker can deduce with certainty that a certain colour must be in the code, even if its position is still uncertain.

Inductive reasoning: The codebreaker observes patterns and outcomes over multiple rounds, forming general theories about the codemaker's strategies and tendencies (e.g. frequently using certain colours or avoiding specific positions).

Abductive reasoning: When deductive and inductive reasoning are insufficient, the codebreaker uses abductive reasoning to develop and refine hypotheses based on partial feedback. This involves inferring the most likely explanation from limited and sometimes ambiguous clues, leading towards uncovering the ultimate code.

For example, Alan Turing, renowned for cracking the Enigma code, combined his deductive reasoning skills with abductive reasoning. He not only used mathematical logic to decode sequences but also made intuitive judgements about human behaviour. Turing speculated whether a young, possibly frightened soldier would always follow the strict rules on starting the message encoding process each day by selecting a random number, or would they be more likely to skip this and use the previous day's starting point for the coding process. By making judgements about likely human behaviour, Turing reduced the number of calculations needed to crack the Enigma code.

This type of reasoning – making judgements and decisions based on partial, sometimes inconsistent, information – also explains the methods of many well-known TV detectives who capture our imagination.

Columbo

Lieutenant Columbo from the classic TV series 'Columbo' exemplifies an abductive thinker. Columbo's approach involved forming hypotheses based on partial information and meticulously arriving at the best possible explanation from his detailed detective work.

Columbo's style was about starting with incomplete observations and gradually formulating the most likely scenario to fill in the gaps. His reasoning included taking into account small clues and limited ambiguous evidence, followed by iterative questioning of people and events to help him eventually pin down the hypothesis that best explained what had happened.

Interestingly, his tagline, 'Just one more thing', epitomises the abductive thinking approach. It encapsulates the process of developing a hypothesis, then constantly revising and adding to it by seeking out new information and being open-minded as new details become available.

Sherlock Holmes

Sherlock Holmes's approach also exemplified abductive thinking. Holmes is attributed as often describing his method to his sidekick Doctor Watson as 'elementary'. This implies the value of deductive reasoning. But his approach frequently leaned more towards abduction. Holmes famously said, 'When you have eliminated the impossible, whatever remains, however improbable, must be the truth' (Agatha Christie, *The Sign of the Four*, published in 1890).

This reflects the abductive process of testing hypotheses against the facts and ruling out those that do not fit, until only the most plausible explanations remain.

Having painted a picture of the fundamental types of critical thinking, let's now review some other thinking styles that have become popular and are valuable in helping knowledge workers shape their personal critical thinking style.

Techniques to cultivate critical thinking prowess

Building on the fundamental reasoning styles of deductive, inductive and abductive, there are various thinking styles and techniques often linked to different personalities and thought leaders. We believe that reviewing these will be helpful to knowledge workers who may wish to consider using or adapting some of these approaches to add an edge to their critical thinking prowess.

Clean thinking: Steve Jobs

Steve Jobs is renowned for his 'clean thinking' approach, which was rooted in his belief that simplicity is the ultimate sophistication. This mindset drove him to create designs that were not only functional but also intuitive and aesthetically simple. Jobs took a minimalist approach, constantly asking what could be removed or simplified rather than adding unnecessary complexity. Here are the distinctive features of his clean thinking.

Clear vision and excellence

Jobs began every project with a well-thought-out vision and the determination to see it through. He was committed to outstanding excellence, which was key to Apple's success.

Intellectual bravery

Jobs was fearless in rejecting the status quo and reframed problems from a new perspective. For example, instead of improving keypads, he proposed eliminating them entirely and using touchscreens.

Integrative thinking

Jobs excelled at holding two opposing ideas in his mind and synthesising them into a new solution. For example, Apple combined art and technology to create products that were both functional and aesthetically appealing, thereby generating a loyal fan base.

Master storytelling

Jobs recognised the importance of storytelling in effectively communicating the benefits of his products. His ability to articulate the end product's value was a crucial element of his clean thinking approach.

These dimensions collectively explain why Jobs's clean thinking was so effective for both him and Apple. We will explore the storytelling aspect of his skill set in more detail in a later chapter, focusing on its power as a stand-alone skill.

Lateral thinking: Edward de Bono

Edward de Bono (1970)[3] pioneered lateral thinking, which involves breaking away from traditional thought patterns and discarding standard solutions to view problems from entirely new angles. This technique emphasises stepping back from the problem and approaching it from a different perspective to generate novel solutions. Here is an illustration of lateral thinking in action.

Illustration: Getting home on a wing and a prayer

During the war, returning planes were examined for damage from anti-aircraft fire. Initially, the decision was made to reinforce the areas of the planes that had been hit. However, a lateral thinker proposed a different approach: gather information on the planes that had been shot down and identify the damage they sustained.

The logic was that reinforcing the areas where damage had caused crashes would reduce the planes' vulnerability. This approach was seen as a better preventative measure than reinforcing the areas on planes that had at least managed to return despite the damage.

Divergent thinking: J. P. Guilford

J. P. Guilford (1967)[4] popularised the distinction between 'convergent thinking' and 'divergent thinking'. Convergent thinking focuses on deriving a single correct answer to a problem using a linear, systematic approach. In contrast, divergent thinking involves generating multiple diverse solutions, often arrived at in a non-linear fashion. Divergent thinking is a hallmark of polymaths because it helps them navigate ambiguity and explore a wide range of often risky possibilities.

Illustration of convergent and divergent thinking

Let's say we want to make business meetings more productive, enjoyable and effective.

The 'convergent thinking' approach would follow the linear route of examining the expertise of the chairman, reviewing how the agenda could be better organised and other practical issues such as the layout of the room.

In contrast, the 'divergent thinking' route would challenge the fundamental meeting concept and suggest ideas, such as the 'walking meeting', where teams discuss topics while walking, rotating who talks to whom. And this thinking could lead to the idea of 'standing meetings' where participants are standing instead of sitting, thereby encouraging brevity and focus.

Divergent thinking opens up innovative and unconventional ways to improve business meetings by considering a broader range of possibilities.

Hidden constraints thinking: Dr Eliyahu Goldratt

Hidden constraints thinking focuses on identifying the primary limiting factor that hinders achieving a specific goal rather than addressing symptoms of the problem. This concept was developed by Dr Eliyahu Goldratt (1990).[5] Here's an illustration to clarify this idea.

Illustration: We need a bigger oven

Consider a business selling takeaway pizzas. The owner has taken several steps to improve profits, including encouraging the chef to speed up pizza preparation, increasing the efficiency of customer service, and exploring ways to lower ingredient costs in the supply chain.

Yes the business owner has done all the tactical thinking around improving profitability. But he had not identified the biggest single constraint to the growth of this takeaway business: he needs a bigger pizza oven!

The current oven can bake only four pizzas at a time. This bottleneck is the primary factor limiting the business's growth.

Phenomenon not default thinking: Lego

Phenomenon thinking involves addressing the core problem rather than just its symptoms. This approach goes beyond superficial analysis to deeply understand the issue at hand. It prompts us to avoid default thinking – automatically going to a familiar way of solving a problem.

Christian Madsbjerg and Mikkel B. Rasmussen illustrate this concept in their book *The Moment of Clarity*, using Lego's revitalisation as an example (2014).[6]

Lego's transformation

Lego's sales had plateaued, and the 'default thinking' response would have been to offer more types of assembly kits.

But Lego realised that 'phenomenon thinking' was called for – it needed to delve deeper and understand what truly made the brand unique. They discovered that Lego wasn't only about assembling plastic bricks – it was strongly associated with creative play. This triggered the idea of inspiring and developing the builders of tomorrow – the theme of the first Lego movie!

This insight led to a new vision: 'Inventing the future of play'.

By shifting from default thinking to phenomenon thinking, Lego was able to revitalise its brand and significantly improve its fortunes.

The jobs to be done concept: Clayton Christensen

Continuing the theme of addressing the core problem, the 'jobs to be done' approach, pioneered by Clayton Christensen and his colleagues at Harvard Business School (2003),[7] provides a valuable framework. This technique focuses on identifying the fundamental tasks or 'jobs' that customers need to accomplish in using a product or service.

Illustration of a 'jobs to be done' analysis

Consider the challenge of improving a health magazine subscription service. Understanding the specific 'jobs' that customers need the magazine to do can guide enhancements.

The analysis might reveal that customers seek the magazine to:

- Provide up-to-date health information
- Entertain and offer a break from daily routines
- Reflect their identity and enhance their self-concept as being informed about health issues
- Connect them with a community of like-minded individuals

This insight about being part of a like-minded community could lead to ideas such as introducing exclusive networking events and online forums for fellow subscribers.

Thus, by identifying 'community building' as a top-level job that customers are seeking, the magazine can now better meet its readership needs.

Lean thinking: Toyota

Lean thinking is a methodology initially pioneered by Toyota. It focuses on identifying what matters most to the customer and improving productivity, efficiency and reducing waste throughout the system. This approach emphasises measuring, assessing and correcting duplication; avoiding over-complication and unnecessary activities; streamlining cumbersome or muddled processes and simplifying labelling and eliminating superfluous elements.

Another example of lean thinking is McDonald's. They are constantly refining food preparation and serving processes to improve efficiency and customer experience. Also, Disney regularly reviews and applies lean thinking to enhance operational effectiveness and the enjoyment of the customer experience.

Here the key lesson is that the well-rounded polymath will be able to deconstruct processes, apply their own creativity and improve them.

The minimal viable product (MVP) concept: Eric Ries

Popularised by Eric Ries, the MVP concept focuses on identifying the most critical and important features of a product (2011).[8] The idea is to create a version requiring minimal investment in time and resources, then test this prototype to determine if it's worth further development. This approach emphasises starting the evaluation process by testing the core assumptions underpinning your idea.

Illustration: Buying shoes online

When Zappos considered selling shoes online, they needed to test the assumption that people would buy shoes without trying them on first. They set up a simple website offering shoes for sale online (without having the full delivery infrastructure in place). By gauging the response, they could see if there was interest. Initially, they sent out shoes sourced from a conventional retailer whilst they then developed the online delivery system.

This approach allowed Zappos to validate their concept with minimal initial investment, demonstrating the effectiveness of the MVP methodology.

The effectual reasoning style: Saras D. Sarasvathy

Effectual reasoning, a critical thinking style closely associated with the entrepreneurial mindset, was advanced by Professor Saras D. Sarasvathy (2001).[9] This approach begins with having a general idea of a goal, which is then refined and evolves as you learn. This is in contrast to classic deductive reasoning that starts with a predetermined goal and follows a set process to achieve it. The key characteristics of effectual reasoning are as follows.

Starting with available resources: Begin with what you have and adapt as you go.
Learning and adapting: Progress through continuous learning and adjustments.
Flexible goals: Set off without full information or a clear end goal, adjusting course along the way.

Let's take an analogy. Classic reasoning is like a train journey from London to Scotland, with a predetermined route and destination.

In contrast, effectual reasoning is like a boat journey across the English Channel to Northern France, where the route is determined by wind and tide, requiring course corrections based on encountered conditions.

Effectual reasoning is vital for those with a polymath mindset, especially when working alongside AI. It introduces a flexible problem-solving approach that leverages human intuition and adaptability – qualities where AI may struggle.

In summary, effectual reasoning is a valuable skill for polymaths, enabling them to navigate complex environments creatively and opportunistically.

Renegade thinking: Rory Sutherland

Renegade thinking focuses on unconventional, 'outside the box' approaches to problem-solving, often employing seemingly illogical methods to find innovative solutions. A notable proponent of this approach is Rory Sutherland, whose book *Alchemy: The Surprising Power of Ideas That Don't Make Sense* (2019)[10] epitomises polymath thinking. Sutherland explores the intersection of behavioural science, marketing and human psychology, advocating for the use of irrationality to drive innovation.

The key features of this style of thinking are the following.

Beyond data-driven solutions: The argument is that validated data-driven solutions are not always the best or most effective.
Understanding context: The importance of understanding the broader context when solving problems.
Counter-intuitive thinking: The value of challenging conventional wisdom and embracing serendipity and chance.
Non-logical reasoning: The power of applying non-logical reasoning to arrive at creative solutions.

Examples from Alchemy

High-speed rail in the UK: Sutherland suggests that instead of focusing on speeding up trains to save 20 minutes between London and Manchester, it would be more effective to use information technology to reduce passenger waiting times on the platform.
Encouraging safe driving in Sweden: Instead of just punishing speeding drivers, Sweden incentivised safe driving by entering non-speeding drivers into a lottery, with rewards funded by the fines from speeding tickets.

The aim of this section has been to encourage knowledge workers to combine different thinking styles. This eclectic approach forms the basis for building a productive symbiotic relationship with AI, leveraging human intuition and adaptability to creatively solve complex problems.

Building a best practice critical thinking mindset

Let's look at three ways to build the thinking skills with work alongside AI.

Complementarity

Complementarity in decision-making involves embracing the strengths of both AI and human capabilities. While AI excels in deductive reasoning, humans possess the ability to interpret nuances and address cultural, emotional and ethical issues in ways that AI cannot.

AI superiority: AI has enormous power and is superior to human capability in many areas of deductive reasoning.
Human strengths: Humans can interpret nuances, understand different cultures, exhibit emotional intelligence and address ethical issues effectively.
Collaborative approach: Begin the critical thinking process by recognising and leveraging the respective strengths of both AI and humans.

By understanding and integrating the strengths of both parties, decision-making becomes more robust and comprehensive.

Know yourself

It is well known that there are those whose dominant thinking style is left-brain in the sense that it favours logical, analytical detailed thinking. This is in contrast to those who have a more right- brain dominant thinking style, which is associated with intuitive, holistic, often more emotional based and creative thinking.

In reality, individuals are a blend of both styles. For instance, Einstein combined brilliant left-brain thinking in physics with right-brain creativity to think outside conventional boundaries.

So it is important to recognise your dominant style – identify whether you are more left-brain or right-brain dominant. Use this self-awareness to develop a thinking style that works for you, reflecting on the approaches we have reviewed earlier.

The aim is to be open-minded, avoid defaulting to a single thinking style. So stay flexible and pragmatic. Throughout, combine analytical and intuitive approaches. And leverage AI – know where it can assist and support you in your decision-making.

Enjoy mastering the thinking craft – honour the struggle

Writer Germaine Greer once listed 'thinking' as her hobby, highlighting the dedication required to be a Critical Thinker. The essence of this anecdote is that critical thinking involves embracing the challenging process of thoroughly examining an issue to ensure the highest quality of thought.

Steve Jobs said, during a 1998 interview with *BusinessWeek*, 'Simple can be harder than complex. You have to work hard to get your thinking clean to make it simple, but it's worth it in the end because once you get there, you can move mountains'.

So the more you can put in the homework to understand the craft of critical thinking the more this will pay dividends. It will give you the frameworks you need to develop the mind of a Critical Thinker who can work alongside AI to bring that forensic human energy to problem-solving.

The cognitive biases that influence decision-making

Understanding critical thinking involves recognising the cognitive biases and influences that can impede sound decision-making. There is an old adage along the lines of, 'People don't so much have a point of view, they just rearrange their prejudices!'

Here, we review some common biases and how they can affect critical thinking, along with strategies to mitigate them. By understanding and mitigating these cognitive biases, you can enhance your decision-making skills and work more effectively alongside AI. Mitigation strategies include the following.

Self-awareness: Be aware of your own biases and actively question them.
Diverse perspectives: Seek input from diverse sources to counteract personal biases.
AI assistance: AI can help prevent suboptimal decision-making by offering unbiased insights and highlighting potential biases.

Twenty mistakes humans often make when arriving at decisions and how AI can help prevent them

1. **Confirmation bias:** Favouring information that conforms to existing beliefs. AI can provide data-driven insights and highlight information that contradicts common biases, encouraging more balanced decision-making.
2. **Anchoring bias:** Relying too heavily on the first piece of information offered (the anchor). AI systems can recalibrate the decision-making process by introducing multiple reference points.
3. **Overconfidence:** Overestimating one's own ability to perform tasks or to make accurate predictions. AI can provide probability-based outcomes and risk assessments to temper overconfidence with realistic data.
4. **Availability heuristic:** Overvaluing information that comes to mind quickly. AI can systematically analyse a broader set of data to ensure decisions are based on all relevant information, not just the most memorable.
5. **Status quo bias:** Preferring options that perpetuate the existing situation. AI models can simulate the outcomes of various change scenarios, demonstrating the potential benefits of different approaches.
6. **Affect heuristic:** Making decisions based on emotions. AI's data-driven approach can help focus decisions on factual information rather than emotional responses.
7. **Bandwagon effect:** Doing things because others are doing them, regardless of personal beliefs. AI can provide personalised recommendations based on individual data analysis, reducing the influence of others' decisions.
8. **Dunning-Kruger effect:** The less knowledgeable or skilled individuals are, the more likely they are to overestimate their own ability. AI can assess skills and knowledge levels objectively, providing feedback and recommendations for improvement.
9. **Framing effect:** Making decisions based on how information is presented rather than just on the facts. AI can reframe the same information in multiple neutral ways to help individuals evaluate situations more objectively.
10. **Sunk cost fallacy:** Continuing a project or consuming more resources because substantial resources have already been spent. AI can provide ongoing cost–benefit analyses to help determine when to cut losses on unprofitable endeavours.

11. **Halo effect:** Allowing one positive characteristic of a person to influence the overall judgement of them. AI algorithms can evaluate individuals based on multiple criteria, ensuring a more balanced view that avoids the halo effect.
12. **Hindsight bias:** Believing after an event has occurred that one could have predicted the event beforehand. AI can document decision-making processes and forecasts, providing clear references for evaluating what was actually known and predicted at the time.
13. **Optimism bias:** The tendency to be over-optimistic, underestimating greatly the probability of undesirable outcomes. AI can simulate worst-case scenarios and generate risk assessments to counteract unwarranted optimism.
14. **Planning fallacy:** Underestimating the time, costs and risks of future actions while overestimating the benefits. AI can analyse historical data to provide more accurate estimates for project timelines and budgets.
15. **Selective perception:** Ignoring information that does not conform to one's beliefs. AI can highlight critical information that might be overlooked due to selective perception.
16. **Groupthink:** The practice of thinking or making decisions as a group in a way that discourages creativity or individual responsibility. AI can provide an external, unbiased perspective to counteract the effects of groupthink.
17. **Gambler's fallacy:** Believing that past events affect the likelihood of something happening in the future. AI can use precise calculations to explain probability and ensure decisions are based on likelihood rather than superstition.
18. **In-group bias:** Favouring one's own group. AI can use anonymised data to ensure fair treatment and decisions devoid of in-group bias.
19. **Neglect of probability:** Ignoring the probability of events when making a decision under uncertainty. AI systems can calculate and present the probabilities of different outcomes clearly to inform decisions.
20. **Information overload:** Facing so much information that decision-making abilities are impaired. AI can filter and prioritise information based on its relevance, helping decision-makers focus on what is most important.

We now move on to creating an overall framework for decision-making.

Towards building a framework for critical thinking and decision-making

To develop a framework that enables effective collaboration between humans and AI in decision-making, we must challenge the tendency to favour the binary, confrontational approach.

Hans Rosling, a polymath comfortable across various fields, was a notable critic of binary thinking. He saw this as a barrier to creative problem-solving. He argued that binary thinking limited possibilities. He advocated for considering a full range of options and avoiding the premature dismissal of exciting opportunities and transformational ideas.

In 2018, he stated:

> Human beings have a strong dramatic instinct towards binary thinking, a basic urge to divide things into two distinct groups, with nothing but an empty gap in between. We love to dichotomize. Good versus bad. Heroes versus villains. My country versus the rest. Dividing the world into two distinct sides is simple and intuitive, and also dramatic because it implies conflict, and we do it without thinking, all the time.

The binary approach helps cultivate a decision paradigm that often involves making a decision and then convincing others to support it. This can lead to dysfunctional behaviours, polarisation of viewpoints and a focus on winning arguments rather than finding informed, evidence-based solutions.

An approach that offsets this premature closing down of opportunities is decision-choice framing. It was Lou Gerstner, the former chairman of IBM, whom we mentioned previously, who emphasised that 'Decision-making is easy once someone has framed the decision choices for me' (2002).

One methodology that underlines the power of the decision-choice framing approach is the CIA's Analysis of Competing Hypotheses (ACH).[11] This decision-making process allows the CIA to critically evaluate complex scenarios to arrive at an informed Point of View (POV). The ACH method involves setting up and framing different scenarios and hypotheses and then applying a rigorous process to evaluate the strengths and weaknesses of each hypothesis. The steps are summarised in the following.

THE CIA ANALYSIS OF COMPETING HYPOTHESES (ACH) TECHNIQUE

Step 1: Identify possible hypotheses

Begin by brainstorming all the obvious and also non-obvious hypotheses about the issue under investigation.

Step 2: Collect information and evidence

Drawing on a broad range of sources, compile the evidence relevant to each hypothesis.

Step 3: Critically and systematically evaluate each piece of evidence with regard to its validity and reliability and relevance to the hypothesis

Each piece of evidence is assigned a rating that reflects its impact on the likelihood of each hypothesis being true.

Step 4: Prepare a matrix. On one axis of the matrix list each hypothesis and on the other the evidence

This visual representation helps build a picture of how the evidence is beginning to stack up in relation to each hypothesis.

Step 5: Refine the matrix and reassess each hypothesis

This phase is about looking for patterns that are beginning to emerge but also inconsistencies and contradictions that could lead you to refine or eliminate certain hypotheses.

Step 6: Analyse the diagnostic value of each piece of evidence

This is about identifying how strongly each item of evidence supports one hypothesis over another and helps with the process of advancing some but eliminating other hypotheses.

Step 7: Draw tentative conclusions

The matrix analysis now allows the analyst to start prioritising the hypothesis that is most likely to be true.

Step 8: Seek disconfirming evidence

Now actively seek out evidence that could disprove the leading hypothesis. This is important to avoid confirmation bias, where the analyst might favour information that confirms their preconceptions.

Step 9: Report conclusions

Once each hypothesis has been tested against the evidence, it is possible to start compiling a report stating which hypothesis is most likely to be true based on the evidence and outline the areas of uncertainty when no conclusive evidence is available.

So, in summary, the CIA approach is a rigorous step-by-step process of ensuring that all hypotheses are closely evaluated without prejudice in an objective way using the best available evidence whilst critically avoiding confirmation bias and the analyst leaping to a preconceived conclusion.

With robust frameworks like the CIA's Analysis of Competing Hypotheses (ACH) being available, it is perplexing that the UK Post Office's management did not adopt a similar approach to avoid the scandal (which came to a head in 2022) and wrongful imprisonment of sub-postmasters. When faced with allegations that postmasters were stealing, the Post Office should have considered the following alterative hypotheses.

Hypothesis 1: A large number of postmasters independently decided to steal money from the post office.
Hypothesis 2: There was a fault in the Horizon IT system, causing money to be taken from local post office accounts without the knowledge of postmasters or management.

Instead, the post office management primarily focused on the theft hypothesis, neglecting the possibility of an IT fault. This failure to adequately investigate the second hypothesis led to wrongful prosecutions and the jailing of innocent postmasters.

So returning to our framework for critical thinking and decision-making, we are arguing for a move away from binary thinking towards adopting a decision-choice framing approach. This allows us to consider multiple valid options, reduces polarisation and achieves more informed and effective outcomes.

A decision framing model to foster human-AI collaboration

So let's look at a possible decision-making framework for knowledge workers – one that spells out the roles played by humans and AI.

With our approach, we begin by framing the strategic choices that are open to deal with this particular issue. The framework involves presenting the pros and cons of each decision option as we proceed to arrive at a final informed choice.

The fundamental benefit of the framing choices approach is that it opens up the opportunity for the human dimension of critical thinking that we've been highlighting earlier whilst also acknowledging the way AI will be playing a role in different parts of the process.

Let us walk through the process outline and review the respective roles played by humans and AI.

Stage 1: Map the decision choices

- Collaborate with AI to identify the initial decision choices. (Typically, there might be around four to six scenarios.)
- Use an initial SWOT analysis, leveraging AI to analyse strengths, weaknesses, opportunities and threats.
- Prioritise the top three options based on this analysis.

Stage 2: Explore the opportunities

- List the pros and cons for each decision choice.
- Use AI for creative prompting to explore different angles and perspectives.
- Add human insight by applying critical and abductive thinking.

Stage 3: Assess risks

- Present evidence suggesting risks for each option.
- Use AI to identify additional risk perspectives.
- Combine AI findings with human intuitive observations to evaluate risks.

Stage 4: Unearth the complexities

- Identify and clarify confusing issues for each option. Here it's helpful to use the Cynefin framework to classify problems.[12]
- Use AI to provide new angles and perspectives.
- Ultimately, apply human judgement to resolve complexities.

Stage 5: Estimate the likelihood of success

- Assess each option's likelihood of success with supporting evidence.
- Use AI for formal evaluation techniques like Bayesian thinking and probability assessments.
- Add human intuition to refine the AI-generated analysis.

Stage 6: Consider the consequences

- Use AI to broaden the understanding of potential consequences for each option.
- Review the interdisciplinary search process (see Chapter 8) and employ 'What If' scenarios to explore impacts.
- Consider AI responses and human insights to gauge consequences.

Stage 7: Review and recommend

- Review all previous steps for each decision choice.
- Use AI to set up decision tree techniques and other decision-making systems like Mini Max Regret Strategy and Multi-Criteria Decision Analysis.
- Now base the final recommendation on human judgement, incorporating empathy and a comprehensive understanding of the nuances in play – the application of detective-like skills that are the sum of the way the polymath will look at the world.

In sum, by following this structured approach, we can ensure a thorough and balanced evaluation of options, leveraging both AI capabilities and human critical thinking.

Practical actions to make leading-edge critical thinking a habit

Let's conclude this chapter with a checklist of actions to build critical thinking excellence.

Apply common sense

Common sense first: Begin by ensuring that you can explain what is happening to yourself in simple terms. Do this before relying solely on an AI-generated outcome.

Sense-checks: Use the sense-checks listed in Chapter 7 to avoid starting with a flawed premise. Remember the advice from statisticians: 'Any figure that looks particularly interesting is probably wrong' – so verify it.

Attention to detail: Combine big-picture thinking with meticulous attention to detail – a key polymath skill.

Work with AI, not against it

Leverage AI strengths: Recognise AI's superiority in logical reasoning. Embrace its capabilities and collaborate effectively.

Embrace simplicity

Occam's razor: Default to the simplest solution first, as it is usually the best. Cut out unnecessary confusion and focus on genuine complexity that needs resolving. This approach requires commitment, energy and hard work.

Touch the human condition

Polymaths approach decision-making with empathy and compassion, seeking angles and perspectives that AI might miss but are crucial for making the right decision.

Polymaths put on their empathetic hat and look beyond the obvious, understanding that emotion can be a powerful driver in decision-making. They understand that in a straight choice between emotion and reason, emotion usually wins.

They act as detectives, piecing together subtle clues that could lead in a different direction. They look for complex contextual interrelationships, counter-intuitive attitudes, unusual outlier behaviour and trending social media narratives.

By linking these clues with their intuition, creativity and flair, polymaths can make a significant difference in achieving the right decision. This holistic approach combines analytical and emotional insights for a more comprehensive understanding.

Sounding board and reflection

Polymaths understand the importance of using a sounding board before making decisions. They value strategic conversations with team members to explore decision choices. This dialogue helps them gain insights and learn from different perspectives. Additionally, they enjoy engaging in one-on-one interrogative 'dialogue' with AI to examine various angles before finalising a decision.

Playing the renegade

Polymaths embrace unconventional thinking. They approach problems from every angle, including sideways and upside down, to see if an unusual or quirky perspective might lead to a better decision. This renegade mindset helps uncover insights that might otherwise be missed, ensuring a more thorough and innovative decision-making process.

Stay curious, ask questions and self-monitor

It is crucial to develop a deep understanding of situations by constantly asking questions. This is a hallmark of quality critical thinking.

To cultivate curiosity, always be seeking a deep understanding of the topic you are investigating. Develop the habit of always getting to the root cause of any situation. Continuously ask questions to ensure you fully grasp what's happening.

Ensure you can convincingly explain the situation to yourself. Ask, 'Do I really believe it?'

Einstein said, 'If you can't explain it to a six-year-old, you don't understand it yourself'.

Apply self-monitoring: after something is explained to you, be honest with yourself to determine whether you have a superficial grasp or if you need to ask more questions to uncover the true causes and fundamental drivers behind a phenomenon.

By following these practical actions, you can cultivate leading-edge critical thinking as a consistent habit.

Summary

In this chapter, we began by outlining various types of critical thinking that can be applied to problem-solving. This is essential in a world filled with misinformation and poorly grounded arguments. The ability to apply critical thinking, especially in conjunction with AI, becomes a crucial skill in discovering the truth.

We then explored specific approaches adopted by academics and business leaders to help you identify your own critical thinking style.

Next, we provided a framework to help knowledge workers apply critical thinking to successful decision-making. This model demonstrated how AI, leveraging its strengths, can work alongside humans who will be contributing context awareness, emotional intelligence and nuance to the decision-making process.

Notes

1. Paul, R. W. (1993). *Critical Thinking: What Every Person Needs to Survive in a Rapidly Changing World*. The Foundation for Critical Thinking.
2. Kahneman, D., Sibony, O., & Sunstein, C. R. (2021). *Noise: A Flaw in Human Judgment*. Little, Brown Spark.
3. De Bono, E. (1970). *Lateral Thinking: Creativity Step by Step*. Harper & Row.
4. Guilford, J. P. (1967). *The Nature of Human Intelligence*. McGraw-Hill.
5. Goldratt, E. (1990). *The Theory of Constraints: What Is This Thing Called TOC and How Should It Be Implemented?* North River Press.
6. Madsbjerg, C., & Rasmussen, M. (2014). *The Moment of Clarity: Using the Human Sciences to Solve Your Toughest Business Problems*. Harvard Business Review Press.

7. Christensen, C. M., & Raynor, M. E. (2003). *The Innovator's Solution: Creating and Sustaining Successful Growth*. Harvard Business School Press.
8. Ries, E. (2011). *The Lean Startup: How Today's Entrepreneurs Use Continuous Innovation to Create Radically Successful Businesses*. Crown Business.
9. Sarasvathy, S. D. (2001). *Causation and Effectuation: Toward a Theoretical Shift from Economic Inevitability to Entrepreneurial Contingency*. Academy of Management Review, 26(2), 243–263.
10. Sutherland, R. (2019). *Alchemy: The Dark Art and Curious Science of Creating Magic in Brands, Business, and Life*. William Morrow.
11. Heuer, R. J. Jr. (1999). *Psychology of Intelligence Analysis*. Center for the Study of Intelligence, Central Intelligence Agency.
12. Snowden, D. J., & Boone, M. E. (2007). *A Leader's Framework for Decision Making*. Harvard Business Review, 85(11), 68–76.

10

THE AUDACIOUS CREATOR

They say that with AI, 'average is now going to come for free'. This means knowledge workers need to enhance their creativity to build on the excellent outputs AI provides in seconds.

In this chapter, we explore how humans and AI can collaborate during the creative process to deliver the bold and distinctive creativity needed in an increasingly commoditised and homogeneous world.

The future will involve a collaborative process where humans work with AI to generate innovative solutions. Humans will remain the creative driving force, but AI will increasingly provide initial creative ideas. Humans can then enhance these ideas with their unique flair, adding that audacious wow factor in the final stages of the creative process.

In this chapter, we start by outlining various approaches to generating creative ideas. We then examine how humans, with their unique understanding of the human condition, can bring fresh creativity to an increasingly commoditised world.

DOI: 10.4324/9781003514879-11

Next, we explore how AI can assist in the creative process, working alongside human creativity. We conclude by discussing how humans can elevate their creative skills in the new AI era. Here the positive message is that AI is our ally, prompting us to go the extra creative mile and leave our distinctive human mark on the foundation that AI provides.

The reality is that many creative outputs will come from productive and innovative symbiotic relationships between humans and AI. So our core message is not about a competition between human and AI performance but about embracing a future where exciting new partnerships allow both to work in harmony to generate creative outputs.

So let us start by briefly reviewing the essence of the creative process.

An overview of the creative process

Creativity is multifaceted and doesn't follow a set formula for enhancing capabilities. However, there's a consensus that creativity often stems from the ability to connect disparate ideas, aligning with the theme of polymath thinking explored in this book.

Steve Jobs, a modern polymath and perhaps the greatest innovator of his generation and someone who changed our relationship with technology, shared this view in a *Wired Magazine* interview in 1996.[1] He said:

> Creativity is just connecting things. When you ask creative people how they did something, they feel a little guilty because they didn't really do it: they just saw something that seemed obvious to them and connected it to their own experiences. They knew how to synthesise. And the reason they were able to do that was because they had a diverse range of experiences. But most people don't have enough dots to connect: they don't have the broader perspective on a problem.

And Vincent Van Gogh said, 'Great things are done by a series of small things brought together'.

However, whilst there is agreement on the importance of connecting ideas, there are many ways to achieve this. As discussed earlier, creativity often flows from looping through various stages of thinking in an iterative process.

Tim Harford, in his book *Messy: How to be Creative and Resilient in a Tidy-Minded World* (2016),[2] explains that many creatives operate in a non-linear, seemingly disorganised way but still achieve great outcomes. This highlights that creativity is influenced by the environment and the unique personalities involved. The key point here is that creative individuals often develop their own working styles.

So we know for example that Isaac Newton celebrated building on what had gone before. 'If I have seen further than others, it is by standing upon the shoulders of giants'. This was said in a letter to his fellow scientist Robert Hooke (1675).

However, we also have examples of people who preferred to start the creative process with a blank canvas. For instance, Clive Sinclair, a polymath and the inventor in the 1980s of the Spectrum computer and the pioneering C5 electric car, did not begin the creative process by researching existing landscapes. He believed that such research could limit his creativity and narrow his vision.

Opportunism and pragmatism also play significant roles in the creative process. Paul Simon, for instance, added a memorable third verse to the classic song *Bridge Over Troubled Water* (1970) at the last minute in the studio, departing from his usual process of spending weeks refining his lyrics at home.

Despite the variability in the creative process due to different circumstances and personalities, it's helpful to recognise that much creativity does follow a fundamental disciplined process.

A framework for thinking about the creative process

Let's outline a framework for enhancing our creative abilities. This framework is useful because it sets the stage for understanding the respective strengths of humans and AI in the creative process. With this framework in place, we can better achieve our goal of maximising creativity.

Here are the stages of the archetypal creative process. Understanding these stages helps us leverage both human ingenuity and AI capabilities effectively in the creative process.

It was Julie Andrews who was reported as saying, 'Creativity is a very disciplined business'.

Triggered by a challenge

Many creative outputs start with a challenge or problem. While some pure creative ideas may seem to drift down mysteriously from the muse, appearing as gifts from the human unconscious, a high proportion of creative ideas are triggered by a specific challenge, problem, or goal.

This process involves a complex interplay between cognitive reasoning and human imagination, shaped iteratively by various personality, emotional, cultural and environmental factors. As Barnes Wallis, the outstanding inventor said, 'I've never had a creative idea in my life; all I do is solve problems'. This was a theme in interviews or public talks given in the 1950s to 1970s.

This highlights that the creative process often begins with a focus on a problem or challenge. Whether it's inventing a new solution, writing a song, or improving a system or process, the journey of creativity frequently starts with addressing a specific need or goal.

Refined by investigation

Following the initial challenge, the next stage typically involves preparation and information gathering. This phase is about fully understanding the problem or assignment through research and knowledge accumulation.

It involves gathering information, conducting research and immersing oneself in the problem space. This includes assembling data about customer needs, examining existing solutions and brainstorming initial new ideas. This thorough investigation lays the groundwork for the creative process.

Fostered by incubation and reflection

Next, there is often an incubation stage where we let our unconscious mind work on the problem. Stephen King, the writer, refers to this phase in his writing process as leaving things overnight for 'the boys in the basement' to do their job – *On Writing: A Memoir of the Craft* (2000).[3]

During this stage, we allow the problem and possible solutions to circulate in our minds, gradually stewing and brewing to help us arrive at a creative solution. This is where ideas begin to subconsciously connect. It's about stepping away from direct problem-solving to give your subconscious mind space to process information.

Activities such as meditating, freeform journaling and taking walks – tasks unrelated to the problem – can often help during this creative incubation stage.

The point of illumination

This process leads us to the point of illumination, that moment of insight or breakthrough that provides a new perspective. We often refer to this as the 'aha moment', where an idea seems to emerge out of nowhere. This stage of illumination can be unpredictable and occur at unexpected times, such as while driving or jogging, with solutions seemingly appearing out of thin air.

However, this moment is often the product of iterations of internal reflection and agonising. The idea surfaces after extensive juxtaposing of concepts and inspired, often subconscious, creative thinking.

Reality checking

The typical creative process then moves to evaluating the sense and validity of the emerging solution and reviewing its practicalities. In the context of knowledge work, this evaluation stage involves assessing your creative idea for feasibility, alignment with business goals, and the reactions of key stakeholders and team members.

Based on the feedback received, this stage might also include another phase of iteration, where ideas are further refined, tested again and a new version of your creative idea is developed.

Learning through implementation

After evaluation, the next step is translating the idea into action. This involves developing implementation pathways that will do justice to the creative idea and deliver a true solution rather than a diluted or modified version.

The implementation phase may include making additional creative adjustments as necessary, ultimately culminating in the idea coming to fruition.

Now, let's explore several dimensions of the human personality that serve as sources of outstanding creativity.

Exploring the creative dimensions of the human personality

Humans possess a unique ability to find flashes of inspiration, pulling ideas seemingly out of nowhere. In contrast, AI lacks self-awareness, personal experiences, emotions and an understanding of the human condition – all crucial elements for sparking creative genius. Let's explore human creativity a little further.

Tap into your emotional intelligence

One significant source of creative inspiration is emotional intelligence (EQ). This ability allows humans to understand, interpret and empathise with others. EQ involves recognising and managing both our own emotions and those of others, with empathy at its core. Empathy enables us to relate to others, sense their feelings and respond appropriately and compassionately.

Unlike AI, which lacks the nuanced understanding of human emotions, humans can interpret complex emotional cues such as humour, irony, pathos and happiness. While AI can mimic some aspects of EQ by analysing sentiment, it falls short of genuine emotional understanding and sentience.

EQ provides heightened sensitivity – the ability to read subtle clues, pick up on hints, and peer deeply into what it means to be human in a way that AI cannot. This human ability to read subtle emotional clues often triggers creative insights and ideas.

For instance, AI would likely miss the significance of Princess Margaret's affectionate gesture towards Group Captain Townsend when she brushed away a piece of fluff from his uniform during Queen Elizabeth II's coronation (1953) – a moment hinting at a secret relationship. But the world's press got the message straight away!

Similarly, AI would not understand the emotion behind a poignant act captured on rare film footage of an older soldier compassionately tapping a younger comrade on the back seconds before the ramp goes down from their landing craft, and they come under enemy fire on Omaha Beach on D-Day, 6 June 1944.

In summary, EQ provides deep sensitivity and understanding of the human condition, which is essential for creative inspiration and should be cultivated.

Seeing the big picture and harnessing serendipity

Another dimension of creativity is the ability to see the broader context and leverage serendipity. The 'panorama principle' tells us that stepping back to view the wider context often yields greater insight than focusing on minute details. By keeping abreast of diverse happenings, you are more likely to spark creative ideas.

Expanding your range of interests and perspectives, or 'hinterland', increases the likelihood of generating innovative ideas. For example, Denis Healey, a former UK Chancellor (1974–1979), had a wide range of interests beyond politics, which enriched his creativity. This was in contrast to his nemesis Margaret Thatcher (UK Prime Minister 1979–1990). She had a much narrower focus which limited her exposure to broader insights and serendipitous discoveries. She did not scan newspapers daily for hints about ordinary people's activities but relied on her press secretary to present selected clippings, making her oblivious to popular culture moments like Gazza's tears during the football 1990 World Cup.

Creativity thrives in environments open to serendipity, embracing diverse influences, subtle clues and contradictions. As Tim Harford has noted, disorder and chaos can foster creativity. While some discipline is essential, embracing a level of chaos can enhance the serendipity factor, leading to unexpected creative breakthroughs.

For knowledge workers, the message is clear: maintaining discipline whilst at the same time embracing diverse experiences and environments increases the likelihood of making significant creative contributions.

Boost your creativity by seeing the world though your personal experiences

To gain a creative edge, knowledge workers should leverage their unique personal perspectives on problems. This approach can unlock innovative solutions. Interestingly, even AI like ChatGPT, acknowledges that exploring anecdotes and personal perspectives, which it lacks, is crucial for human creativity.

A key factor here is 'cognitive flexibility'. This ability allows individuals to break down complex problems and explain them through personal experiences, adding significant creative value. Sharing personal and possibly unconventional views promotes new ways of thinking and understanding in others.

Accounts from those with direct experience, although anecdotal, help others consider issues in new ways, often leading to innovative solutions. Personal narratives filled with emotion, passion and relatability make challenges more vivid and stimulate the exploration of creative alternatives.

For example, consider the value of cognitive flexibility if we were to set ourselves the challenge of switching from driving on the left to the right in the UK. AI like ChatGPT would provide a comprehensive analysis in seconds, covering infrastructure changes, vehicle modifications, legal adjustments, public education and more.

However, an individual from a small village in Norfolk might notice a unique issue overlooked by AI. Living on a 'quiet lane' prioritised for wildlife and shared by pedestrians, cyclists and horse riders, they would realise this specific context needs special consideration. Additionally, there's a unique case in the UK: Savoy Court in London, where driving on the right is officially authorised to facilitate traffic flow – again highlighting the importance of specific local insights.

In summary, embracing and sharing your personal experiences and local perspectives can significantly enhance your creative capabilities, offering insights that even advanced AI might miss.

Dial up your creative polymath mind

A polymath's mind offers unique advantages for creativity, combining interdisciplinary connections to inspire innovative solutions. These include the following.

Broad context and diverse perspectives: Polymaths excel in seeing the broader context and making connections across various fields. They embrace the 'panorama principle', valuing insights from the periphery of a problem as much as the core issue.

Cross-disciplinary approach: Polymaths transcend traditional disciplinary boundaries, viewing problems from multiple angles. They employ diverse reasoning methods – both inductive and abductive – to interpret emerging evidence. This flexibility enables them to approach issues both logically and unconventionally.

Connecting the dots: At the heart of the polymath mindset is the ability to link seemingly unrelated clues and signals, creating fresh perspectives.

Their insatiable curiosity drives them to understand the world's workings, uncovering cause-and-effect relationships.

Polymaths and AI – a creative synergy: Polymaths are naturally positioned to add creative value, and the integration of AI amplifies this potential. In the following section, we'll explore how AI can enhance the creative process by building on the strengths of a polymath.

Now, let's delve into the AI tool bag for ideas to aid the creative process, enhancing the polymath's ability to innovate.

AI's contribution to the creative process

Let's explore how AI can turbocharge our natural human creativity. Here are six areas where AI plays a powerful role in the creative process. For each area, we provide examples of AI-driven creativity in action and list specific AI-powered tools that knowledge workers may wish to check out.

One: AI as an organising platform for human creativity

Creativity sometimes emerges from a messy, hard-to-define process where ideas seem to drift down from a muse in an almost illogical way. However, many creatives describe a highly organised approach to their creative process. Few simply wait for inspiration to strike; instead, they structure their days to maximise creative output.

Most creatives identify the times of day when they are most productive and establish routines that support their creative process. These routines become habits they rely on daily to produce creative work.

The following are illustrations of how some famous creative individuals organised their day, time and logistics to maximise their creativity. By establishing such routines, these creatives ensured consistent productivity and harnessed their creative potential effectively.

EXAMPLES OF THE WAY WRITERS GO ABOUT ORGANISING THEIR CREATIVE DAY

Stephen King writes 2,000 words a day typically in the morning no matter how long it takes and doesn't stop writing till he meets his word count goal.

Virginia Woolf devoted the mornings to writing and then took long walks in the afternoon to reflect on her output.

Maya Angelou was known for renting a local hotel room, where she would write free from interruption from 6 a.m. to 2 p.m. without any distractions.

Ernest Hemingway used to write in the morning and keep going until he knew what would happen next in his plot thereby leaving a thread that will provide a trigger for him to pick up the story the next day.

Will Self tells the story of writing what he calls a 'Conrad' every day after he read that Joseph Conrad, who was a highly successful writer, managed to sustain a very lavish lifestyle based on writing 500 words a day.

Franz Kafka, in contrast to many writers who tend to favour early morning writing, wrote from 11 p.m. to 6 a.m. where his nights were dedicated solely to his creative endeavours.

So knowing that creativity is a disciplined process, not a random affair, let's now explore how AI can significantly enhance human creativity by organising and developing new ideas and supporting the creative process. Various AI tools are now available to automate the organisational and administrative aspects of creative projects, helping to declutter the initial muddle of ideas and organise them into actionable concepts.

AI tools for structured creativity

AI tools can provide structure and assist in managing incoming ideas, organising them into mind maps or other frameworks to prioritise and prevent them from becoming a disorganised stream of consciousness. Additionally, AI tools can manage workflows, ensuring effective collaboration within creative teams.

Throughout this book, we mention specific AI tools. But given the rapid pace of new tool development, consider these as illustrative examples rather than the latest or best options. Our goal is to showcase how AI can assist in the organising phase of creativity and not necessarily to recommend the latest cutting-edge tools. So some suggestions include the following.

Asana: Provides AI-assisted automated suggestions for optimising workflows, organising deadlines and prioritising creative tasks.

Trello: Offers versatile AI-powered project management solutions that aid creativity.

Canva's Magic Design: Uses AI-powered features to help streamline the creative design process.

These tools and others like them are invaluable because they automate repetitive tasks and handle administrative elements, freeing up more space for human creative thought.

By handling straightforward tasks, AI allows humans to focus on the core of creative thinking, such as ideation and innovation, which rely on human intuition, flair and experience. So embrace the support that AI can provide to the creative process, allow it to do the heavy lifting in more administrative areas thereby leaving the core creative tasks to us humans.

Two: AI's contribution to the problem framing and crystallisation phases of the creative process

AI plays a crucial role in the initial problem definition phase of the creative process, helping to clarify, refine and expand our understanding of the problem at hand. Here's how AI aids in these stages.

Analysing data for insights: AI can analyse vast amounts of data to identify trends and patterns that might not be visible to the human eye. This helps in uncovering hidden insights and understanding the problem more comprehensively.

Exploring related data: AI can explore data from related areas, suggesting analogies and connections that human analysis might overlook. This broadens the scope of understanding and opens up new avenues for problem-solving.

Formulating clear problem statements: Using its advanced natural language processing capabilities, AI can help formulate clear and concise problem statements. This ensures that the problem is well-defined from the start, providing a solid foundation for subsequent creative efforts.

Specific AI tools for problem definition you may wish to explore include the following.

OpenAI's ChatGPT: Assists in answering questions to deepen understanding and works with human analysts to refine initial problem statements.
IBM Watson: Analyses unstructured data from various sources to uncover new angles and perspectives, aiding in the problem definition process.
Google DeepMind: Helps define and refine problems by setting up different scenarios and examining likely outcomes.

By leveraging these AI capabilities, the problem framing and crystallisation phases of the creative process become more efficient and effective, setting a strong foundation for teasing out innovative solutions.

Three: AI as a sounding board and critical friend to support human creativity

AI plays an essential role as a sounding board, helping to critique and refine initial human creative ideas. Here's how AI can support the creative process.

Providing feedback and alternative perspectives: AI can offer unbiased feedback, free from personal bias or emotional influences. It suggests improvements and alternative perspectives, which can enhance the human creative process. AI provides honest, robust feedback, helping to refine ideas and take them to the next level.
Real-time responses for quick iterations: AI can deliver real-time responses to creative ideas, enabling quick iterations and improvements. This immediate feedback allows creators to rapidly develop and enhance their concepts.
Drawing on an eclectic mix of knowledge: AI can access extensive databases of knowledge, including diverse cultural perspectives. It can suggest various viewpoints, challenging creators to think outside their usual frames of reference and prompting more innovative thinking.

Specific AI tools for creative support to consider include the following.

OpenAI's ChatGPT: In addition to refining problem statements, ChatGPT can act as a sounding board, providing feedback and suggestions for creative ideas.

AI tools for marketing copy: These tools can evaluate marketing content and suggest adjustments to improve engagement, prompting creators to revisit and enhance their drafts.

Enhancing brainstorming sessions and visual mapping: AI can feed gathered information into brainstorming sessions and provide tools for organising ideas. For example, Miro is an online collaborative whiteboard platform that integrates AI features for brainstorming and visual mapping, helping to organise and visualise creative outputs.

By leveraging these AI capabilities, knowledge workers can refine their initial ideas, transforming raw concepts into polished, ready-for-development creative solutions. AI's role as a critical friend ensures that the creative process is both efficient and effective.

Four: AI as a catalyst in the creative process

As we have said, think of AI as being your sparring partner. AI is revolutionising creativity by acting as a catalyst, trigger and co-creator. AI can support and enhance human creativity in the following ways.

Catalyst for creativity: AI tools can remove creative blocks, kicking in when human creativity hits a mental roadblock. These tools analyse large data sets, identifying patterns and anomalies that inspire new angles and insights, prompting creative solutions.

Creative synthesis: Modern AI tools operate in creative synthesis mode, suggesting ideas that might not naturally occur to human thinkers, who often have a narrower perspective. AI can build 'what if' scenarios that stimulate creative thinking and new ideas.

Facilitating brainstorming: AI can turbocharge brainstorming sessions by prompting semantic associations and bringing together disparate concepts and ideas. AI facilitates constructive, iterative idea-building without critique, enhancing traditional brainstorming techniques.

Some AI tools to review to aid the creative process include the following.

DALL-E: Generates images from textual descriptions.
Google DeepDream: Offers unique visualisations to inspire creativity.
Runway ML: Assists in visualising concepts and generating new insights.
Sudowrite: An AI writing assistant that provides creative suggestions and helps overcome writer's block.

And we need to specifically address the power of 'creative prompting'. This involves crafting input prompts that guide AI to produce specific, innovative outputs. This technique leverages AI's capacity for creativity and novelty, adding a new dimension to human thinking. Remarkably, the concept of creative prompting has emerged as a valuable skill within a short time.

And interestingly, even before AI, creative individuals used external stimuli to nudge them to the next level of creativity. Perhaps, most famous of all is the way David Bowie used to work with Brian Eno to take an initial Bowie song idea and apply what they called the *Oblique Strategies* technique to refine and enhance – turbo boost – the original idea. This is explained in the following.

BOWIE AND ENO: TURN AND FACE THE STRANGE

The Oblique Strategies technique was developed in the mid-1970s by Brian Eno and Peter Schmidt and is designed to help individuals overcome creative blocks.

The technique involves a deck of cards each with a cryptic or aphoristic remark designed to challenge the initial creator to rethink their opening creative output.

So for example: One of the cards could contain the statement 'Consider changing the middle eight' which could have led to possibly a guitar piece being replaced by a French horn – you get the idea.

And one interesting prompt was 'honour the error as a hidden intention'. Here, in response, the creator might see something as being wrong but actually the prompt is to suggest leaving it in the final version.

David Bowie famously used this technique on a number of his albums in the late 1970s whilst recording in Berlin. He found it a great way of breaking from conventional thinking and inspiring innovative production and musical techniques that were unexpected and unconventional.

Let's now delve into how the creative prompting process works.

Creative prompting

We have already introduced the idea of creative prompting. We stressed that the key to successful prompting is being specific and detailed in your request, ensuring it aligns with your intentional purpose.

When prompting AI to generate creative output, it's essential to convey not just the subject matter but also the context. For example, if you need an image to support an idea, describing the subject alone isn't enough. You must also provide the context.

For instance, if you want an image of a seaside pier to promote a holiday destination, specify an image with lots of smiling tourists. Conversely, if you need an image to illustrate a fisherman enjoying solitude on a winter's day for a specialist fishing magazine, provide that context.

As we have shown, creative prompting is an iterative process. So review your initial outputs and refine your prompts to better align the AI's responses with your creative goals. Let's take the example of how AI can help a human analyst develop a new hardcopy magazine focused on holistic health. The magazine aims to cover various aspects of staying healthy, eating well, managing mental health and promoting overall well-being.

By refining your prompts and iterating based on initial outputs, you can effectively use AI to enhance your creative projects and achieve your desired outcomes. For our illustration here, we used ChatGPT, but other large language models are available!

Illustration of creative prompt engineering at work

The following are seven creative prompting iterations using ChatGPT for our holistic health magazine example.

Iteration 1

Prompt: What would be a unique theme for our new holistic health and wellness magazine that distinguishes it from existing publications?

Response: A unique theme could be 'Seasons of Wellness' where each issue focuses on health and wellness practices that are best suited for the current season. This could include seasonal diets, exercises and mental health strategies that align with the changing weather and lifestyle adjustments throughout the year.

Iteration 2

Prompt: How could we structure the content for each seasonal issue to engage readers?
Response: Each issue could be structured around four main sections: Nutrition (seasonal recipes and foods), Physical Activity (seasonal exercises and sports), Mental Health (season-specific stress management and self-care practices), and Holistic Practices (like ayurveda or traditional Chinese medicine that align with the season). This structure ensures comprehensive coverage of wellness.

Iteration 3

Prompt: Can we include interactive elements in each issue to increase reader engagement?
Response: Yes, we could include QR codes next to major articles that lead to online interactive content like video workouts for physical activities, cooking demonstrations for seasonal recipes, and guided meditations for mental health. Additionally, including a monthly challenge related to the season could motivate readers to actively participate.

Iteration 4

Prompt: What type of monthly challenges could we incorporate that would align with the seasonal themes?
Response: For winter, a challenge could involve a Danish-inspired 'Hygge Lifestyle Challenge' focusing on mindfulness and creating a cosy environment. Spring might feature a 'Spring Clean Your Life Challenge', involving physical, mental and environmental decluttering. Summer could have a 'Get Active Outdoors Challenge', and Autumn could focus on 'Gratitude and Harvest', which encourages reflection and thankfulness.

Iteration 5

Prompt: How can we utilise expert contributions to enhance credibility and variety in our magazine?
Response: We could feature monthly columns by a diverse panel of experts, including dietitians, fitness coaches, mental health professionals, and holistic healers. Each expert could provide insights and tips that align with the seasonal theme of the issue, such as a dietitian offering advice on seasonal superfoods or a coach discussing how to adapt workouts to weather conditions.

Iteration 6

Prompt: What could be an innovative approach to the magazine's visual and material design to attract readers?
Response: Opting for a bold, vibrant design that changes with each season could visually attract readers. Using eco-friendly materials for the print editions would not only appeal to environmentally conscious readers but also reinforce the holistic health message of the magazine.

Iteration 7

Prompt: How can we integrate community involvement in our magazine?
Response: We could invite readers to submit their own stories and tips related to the seasonal themes, which could be featured in a dedicated 'Community Corner'. Additionally, hosting a reader photo contest related to the monthly challenge could foster a sense of community and participation.

We will stop at this seventh iteration, but just to confirm, ChatGPT did as it was asked and ended up producing 20 really helpful iterations. These took us into ideas such as creating spin-offs from the magazine, including offering interactive tools such as wellness trackers and much more.

Five: AI as evaluator of creative ideas

AI can play a valuable role in evaluating the potential success of human creative ideas. Utilising its immense data analysis, predictive modelling and machine learning capabilities, AI offers several techniques to aid in this assessment process including the following.

Predictive analytics and sentiment analysis: AI can use predictive analytics to forecast the success of creative ideas. By reading social media reviews and other online platforms, AI can perform sentiment analysis to gauge immediate feedback and the likely acceptance of a creative idea.
Simulation and testing techniques: AI also provides various simulation and testing techniques to give creators an initial feedback on how well their ideas might be received. These simulations help in understanding potential outcomes and refining ideas before full implementation.

And there are several AI tools for evaluating creative ideas including the following.

Google analytics predictive metrics: Helps predict user behaviour and the potential success of marketing campaigns.

HubSpot predictive lead scoring: Assists in forecasting which leads are most likely to convert, useful for evaluating marketing and business initiatives.

IBM Watson Studio: Offers a suite of tools for data analysis and predictive modelling, helping assess the potential of creative and business initiatives.

By leveraging these AI capabilities, creators can make informed decisions about which ideas to pursue, ensuring a higher likelihood of success in their endeavours.

Six: AI as supporting implementation

AI plays a crucial role in implementing new creative ideas by organising workflows and helping teams refine ideas to perfectly meet end-user needs. AI can support this process in the following ways.

AI handles the heavy lifting of workflow automation and performance monitoring, freeing up human time for adding final touches to creative outputs. AI tools streamline tasks, allowing teams to focus on creativity.

In addition, several AI-driven tools facilitate collaboration and ensure that creative projects reach completion including the following.

Slack: Enhances team communication and collaboration, using AI features, ensuring creative ideas are executed efficiently.
Monday.com: Monitors timelines and helps teams tweak outputs to meet end-user needs.

Furthermore, AI can rigorously evaluate new ideas against existing ones, ensuring they are viable and innovative. For example:

RebeccAi: Can help evaluate and validate business startup ideas.

AI supports different stages of the creative process, from defining problems to implementing innovative ideas. While AI enhances various stages, humans remain essential for capturing that elusive flash of inspiration leading to groundbreaking ideas.

It's important to recognise AI's evolving capability through deep learning to play a role in the creative process. As AI continues to improve, it becomes an increasingly valuable tool for knowledge workers, helping with everything from initial idea generation to final implementation.

AI is an invaluable tool in the creative context, supporting and enhancing human creativity at every stage. By automating tasks and facilitating collaboration, AI allows humans to focus on the elements of creativity that require intuition and inspiration.

Build your audacious creativity mindset – make creativity a habit

Here we provide some practical suggestions for encouraging knowledge workers to go to the next level with their creativity by setting up triggers that build world-class creativity habits.

Embrace AI as a co-creativity partner

Recognise that we are at an inflection point in history, requiring a new mindset to appreciate the power and value of AI. To fully embrace AI as a co-creative partner, it's crucial to adopt a mindset that integrates AI into your creative process rather than viewing it as a separate or inferior contributor. Engage with AI, don't be fearful of it.

Begin by reading about and experimenting with AI. Explore its possibilities and understand how it works. Use AI to enhance your creativity, not replace it.

It's about applying the 'virtuous confidence circle' concept. By using AI you build your confidence, which in turn improves your comfort and enjoyment in working with AI, creating an upward spiral of growth. The steps to embrace AI in creativity include the following.

Educate yourself: Learn about AI technologies and their applications in creative fields.
Experiment: Play with AI tools to understand their capabilities and how they can augment your creative process.
Integrate: Find ways to incorporate AI into your workflow, allowing it to assist and enhance your ideas.
Reflect: Continuously reflect on how AI is impacting your creativity and adjust your approach as needed. By embracing AI as a partner, you can unlock new levels of creativity and innovation.

Why not start a creativity journal?

To build your confidence in working with AI, consider keeping a creativity journal. This journal can serve multiple purposes including the following.

Observation: Note down observations about AI and how it can help you become more creative. Review how you can collaborate with AI in a co-creative mode.
Self-reflection: Regularly self-reflect to adjust to working with AI. Record your creative skills and how AI complements them, highlighting both positive points and any concerns. This will help you avoid self-sabotage through negative thoughts and instead build self-belief and confidence in working with AI.
Opportunity identification: Use the journal to explore opportunities to boost your confidence in your own creativity and your ability to work alongside AI. This practice can enhance your emotional intelligence.
Progress tracking: Track your progress and identify the improvements you could make.

Some practical steps to follow in maintaining a creativity journal include the following.

Daily entries: Make daily or regular entries about your experiences with AI and creativity.
Focus on your skills: List your creative skills and how AI can enhance them.
Celebrate wins: Record successful collaborations with AI to reinforce positive outcomes.
Reflect on emotional intelligence: Use the journal to evaluate and improve your emotional intelligence in the context of AI collaboration.
Track concerns and solutions: Note any concerns about AI and brainstorm potential solutions.

By maintaining a creativity journal, you'll develop a habit of reflection and self-improvement, ultimately making AI your ally in your journey towards greater creativity. Embrace this lifelong journey of self-learning and exploration, making AI your companion rather than something to fear.

Identify the best environment for your creativity to flourish and protect this space

To foster creativity, it's important to identify and protect the environment where your creativity thrives. Here's how to ensure your creative space supports your best work.

Identify your creative space: Determine where your creativity flows best. This could be a specific room in your home, a favourite café, or a special place overlooking the ocean. Recognise the environment that works best for you.
Create a mindful environment: Choose a space that encourages mindfulness and meditation. This helps to maintain focus and enhances creative thinking.
Protect your space: Take steps to ensure you can consistently operate in your optimal creative space. Avoid distractions and resist getting pulled away from the environment that fosters your creativity.

By identifying and protecting your ideal creative environment, you can enhance your productivity and creative output.

Don't let crazy makers rob you of your time and energy

To maximise your creativity, it's essential to protect your time and energy from disruptions. Here's how.

Identify optimal time periods: Determine the time periods and work patterns that are best for your creativity. Protect these periods from interruptions and distractions, such as demanding inboxes and 'crazy makers' who disrupt your day.
Manage energy flow: Be mindful of how your creative energy fluctuates throughout the day. If you feel your energy waning, take a break to recharge. Einstein and Charles Dickens were known for taking walking breaks to regain their creative focus.
Establish a personal system: Develop a system that works for you to manage your creative energy. Some creatives prefer working in block time in the morning, dedicating specific periods solely to creative activities and leaving administrative tasks for later.
Personalise your approach: There is no one-size-fits-all solution. The key is to organise your schedule in a way that aligns with your unique creative flow and energy levels.

By identifying your optimal creative environment and protecting your time from distractions, you can enhance your creative productivity and maintain your energy throughout the day.

Identify opportunities to collaborate and stimulate the creative juices

Collaboration in the creative process can be a powerful stimulus, although opinions on its value vary. John Steinbeck favoured working alone, whereas T. S. Eliot benefitted from a collaboration with Ezra Pound.

It's a matter of deciding what works best for you. If you choose to collaborate, seek out a critical friend and work out a system for successful collaboration. For example, Lennon and McCartney's partnership often involved one taking the lead on a song and the other refining it, though they sometimes worked independently.

Today, AI can serve as a collaborative 'critical friend'. Tools such as ChatGPT can prompt and nudge you towards more creative outputs. AI can offer constructive feedback and new ideas, making it a valuable partner in the creative process.

By leveraging collaboration, whether with humans or AI, and using creative thinker tools, you can enhance your natural creativity and produce innovative solutions.

Develop creative rituals that work for you

Julia Cameron, in her book *The Artist's Way* (1992),[4] recommends various daily rituals to boost creativity and sticking to them. Here are some key ideas from her and others.

Morning pages: If you are a creative, commit to writing a few pages every morning, regardless of how you feel. This daily practice can help spark new ideas and maintain creative flow.

Social media posts: Regularly write and share posts with peers, inviting feedback to refine your ideas.

Detoxing: Eliminate time-wasting activities, like watching toxic reality TV or engaging in negative social media. Instead, use this time more productively to conserve and channel your creative energy.

Artist dates: Set aside time to go alone to a fun, interesting, or different experience. Reflect on this experience to draw out creative inspiration.

Cross-disciplinary events: Attend events outside your usual interests to prompt new connections and ideas.

Safe experimentation: View the creative process as a chance to play and experiment in a non-threatening environment. Consider joining a creative writing workshop or a similar group.

Regular creative activities: Set aside regular time each month for activities that stimulate your creativity, such as theatre visits, poetry readings, or scientific presentations.

Mindfulness and meditation: Incorporate mindfulness and meditation into your daily routine to boost creativity and overcome blocks.

Cultivate metacognition: Take an evening class on metacognition to understand how you think, which can enhance your creative process.

Step out of your comfort zone: Challenge yourself by joining a debating or speaking club to refine your ability to articulate creative ideas.
Work with constraints: Boost creativity by setting clear, tight objectives. For example, writing within the framework of a poem forces concise and creative expression.
Reflective thinking: Regularly reflect on whether you're doing enough to boost your creativity. Use a journal to note down actions you can take to enhance your creative output.
Sleep on it: Allow your subconscious to develop ideas overnight by 'sleeping on it'.

By integrating these rituals into your routine, you can create a supportive environment that nurtures and stimulates your creativity. Find what works best for you and stay with it, constantly evaluating and adjusting your practices to maintain and enhance your creative output.

Go full polymath – embrace diverse creative thinking

The central thesis of this book is that the future belongs to knowledge workers who embrace an interdisciplinary polymath approach to creativity, particularly when working alongside AI. These individuals have an insatiable curiosity and a keen interest in exploring the edges of AI-generated outputs. They are also attentive listeners who value diverse perspectives.

Many of the characteristics of polymaths – reviewed here – promote creativity.

Eclectic knowledge: Polymaths draw inspiration from a wide range of disciplines, enjoying the challenge of devising creative solutions and resisting default thinking.
Curiosity and enjoyment: Polymaths approach thinking as a hobby rather than a burden, finding joy in the process of learning and exploring new ideas.
Constructive feedback: Polymaths value feedback, gracefully accepting criticism and learning from it to improve continuously.
Goal setting: Polymaths set personal goals and milestones to enhance their creative collaboration with AI.
Building on this, some practical tips for embracing a polymath mindset include the following.

Approach problems creatively: Always ask, 'Is there a better way of doing this?' Cultivate a habit of innovative thinking.
Diverse reading: Engage with a diverse range of books and materials. For example, in the book *Will It Make the Boat Go Faster* (2011),[5] Ben Hunt-Davies explores how the Olympic rowing team implemented a series of creative ideas to achieve gold. Such reading habits can inspire new ways of thinking and problem-solving.
Interdisciplinary exploration: Apply knowledge from various fields to create a rich tapestry of insights that can lead to innovative solutions.

By following these tips and developing a polymathic approach, you can enhance your creativity and effectively collaborate with AI.

Summary

In this chapter, we reviewed the fundamental creative process. We then highlighted areas where humans have a distinct creative advantage. Following this, we identified how AI can make significant contributions to this process.

Next, we explored opportunities for creative AI-human collaboration. We looked at the power of creative prompting and provided various tips for being more creative.

In the upcoming chapter, *The Forward Thinker*, we will focus on how humans can shape the future they desire, leveraging their unique ability to envision and create.

Notes

1. Wolf, G. (1996). *Steve Jobs: The Next Insanely Great Thing*. Wired Magazine. www.wired.com/1996/02/jobs-2/
2. Harford, T. (2016). *Messy: The Power of Disorder to Transform Our Lives*. Riverhead Books.
3. King, S. (2000). *On Writing: A Memoir of the Craft*. Scribner.
4. Cameron, J. (1992). *The Artist's Way: A Spiritual Path to Higher Creativity*. TarcherPerigee.
5. Hunt-Davis, B., & Clegg, H. (2011). *Will It Make the Boat Go Faster? Olympic-winning Strategies for Everyday Success*. Troubador Publishing Ltd.

11

THE FORWARD THINKER

In this chapter, we focus on a crucial skill for knowledge workers that will significantly enhance their ability to support senior management in the AI era. This skill involves identifying plausible possible future scenarios and making informed judgements on managing potential uncertainties.

This challenge – handling disruption and volatility – is one of the most significant issues organisations face today. A critical task in this process is classifying uncertainties based on their likelihood of occurrence and the impact they would have.

We look at a framework for understanding the future that enables senior decision-makers to act intelligently on changes and disruptions. Specifically, we explore how humans, working alongside AI, can identify the most probable uncertainties we face.

We will also highlight a unique human characteristic that AI lacks: the ability to perform 'mental time travel'. Humans can reach into the past, learn from deeply embedded emotional and visceral experiences and apply these lessons to future decision-making. This ability to create 'future histories' that engage others is something that AI does not possess.

DOI: 10.4324/9781003514879-12

In the AI era, a key role for many knowledge workers will be helping their organisations understand the future and navigate disruption and change. This chapter focuses on the roles of AI and humans in interpreting likely future events and projecting their impact on people, organisations and society.

We call this power skill the Forward Thinker – a kind of strategic envisioner. This skill is more comprehensive and nuanced than traditional terms like forecaster or trend predictor. It encompasses a broader and richer understanding of potential futures.

To begin, let's review some terminology and concepts related to understanding likely future events and their implications.

Defining the Forward Thinker power skill

Let's open by looking at some elements of being a Forward Thinker – starting with forecasting.

Forecasting

Forecasting involves making predictions about future events based on historical data trends and analysis. A key part of the forecaster's role is to collect relevant data from various sources and identify patterns and trends. This is typically followed by model development using statistical tools to predict likely future outcomes.

In essence, forecasting is about interpreting past data and projecting it into the future using modelling techniques. It includes providing commentary on the underlying risks and uncertainties that may affect the forecast's accuracy.

Super forecasters

The concept of super forecasters was introduced by Philip E. Tetlock and Dan Gardner in their book *Superforecasting: The Art and Science of Prediction* (2015).[1] They identified an elite group of individuals known as super forecasters who consistently produced highly accurate predictions about future events, outperforming both average participants and many experts.

This concept is fascinating as it sheds light on the traits associated with exceptional predictive abilities. Tetlock and Gardner argue that super forecasting excellence is not due to a special gift but rather a process that many super forecasters initially followed intuitively.

The key characteristics of super forecasters include the following.

Thinking in probabilities: Super forecasters assess the probability of various competing events rather than prematurely eliminating options or fixating on certain outcomes without sufficient evidence. They assign numerical probabilities to their predictions.

Intellectual humility: They are open to revising their positions when confronted with powerful contradictory views, demonstrating a willingness to learn from mistakes. This aligns with Korzybski's idea (writing in the 1930s) that 'However thin you slice it, there are always two sides' (which some attribute to Spinoza).

Integration of information: Super forecasters appreciate the power of integrating information from diverse sources and fields, using this broad knowledge base to inform their predictions.

Chunking down: They enhance their analytical abilities by breaking down problems into smaller, more manageable parts, allowing them to analyse these from multiple perspectives.

Incremental adjustments: Super forecasters make ongoing, incremental adjustments to refine their initial thinking rather than stubbornly clinging to their original viewpoints.

In summary, super forecasters work with probabilities and scenarios to quantify the likelihood of different outcomes. They are open-minded, willing to challenge their own beliefs, and have the mental flexibility to hold conflicting ideas without this causing any stress. They possess the intellectual capacity to consider multiple scenarios and outcomes, including less likely ones with significant consequences.

Thus, Tetlock and Gardner argue that good forecasting relies on a rigorous intellectual process combined with high levels of self-awareness and sensitivity to human biases. These traits help counter Warren Buffet's observation that 'Forecasts tell us more about the forecaster than the future' (Buffett's 1992 letter to Berkshire Hathaway shareholders).

Strategic foresighter

The strategic foresighter approach incorporates much of the super forecaster's methodology by analysing core trend data and using human intuition to sensitively interpret these trends. However, strategic foresighters add an extra dimension by providing a clear strategic picture of the future by outlining different scenarios.

Strategic foresighters paint pictures of various 'future histories', offering narratives of potential scenarios to help senior decision-makers better understand and navigate future complexities and uncertainties. They help organisations visualise different ways the future could unfold, enabling senior management to plan flexibly around these possibilities.

The primary goal of the strategic foresighter is to lay out a range of potentially disruptive scenarios, detailing the strategic opportunities and threats each poses. They present these scenarios vividly to galvanise decision-makers into action, playing a crucial role in the fast-moving world of AI.

Learning from the past and building future histories

Our Forward Thinker, or strategic envisioner, in the AI era combines the following essential elements.

Traditional forecaster: They apply the rigor of conventional forecasting by analysing historical data and trends.
Super forecaster: They incorporate the open-mindedness and intuitive, human-centred skills of super forecasters.
Strategic foresighter: They adopt the ability to create vivid pictures of potential future scenarios, helping organisations visualise and prepare for different possible outcomes.

An additional, crucial ingredient of the Forward Thinker is the uniquely human ability to undertake 'mental time travel'. Unlike AI, humans can draw on rich past experiences to humanise and enliven future scenarios. This involves creating future histories by using past experiences to inform and enhance the understanding of future possibilities. This ability to connect the past with the future adds depth and context to the Forward Thinker's role, making their insights invaluable for the success of future ventures.

Let's now look more closely at mental time travel.

Mental time travel

Mental time travel involves envisaging possible future scenarios based on past experiences. This cognitive ability allows individuals to simulate different outcomes before they occur, thereby making more informed decisions about the future.

In the world of knowledge work, where organisations face constant disruption and a relentless demand for innovation, there is pressure on individuals to create future scenarios that have consensus and are likely to work. And critically this vision is often shaped by drawing on past experiences.

Thus, the primary function of mental time travel is to analyse past events and learn from them. It helps avoid repeating past mistakes and reinforces successful practices. Mental time travel allows humans to think more clearly about the future they want by reflecting on past experiences and projecting into the future. This capability is an invaluable asset that AI cannot match.

While AI can perform predictive modelling and set up planning algorithms based on historical data, it lacks the ability to imagine or experience the future based on an emotive and visceral understanding of the past.

Therefore, mental time travel, the ability of humans to recall past experiences vividly and imagine future scenarios, is unique to the human species. It is a complex cognitive process deeply intertwined with our consciousness, memory and sense of self.

Dean Buonomano, in *Your Brain is a Time Machine: The Neuroscience and Physics of Time* (2017),[2] stated,

> Memory did not evolve to allow us to reminisce about the past. The sole evolutionary function of memory is to allow animals to predict what will happen, when it will happen, and how to best respond when it does happen.

Other important contributors to the concept of mental time travel include:

Endel Tulving: Introduced the concept of episodic memory in the 1970s, which is the ability to recall personal experiences in a temporal context.
Daniel Schacter: Argued that the same neural mechanisms used to recall past events can also be used to envision future scenarios, helping humans prepare for the future.

Michael Corballis: Emphasised that mental time travel involves understanding narratives, which is foundational for language and how we make sense of the world.
Karl Friston: Viewed the brain as a prediction machine that constantly reconciles differences between its predictions and new inputs.
Martin Seligman: One of the architects of positive psychology, he emphasised that the ability to think about the future and anticipate possibilities is crucial for well-being.
Thomas Suddendorf: In *The Invention of Tomorrow: A Natural History of Foresight* (2023),[3] he argued that mental time travel differentiates humans from animals and is essential for innovation and adaptation.

Suddendorf explained that humans, as mental time travellers, can prepare for future opportunities and threats, shaping the future according to our design. Foresight allows us to anticipate events based on past experiences and act accordingly. While we can't predict the future with certainty, human foresight alerts us to potential dangers and prompts preventive action.

Our brains can review the past, consider the future, and plan ahead without moving a muscle. This ability helps build our sense of self over time. Suddendorf[4] noted in 2013, 'We are alone on this planet in our mental access to this fourth dimension – mental time travel'.

Thus, while many animals can plan for the future, such as stockpiling food, humans uniquely incorporate emotions and experiences from the past into this process. This ability helps shape how we want our future histories to look, using past impressions to steer us towards universally desired goals.

Let us illustrate the point of past experience guiding decision-making with some examples.

EXAMPLES OF HOW MENTAL TIME TRAVEL HAS SHAPED MOMENTS IN HISTORY

John F. Kennedy served as a naval officer in the Pacific during World War II where his patrol boat was rammed and sunk by an enemy destroyer leading to a very harrowing survival story.

It could be argued that his management of the Cuban missile crisis in October 1962, when the world teetered on the brink of nuclear war, was guided by his deep appreciation of the gravity of war and the consequences of him failing with his diplomacy.

Kennedy's handling of the Cuba missile crisis is often cited as a quintessential example of using personal experience and foresight to temper emotional reactions and apply restraint.

Kennedy would have been able to use mental time travel by envisioning possible outcomes of different military engagements such as a US strike on Cuba or a full-scale invasion of Russia. His actions were all tempered by his experience of having been in a theatre of war.

Martin Luther King is another example whose actions were influenced by mental time travel. He frequently drew on historical content, including citing the way he advocated non-violent resistance in shaping America's response to racial prejudice and fostering the civil rights movement in the 1960s. He modelled himself on Gandhi and his approach to Indian independence (1947).

King's ability to understand the past was articulated brilliantly in his 'I have a dream' speech where he promoted the idea of a world where people lived in harmony. He was able to recall the lessons of the past and combine these with a compelling vision of the future.

Nelson Mandela was able to reflect while imprisoned on Robben Island on the decades of adversity that black South Africans had suffered and harness this into his future vision of a racially harmonious South Africa. This was so eloquently summed up in his reference to Marianne Williamson's words: 'Your playing small does not serve the world. . . . We are all meant to shine' (1992).[5]

A framework for forward thinking

Let's explore a framework for forward thinking, starting by revisiting the concepts of scenario planning.

Scenario planning

Earlier, we touched on how scenario planning involves developing detailed, plausible scenarios based on different assumptions about the future. This method helps organisations explore how varying conditions could impact their strategies and operations, enabling them to plan for a range of possible futures.

The fundamental idea behind scenario planning is not to make precise predictions but to outline plausible futures. This approach helps organisations prepare for various possibilities, identify and manage uncertainties, and remain flexible and adaptive in today's fast-paced AI-driven business environment.

Alan Kay, a pioneering computer scientist, said in the 1970s, 'The best way to predict the future, is to invent it'.

At a high level, scenario planning involves collecting all available information to identify fundamental uncertainties that could impact the future. This is followed by developing multiple diverse future scenarios that could affect the organisation. Then there is an assessment of the likely impact of different scenarios and formulating strategies to handle various situations.

An example of scenario planning in action is the approach taken by South African stakeholders at the end of Apartheid (1994) to transition to a majority rule democratic government. They considered the following scenarios.

The Ostrich Scenario: No negotiated settlement is achieved, and the government continues to ignore or suppress individual rights.
The Lame-Duck Scenario: A transition occurs, but the new government is too weak and indecisive to address the country's challenges effectively.
The Icarus Scenario: A new government comes to power with strong support but implements unsustainable short-term policies, leading to economic and social collapse.
The Flight of the Flamingo Scenario: All groups in South Africa participate in lifting the country, leading to inclusive policies and sustainable growth, resulting in a thriving democratic society.

Scenario planning is particularly powerful in the AI era, where there are many differing viewpoints on the medium- to long-term impact of AI. This includes debates on whether AI will enable or substitute certain jobs, as well as discussions on the extent to which AI will drive growth and productivity versus posing a threat to jobs and social stability.

By mastering scenario planning, knowledge workers can help organisations remain agile and responsive to the volatile, uncertain, ambiguous and complex world shaped by AI.

Three arrows in time

The concept of scenario planning introduces the idea of three arrows in time, which can be used to identify plausible possible futures. We have adapted this concept from the work of Ramirez and Wilkinson (2016),[6] refining it for our framework.

By integrating the three arrows in time, organisations can better navigate uncertainties and make informed decisions in a rapidly changing environment.

Let's start by looking at the first arrow in time – power trends.

Power trends

Power trends refers to significant linear trends from the past that are almost irreversible, making them predictable and providing a solid picture of a particular phenomenon's trajectory. This is all about the past catching up with us.

For example, household car ownership is closely linked to rising disposable income. Basic econometric modelling, considering factors like demographic changes, urbanisation rates and vehicle ownership costs, can predict the steady increase in car ownership. In the UK, car ownership rose from around 22% of households in the 1960s to nearly 50% by 1970, continuing to around 75–80% today. Such trends fuel traditional forecasting and trend analysis.

Various techniques help in power trend analysis, where AI plays a significant role by handling large data sets, identifying patterns, running simulations and providing data-driven insights. Meanwhile, humans contribute strategic thinking, contextual understanding and qualitative judgement. This synergy effectively identifies and maps future uncertainties.

Here are some techniques to check out for generating future scenarios.

Historical trend analysis: AI has the capability to analyse past data to identify patterns and trends, helping understand long-term changes and make informed predictions.
Predictive analysis: AI uses powerful statistical algorithms and machine learning to predict future outcomes based on historical data.
Pattern detection: AI excels at identifying patterns and anomalies in large data sets. AI methodologies, like neural networks, recognise complex

patterns not evident to human analysts, aiding scenario planning by highlighting potential risks and opportunities.
Analysis of expert reports: AI can now synthesise large volumes of expert reports, extracting key insights and identifying consensus or conflicting opinions using natural language processing (NLP).
Horizon scanning: AI can enhance the systematic examination of potential threats, opportunities and future developments – scanning various sources and identifying relevant signals.
Backcasting: This is about defining a desirable future and then working backward to identify the steps needed to achieve it. AI can assist by modelling these steps and evaluating different pathways.
Monte Carlo simulation modelling: AI can model the probability of different outcomes in processes involving random variables by running numerous simulations efficiently.
Sentiment analysis: AI is now capable of embracing natural language processing to analyse public opinion from social media, news articles and other sources, helping understand and predict public attitudes.
Risk assessment: AI is able to evaluate potential threats and their impacts. Machine learning algorithms predict the likelihood and severity of risks, aiding in effective preparation and mitigation.

These AI tools collectively enhance the ability to predict, analyse and plan for various future scenarios, providing a comprehensive approach to scenario planning.

The accelerating present

The second arrow in time, adapted from Ramirez and Wilkinson's work, is the notion of the 'accelerating present'. This concept focuses on prominent current trends. These trends provide insights into what is happening in the present moment. This is the present leaping forward.

By examining these current happenings, we can learn from early adopters and project what will happen when these trends reach mainstream society. For example, we might look at how leading-edge adopters are using augmented reality today. From this, we can predict the likely adoption rate of augmented reality in a few years when it becomes more widespread.

Specific techniques for analysing the accelerating present include the following.

Interactive workshops with leading edge adopters: Engaging with current users at the forefront of technology to understand their experiences and insights.
Pathfinding workshops: Collaborating with subject experts across various disciplines to explore and anticipate future developments.
Leaps to future visualisations: Creating visual representations of potential future scenarios based on current trends.

These techniques help us understand the accelerating present and make informed judgements about the likely impact of emerging trends.

Uncertainty mapping

The third arrow in time in our framework for understanding the future is uncertainty mapping. This involves identifying significant uncertainties, assigning probabilities to their occurrence, and assessing their potential impact on our business. This is the future heading in our direction. The ultimate goal is to prioritise uncertainties with the highest probability of occurrence and the greatest potential impact.

Mental time travel can play a crucial role here, as it allows us to draw on past experiences to help interpret future uncertainties.

Some techniques for reviewing uncertainties that combine human-focused methods with support from AI include the following.

SWOT analysis (Strengths, Weaknesses, Opportunities, Threats)

Human role: Identifying and analysing internal and external factors.
AI assistance: Collecting and summarising relevant data from various sources to inform the SWOT components.

PESTLE analysis (Political, Economic, Social, Technological, Legal, Environmental)

Human role: Analysing the impacts of each factor on the organisation.
AI assistance: Scanning and analysing large volumes of data from news articles, reports and other sources to provide insights into each PESTLE category.

Delphi method

With this technique, a group of experts each independently offer their point of view about possible uncertainties. The group then share their points of view and are then able to reflect on their position relative to other experts.

Human role: Facilitating the process, gathering expert opinions and synthesising the results.
AI assistance: Analysing large sets of complex qualitative data from expert responses, identifying common themes and highlighting divergent views.

Panorama scans

Panorama scans involve a comprehensive review of a wide range of factors (economic, political, technological, social, etc.) to identify emerging trends and potential uncertainties.

Human role: Applying Sensemaker skills to the interpretation of results of the scan – integrating diverse information into a coherent strategic overview and making informed decisions.
AI assistance: Conducting extensive data collection and analysis across multiple domains, identifying emerging trends and highlighting areas of potential uncertainty.

Brainstorming

Brainstorming sessions generate a wide range of ideas and perspectives, helping to uncover potential uncertainties and unexpected issues.

Human role: Facilitating the brainstorming session, contributing creative ideas and synthesising the outputs into actionable insights.
AI assistance: Summarising discussion points, identifying common themes and generating additional ideas or questions based on existing data and patterns.

Risk workshops

Risk workshops bring together stakeholders to identify, assess and prioritise risks, providing a structured approach to uncovering uncertainties.

Human role: Facilitating the workshop, contributing expertise and interpreting risk assessments to inform decision-making.

AI assistance: Aggregating and analysing risk data, providing data-driven risk assessments and generating risk scenarios for discussion.

Wildcards

Wildcards are low-probability, high-impact events that could dramatically alter the future. Identifying wildcards helps in preparing for unexpected disruptions.

Human role: Speculating on possible wildcards, assessing their potential impact and incorporating them into scenario planning.

AI assistance: Analysing historical data and trends to suggest potential wildcards, and simulating the impact of these events to evaluate possible outcomes.

Future wheels

Future wheels visualises the ripple effects of a particular change or event, helping to map out its potential consequences and related uncertainties.

Human role: Identifying the initial change/event, mapping out the immediate and secondary impacts, and interpreting the broader implications.

AI assistance: Generating possible consequences and secondary impacts based on data trends and visualising complex interdependencies in the future wheel.

At the end of the process, the aim is to identify those uncertainties with the highest probability of occurrence that will also have the greatest impact on our business.

Building future histories

Once we've identified the most likely scenarios, the next element of the framework for developing forward thinking is to create future histories that people can relate to and support. This involves projecting forward and gaining buy-in for a vision of the future.

This element of our framework involves two interrelated concepts: mental time travel and the creation of future histories.

As previously introduced, humans possess the unique ability to be mental time travellers. This ability allows us to project ourselves into the future, drawing on past experiences to imagine and plan for various scenarios.

The term 'future historics' has its roots in a genre of academic thinking and writing where authors present imagined future events as if they were historical facts. Examples include H. G. Wells's *The Shape of Things to Come* (1933),[7] which envisions a world descending into chaos before emerging into a utopia governed by a world government, and Aldous Huxley's *Brave New World* (1932),[8] which presents a dystopian future.

To help knowledge workers enhance their forward-thinking skills and better understand the future we're shaping, we aim to expand the concept of future histories beyond science fiction. We explore how individuals use visualisations of the future to guide their attitudes and behaviours towards achieving specific goals.

Muhammad Ali is a prime example of this concept. He famously declared, 'I am the greatest' before winning the World Heavyweight boxing title in 1964. This was not out of arrogance but to create a mental image of his future success as the heavyweight champion of the world. Ali visualised the moment when the referee would raise his hand and announce him as the new heavyweight champion, vividly imagining the sights, sounds and emotions of that victory.

This mental picture, or future history, motivated him to train harder and achieve his goal. Ali believed *that* 'It's the repetition of affirmations that leads to belief. And once that belief becomes a deep conviction, things begin to happen'. This approach of visualising future success helped him turn his vision into reality.

By learning to create and communicate future histories, knowledge workers can better guide their organisations and themselves towards desired futures, using vivid and relatable narratives to inspire action and commitment.

Encouraging action taking

The final dimension of the framework for operating as an effective Forward Thinker focuses on knowing how to communicate future scenarios in a way that encourages action. The following are specific storytelling techniques to help paint pictures of the future.

The time machine: This technique illustrates what the future would look like if the audience followed a particular course of action, providing a clear picture of the likely outcome.
The parallel universe: This approach reviews the implications of different scenarios side-by-side. For example, one scenario could explore the future if the company expands into the US, while another examines increased investment in the UK.
The mythbuster: Introduce an element of surprise by debunking common beliefs and challenging established myths. This counterpoint story can jolt management into new ways of thinking about the future.
Through the eyes of the hero: Explain future scenarios through the perspective of individual protagonists. For instance, illustrate a day in the life of a knowledge worker who lacks new AI skills (the villain) versus one who acquires these skills (the hero). This technique vividly brings future scenarios to life and motivates stakeholders to act.
The 'what if' technique: Guide the audience through a series of 'what if' questions about the current business scenario to explore future implications. For example, 'What if our leading competitor cuts their operating costs in half using AI technology? What do we do?'
Personal storytelling episodes: Share how you personally feel about the impact of likely future events. This isn't about unsubstantiated anecdotes but about conveying your understanding in a personal and compelling way. Bring your 'original voice' to the party.

These techniques help sharpen how you communicate identified scenarios and uncertainties. Effective communication is critical, as illustrated by the story of Semmelweis, the medical practitioner who made a groundbreaking discovery but failed to convince the world of its importance, leading to many lost lives before his forward-thinking discovery was recognised.

THE SEMMELWEIS STORY

In 1847, Dr Ignaz Semmelweis was the first to identify that diseases could be transmitted through contact, not just through the air. He realised that handwashing between operations could significantly reduce death rates. However, Semmelweis was not an effective communicator or storyteller. It was Louis Pasteur, years later, who successfully communicated Semmelweis's findings and received most of the credit. If Semmelweis had been able to clearly convey his vision and findings, many lives could have been saved.

A summary of the Forward Thinker framework

The following is a quick recap on the framework we've been proposing to facilitate imaginative forward thinking.

One: Scenario planning

The framework starts with identifying plausible possible futures by assembling evidence drawn from the notion of there being 'three arrows in time':

Power trends: The past catching up with us.
The accelerating present: The present leaping forward.
Uncertainty mapping: Possible futures heading in our direction.

Two: Building future histories

This is about constructing future histories – describing plausible possible scenarios – in a way to which people can relate, including drawing on power of mental time travel.

Three: Encouraging action taking

This is about using techniques that will secure buy-in to your work as a Forward Thinker and prompt action – drawing on a range of storytelling techniques.

Actions to sharpen your Forward Thinker power skill

To sharpen your ability to be a Forward Thinker, consider these specific actions.

Cultivate a growth mindset

Start by exploring Carol Dweck's (2006)[9] book on the growth mindset, which highlights the importance of developing a growth mindset over a fixed mindset. A growth mindset is essential for proactive forward thinking and includes:

- Receptiveness to innovation, change and new ideas
- Enjoyment in adapting for ongoing success
- Continuous learning from past failures and experiences
- Finding lessons and inspiration in others' successes
- Passion for lifelong learning
- Viewing effort as a path to mastery

In contrast, a fixed mindset involves:

- Belief that abilities are static and unchangeable
- Resistance to transformation and change
- Ignoring critique and constructive feedback
- Viewing effort as fruitless or not worthwhile
- Feeling threatened by others' success
- Low curiosity about improvements and reluctance to take personal responsibility for challenges

Embrace the polymath philosophy

Developing a polymath mindset is crucial in today's complex world, enabling you to see the bigger picture and envision future possibilities. Polymathic thinking involves:

- Acquiring wide-ranging knowledge across different disciplines
- Understanding when to delve deeply into specific areas
- Integrating breadth and depth of knowledge to create a comprehensive view of the future

Cultivate curiosity about how the wider world works and take time to understand issues in depth rather than settling for superficial insights. Honing your integration skills will enhance your forward-thinking capabilities.

Michael Araki, who we mentioned earlier as a leading proponent of polymathic thinking, emphasises that it drives innovation and critical thinking by transcending boundaries and limitations. So invest time in broadening and deepening your knowledge and your ability to integrate it.

Build your status as a trusted strategic advisor

Integrate the principles of a growth mindset and polymathic thinking to become a forward-thinking strategic advisor in the AI era. This involves:

- Being open-minded and receptive to AI, learning how to work symbiotically with it
- Regularly scanning the horizon to enhance sensemaking skills
- Developing abductive thinking skills to interpret uncertainty
- Connecting the dots and adding a creative dimension
- Identifying plausible possible futures and communicating them effectively
- Taking personal responsibility for making things happen

By mastering these skills, you will earn recognition as a trusted strategic guru with a polymath mindset, capable of guiding senior management through future disruptions.

Summary

In this chapter we have focused on the ability to strategically envision the future and identify scenarios for senior management so that they are better able to navigate disruption.

Specifically, we've dialled up the importance of the mental time travel capacity of humans which is something that AI cannot provide. Thus, AI will be doing the heavy lifting by identifying fundamental trends and patterns using its massive data analysis power.

But it will be us humans – through our understanding of what has worked in the past and what did not – who will be best able to dial up this past experience and paint a picture of the future histories heading in our direction.

In sum, humans working with AI will be best able to progress ideas that reflect what we want as a society.

In the next chapter we look at how to be an Inspiring Communicator.

Notes

1. Tetlock, P. E., & Gardner, D. (2015). *Superforecasting: The Art and Science of Prediction*. Crown.
2. Buonomano, D. (2017). *Your Brain Is a Time Machine: The Neuroscience and Physics of Time*. W.W. Norton & Company.
3. Suddendorf, T., Redshaw, J., & Bulley, A. (2023) *The Invention of Tomorrow: A Natural History of Foresight*. Basic Books.
4. Suddendorf, T. (2013). *The Gap: The Science of What Separates Us from Other Animals*. Basic Books.
5. Williamson, M. (1992). *A Return to Love: Reflections on the Principles of 'A Course in Miracles'*. New York: HarperCollins.
6. Ramirez, R., & Wilkinson, A. (2016). *Strategic Reframing: The Oxford Scenario Planning Approach*. Oxford University Press.
7. Wells, H. G. (1933). *The Shape of Things to Come*. Hutchinson & Co.
8. Huxley, A. (1932). *Brave New World*. Chatto & Windus.
9. Dweck, C. S. (2006). *Mindset: The New Psychology of Success*. Random House.

12

THE INSPIRING COMMUNICATOR

For knowledge workers, the ability to communicate concisely, economically and memorably to convey their message and turn ideas into action has always been crucial. However, the need to be an Inspiring Communicator has intensified as everyone vies to be heard in a crowded communication landscape filled with similar and commoditised messages.

So, in this chapter, we focus on the essential skill of creating compelling business narratives, working alongside AI. We know that stories that tap into people's emotions have become a powerful way to deliver messages. We can replace the tedious march through dull facts with compelling storytelling. And today AI can serve as our assistant in constructing narratives to convey complex ideas.

We explore in this chapter the value of knowledge workers who collaborate with AI to craft engaging stories in a business context. We emphasise leveraging AI to handle the groundwork while recognising the importance of human qualities in telling memorable stories.

DOI: 10.4324/9781003514879-13

Those who master the art of evoking the emotional power of a story will wield significant influence. This skill will benefit a range of business communications, from major presentations to everyday posts, blogs and emails.

As Daniel Pink said:

> The future belongs to a very different kind of person with a very different kind of mind – creators and empathisers, pattern recognisers, and meaning makers. . . . The right brain qualities of inventiveness, empathy, joyfulness, and meaning increasingly will determine who flourishes and who flounders.
>
> (A Whole New Mind, 2005)[1]

As marketing guru Seth Godin said, 'Today marketing is no longer about the stuff you make but the stories you tell' (*All Marketers Tell Stories*, 2012).[2]

Let's begin by examining the importance of narrative in business.

The power of narrative in business

The business world eventually recognised storytelling as a powerful communications tool. Stories capture attention, create emotional connections and foster trust and empathy with the audience. They are particularly effective at presenting the bigger picture and simplifying complex concepts.

Stories make information easier to retain and have the power to influence and persuade audiences. They are often entertaining, making them more memorable and likely to be shared.

Consider Steve Jobs, who made storytelling his signature presentation style. His iconic 2001 iPod presentation exemplifies his mastery of story structure. He first identified the problem: for people who wanted to carry their entire music collection with them, existing MP3 players were bulky and difficult to use.

Then, he introduced the solution by dramatically revealing the iPod, with his punchline, '1000 songs in your pocket'. Finally, there was his call to action encouraging people to buy the iPod.

For a review of Steve Jobs's prowess as a storyteller, see *The Presentation Secrets of Steve Jobs: How to Be Insanely Great in Front of Any Audience* by Carmine Gallo (2009).[3]

Richard Branson also excels at storytelling. His adventurous exploits through the late 1990s to today, such as around-the-world balloon trips and space exploration, highlight his renegade spirit. These stories attract followers to the Virgin brand, appealing to those who see themselves as unconventional and adventurous.

Similarly, James Dyson tells the story of challenging the traditional vacuum cleaner market in the 1970s with innovative technology, then facing years of failure and perseverance before finally achieving success in the early 1990s and subsequently creating a billion dollar empire.

Having explored the power of narratives in business communication, let's now look at a process for constructing a story with AI as your assistant.

A framework for constructing business narratives

When faced with large, complex creative tasks, breaking them into distinct parts is helpful. Constructing a business narrative is no different. Here, we introduce seven story tools that map out the storytelling craft. See *The High Performance Customer Insight Professional* (DVL Smith, 2019).[4] We have the Audience and Purpose tools, together with our Evidence and Message tools, followed by the Structure, Narrative and Impact tools.

Each tool's role, importance and practical examples are explained, highlighting where human sensibilities lead the way but where AI can provide assistance.

The Audience tool

First, we'll review the role of the Audience tool. Next, we'll discuss the strengths humans bring in understanding audience expectations. Finally, we'll explore how AI can assist us with our storytelling.

Due to space constraints, we can cover only a few techniques and actions from our comprehensive training programmes. However, the selected ideas and techniques will help readers begin developing the art of telling a story with support from AI.

The role of the Audience tool

The Audience tool ensures you clearly understand your audience's expectations of your communication. Whether it's a major business presentation, a blog post, or an internal email, it's crucial to gauge the audience's likely receptivity, resistance, or acceptance of your message.

Abraham Lincoln is reported as saying, 'When I get ready to talk to someone, I spend two-thirds of the time thinking about what they want to hear and one-third about what I say'.

Understanding your audience helps you make your communication relevant and aligned with their perspective. It allows you to use familiar business language and choose a story structure that resonates with them.

Although understanding your audience may seem like common sense, it's often not common practice. The early 20th-century philosopher and writer Bertrand Russell highlighted the frequent gap between the intent of communication and its actual success. A recurring theme of his was that 'many believe they have communicated their thoughts effectively when they have not'.

One common mistake is creating a communication 'about' an issue rather than writing 'for' the audience. Your communication should address the problems your audience faces and guide them to a resolution.

For example, if your business aim is to identify actions a highways authority should take to provide electric car charging points, your presentation should not be 'about' motorists' anxieties about battery life. The presentation should be 'for' your audience – specifically focusing on whether the highways authority should introduce more charge points on motorways, in rural areas, or in high-density city areas with apartments without direct road access.

To ensure you're writing for your audience, ask yourself on their behalf, 'What's in it for them?' and 'So what?' This approach will help you provide actionable substance.

The Audience tool helps keep your message relevant, ensuring your audience doesn't wonder, 'Why are they telling me this?' It ensures that you align your communication with the audience's needs.

The human dimension in understanding audience expectations

An experienced business storyteller knows to research the overall profile of their audience, including job titles, roles and involvement with the project.

They use judgement and creative imagination to see the presentation through the eyes of their clients and stakeholders, always asking themselves key questions to deepen their understanding of the audience.

Additionally, asking the audience directly can ensure you meet their expectations. Consider these powerful questions:

- What do you expect to do with the results at the end of the presentation?
- What is it that you don't you know now, but if you did, it would significantly improve your decision-making and next steps?
- What is it that's unclear now, but if clarified, would make you feel you've received excellent value from this project and presentation?

How AI can help identify your audience's expectations

AI can assist in understanding your audience's expectations. Begin by using tools like *Google Analytics* to profile your audience's overall characteristics. Then, go deeper by engaging with ChatGPT (or another LLM) to identify different information sources about your audience. It can also help you delve further by suggesting probing questions to ask yourself or your audience before a presentation.

Use ChatGPT to role-play a target audience member: ask it questions to help you establish if you are meeting audience expectations.

In this way, by combining traditional questioning techniques with AI-generated insights and analytics you will create a comprehensive profile of your audience's expectations.

The Purpose tool

Let's now look at the role of the Purpose tool and then look at understanding how both experienced professionals and AI can contribute to this process.

The role of the Purpose tool

When preparing a communication or business presentation, it's crucial to go beyond understanding your audience's business objectives and expectations. You need to grasp the fundamental 'purpose' of the communication, which involves knowing the change you want to bring about in your audience.

Your purpose focuses on the emotional and psychological state you want to leave your audience in after your presentation. This requires you to reflect on your stance on the issue – your point of view – and what's at stake for both you and your stakeholders once your message is delivered. Your purpose must be clear to you, though it doesn't always need to be explicitly stated to your audience.

For example, if your aim is to advise a local authority on increasing tourism and business revenue in a seaside resort, you might suggest improving tourist attractions or offering grants to local start-ups. However, beyond this aim, your purpose might be to inspire and motivate the authority to take action rather than maintaining the status quo.

So, in this case, your purpose is to create a sense of urgency and emphasise that procrastination is detrimental. Your purpose is to galvanise your audience into action, build their confidence in implementing your ideas, and assure them that in supporting your proposed strategy their decisions won't harm their careers or reputations.

The human role in identifying your purpose

Human analysts excel at identifying the purpose of a communication due to their ability to understand context, apply emotional intelligence, and envision the future. This gives them a significant advantage in defining the communication's purpose.

To establish the underlying purpose of a presentation, experienced knowledge workers draw on key skills. They use sensemaking skills to understand the broader context, identifying subtle, unresolved dilemmas and tensions within the client organisation. Their critical thinking will help them recognise biases and preconceptions in the audience, enabling them to strategise effectively. And their creativity and forward-thinking skills are crucial for leveraging emotional intelligence, which is essential for truly understanding the audience and determining what they seek from the presentation.

One effective technique for clarifying the purpose is to habitually ask at the beginning of every communication, 'What ultimate outcome do I want to achieve with this presentation?' This prevents getting sidetracked by immediate business aims and keeps the fundamental purpose in focus.

Let's now look at how AI can help you achieve clarity around the purpose of your communication.

The support role of AI in crafting your purpose

In using the Purpose tool, humans take the lead, leveraging emotional intelligence, empathy and compassion to understand and deliver the communication's purpose. However, AI can significantly aid this process through tools like ChatGPT.

AI can help ensure that you have thoroughly considered the true purpose of your communication by using creative prompting techniques. For instance, after setting the business context, you might ask ChatGPT:

I want to understand the anxieties, concerns, and fears my audience might have about what I'm going to say about X. What tips and advice do you have?

ChatGPT might suggest:

Why not conduct informal discussions with friendly client contacts to gauge potential anxieties or concerns.

Then through further iterations, you might receive more detailed advice, such as:

Consider if you fully understand the hidden agendas behind the project.

Identify any major issues you might be avoiding due to their complexity.

Check if there's anything about your presentation that does not feel quite right and validate this with stakeholders.

Are you sure you really understand what your audience is expecting.

Look out for anything that could be confusing in the way you are communicating with your audience.

In summary, AI can act as a critical friend and sparring partner, encouraging you to rigorously analyse and refine the purpose of your communication. This collaboration between human insight and AI ensures total clarity around the purpose, ultimately determining the success of your communication by not only meeting audience expectations but also driving the desired change.

The Evidence tool

Let's begin by looking at the role played by the Evidence tool in the process of constructing a business narrative.

The role of the Evidence tool

The Evidence tool plays a crucial role in constructing a business narrative by delivering just the right amount of supporting data. It involves providing enough evidence to support your argument but without overwhelming your audience with too much information. The principle to follow here is 'less is more'.

For most business presentations, you can achieve your objective and deliver a compelling storyline using only about 20% of the available evidence. So focus on the most compelling evidence to which your audience can immediately relate and eliminate unnecessary details that do not drive your story forward.

The analyst's role in selecting powerful evidence

Experienced business analysts are adept at focusing on critical evidence through concepts like data reduction. They understand that the fundamental story is often evident from the total sample, as subgroup variations usually refine rather than redefine the overall narrative.

Expert analysts also have an instinct for identifying headline evidence that captures the audience's attention, much like top journalists. First-class journalists skillfully support their arguments with just the right amount of compelling evidence, ensuring readers find the story convincing without needing more information. Poor journalism, on the other hand, leaves readers doubtful and demanding more evidence.

In summary, human analysts use intuition and their power skills to find the sweet spot – winning the rational argument with hard evidence whilst engaging the emotional argument with subtle insights. For example, illustrating the rise of billionaires by stating that the richest 1% of people in the world have attracted two-thirds of all new wealth since 2020 – effectively drives home the point.

With the advent of AI, there are now tools that can assist in creating the optimal evidence set for storytelling, enhancing the analyst's ability to present powerful and convincing evidence.

The role of AI in the evidence context

AI can greatly assist in gathering the right evidence to build your story. Various AI tools serve as platforms for organising and constructing stories, streamlining the workflow and allowing you to focus on creative aspects rather than administrative tasks.

Using ChatGPT – after providing the necessary context and data – to refine your evidence selection you can ask questions like, 'What is the most compelling evidence to support my point?'.

Microsoft Azure Cognitive Services can be used to process large datasets, identify patterns and extract key insights. And, *Google Cloud Natural Language API* is available to analyse textual data and facilitate the construction of coherent storylines.

Thus, AI significantly reduces the time required for evidence assembly, handling much of the heavy lifting. However, the final, critical judgements about which evidence will be most persuasive still rely on human intuition and skill.

The Message tool

Let's explore the importance of creating a powerful message, review the human role in crafting it, and examine how AI can support this process.

The importance of creating a powerful message

Your message is what your audience would convey to someone who did not attend the presentation and asks, 'What was that presentation about?' It needs to clearly state how you've addressed the business challenge or question presented to you.

For example, if tasked with improving the productivity of a team of knowledge workers, your message shouldn't be a lengthy, ambiguous account of a host of productivity-related factors with vague suggestions. Instead, it should be concise and specific, like 'Productivity will increase with stronger leadership providing a clear vision, coupled with transparent communication to enhance accountability'.

Remember what they say: 'If you can't sum up your story in a few sentences, you don't know what you're talking about!'

Crafting powerful messages applying human insight, judgement and imagination

Creating a powerful message relies on human instinct to know what will resonate. Here are three suggestions for helping to land your message.

The Commander's intent: Leaders, notably General Dwight D. Eisenhower during World War II, ensured that in the chaos of war, there is one clear objective that every soldier can remember and act upon. In business communications, this means having a clear and simple message at the heart of your communication to which everyone can relate.
The George Orwell test: George Orwell would ask himself after writing each sentence, 'Could I have said this more clearly, in fewer words, and in a more memorable way?' These principles were outlined in his famous essay 'Politics and the English Language' (1946)[5] in the literary magazine *Horizon*. Applying this ensures your message is concise and impactful.
The Authenticity test: Your message must ring true and be perceived as authentic and genuine. People can easily detect insincerity. There's an old saying that 'the man on the street is the first to smell the rat!'

For example, Wells Fargo faced a backlash for fabricated customer satisfaction stories whilst Starbucks received praise for closing 8,000 stores to conduct racial bias training, after a customer incident – this was seen as a genuine response not a token gesture.

And the good news is that AI can support these human instincts by helping to refine and test messages for clarity, impact and authenticity.

AI's role in crafting engaging messages

So let's explore how AI can assist in crafting compelling, genuine and memorable messages.

Copy.ai can be used to help overcome writer's block to create compelling marketing content. *Jasper* is an AI writing assistant that can help you craft engaging messages. And, *Grammarly* is an AI enhanced tool for grammar checking and writing suggestions.

Additionally, iterative creative prompting with LLMs like ChatGPT can significantly aid in honing your message.

Here's how the process could work, after setting the context for say ChatGPT and providing your initial copy:

Question: How can I make the following message clearer?

Answer: Are you sure this is the key takeaway you want your audience to remember?

AI can then suggest alternative ways to improve your message. Then iterate on AI's suggestions to enhance clarity, conciseness and memorability.

You might input: 'Please provide a brand message for our hospital that emphasises high levels of professional patient care, availability whenever needed, and consistent delivery over time'.

Through various iterations – with AI providing a series of ideas – you could make the creative leap to 'The best patient care to every patient, every time'.

The point is that AI, when used intelligently and creatively, can help avoid boring clichéd, standardised communications and instead assist you in generating fantastic, original copy.

So, in sum, the Message tool helps ensure your communication is clear, concise and impactful. Here AI can assist in refining messages, but human intuition and judgement of course remain crucial for authenticity and engagement.

The Structure tool

Now, let's move on to our next tool – the Structure tool.

The importance of structure

Structure is vital in communication. When it's present, we take it for granted, but its absence results in a jumbled mess. A strong structure ensures a coherent delivery of key messages. In business, structure goes beyond presenting facts; it integrates ideas into a compelling narrative.

The Structure tool helps us ensure we have a coherent architecture in place to deliver and land our key message. Our tool provides principles and techniques to create an elegant story structure, guiding your audience through arguments rather than overwhelming them with data.

For an illustration of brilliant storytelling, we need to look no further than Martin Luther King Jr.'s iconic 'I Have a Dream' speech (1963). This speech, which we mentioned earlier, exemplifies masterful story architecture.

First, King presents the 'challenge': the unfair treatment of the Black community in the US.

Next, he discusses the 'solution': the civil rights movement's campaign for equality.

He then delivers a compelling call to 'action' with his repeated and powerful 'I have a dream' message, creating a chorus-like effect throughout the speech.

This story structure creates a rhythm that showcases King's exceptional oratory skills.

The fundamentals of story structure

Understanding the fundamental tenets of storytelling is crucial when constructing a story. At a high level, many stories in novels, dramas and films follow a basic three-part structure.

They begin by establishing a status quo – the current situation and setting where the drama will unfold. Here, a challenge or problem is introduced, creating initial tension and dilemmas.

Next is the 'messy middle', where rising action develops with various complexities and nuances. The characters or organisations face deeper challenges and explore potential solutions, building to a climax. This climax often features a major turning point or urgent issue that must be addressed, keeping the audience engaged and eager to see what happens next.

Finally, the story moves to the resolution, where all loose ends are tied up. In business storytelling, this might include suggested actions and pathways forward.

This three-act structure is evident in many classic plays and films. For instance, in Noël Coward's *Private Lives* (1930), Act One introduces the protagonists, a honeymooning couple who encounter their ex-spouses at the same hotel. Act Two delves into the complexities of their volatile relationships, as they reconsider their divorces and contemplate leaving their new partners. In Act Three, the storyline concludes with our newly divorced couple reuniting and deciding to elope together.

Similarly, in the film *The Godfather* (1972), we see this three-part structure unfold. We begin with the head of a mafia family being tempted by a narcotics dealer to enter the drug trade. In the middle, the son is trying to distance himself from the family's illegal activities and faces a dilemma, ultimately deciding to protect his father by killing the drug dealer thereby making an irrevocable commitment to the family's illicit enterprises. The film concludes with the son becoming the new Godfather.

Understanding the concept of structure in film, drama and literature will help create engaging and coherent stories in the business context.

Continuing with our Structure tool, let's now overview some fundamental story structures for business presentations. But these are not prescriptive. They are suggestions for you to then add your creativity and originality.

For instance, Harold Pinter's play *Betrayal* (1978) starts at the end and works backward, illustrating a reverse story approach that can be applied creatively in business storytelling. For example, starting with where an organisation ended up and explaining what happened leading up to that point. The key is to adapt and tweak standard structures to suit your specific needs.

Here is an overview of some popular story structures

One: Background/Confrontation/Resolution

This structure starts by outlining the critical Background needed to understand the story you are about to tell. It then deals with the central conflict or Confrontation at the heart of the business question. It then moves to ways of Resolving this issue.

Two: Challenge/Solution/Call-to-Action

This structure starts by focusing on a specific Challenge – rather than first talking about the background to the problem. Then you present the Solution that then leads to a Call to Action. This approach, as we have seen, was Steve Jobs's simple but effective go-to structure. Typically, he would present a challenge/problem, then provide the solution and then set up a call to action.

Three: Situation/Complexity/Resolution

The Situation/Complexity/Resolution structure sets out the business Situation and then deals with important Complexities, before outlining the Resolution. The Resolution is often addressed in the form of questions that are then answered.

Four: Lead/Support/Tail

The Lead/Support/Tail structure pivots around there being a killer statistic (or central argument) that essentially tells the story. This structure centres around a few key statistics. It zeros in on a killer statistic which is followed by a key piece of supporting data and selected additional data. These statistics drive the entire story. This structure is popular with newspaper journalists.

Five: High-Level Concept

The High-Level Concept structure has a central concept sitting at the heart of the presentation with there being different perspectives that you then address. So let's say you're presenting on how to drive growth in the UK economy and your central concept is that the UK should invest in AI technology – this is the message that lies at the heart of the presentation.

So having set out this core message you could then outline the increasing power of AI technology, after which you return to your central message about AI being pivotal in driving growth.

Next you could introduce examples of how various countries that have invested heavily in AI are enjoying successful growth. After this you again return to your central message about AI being a growth driver.

You get the idea: the key is that you cover different topics but keep returning to the golden thread – the big high-level concept underpinning your core message – how to drive growth by investing in AI.

Six: Interactive

Another structure is the Interactive storytelling technique. This involves starting by presenting your fundamental message. You will have all the material pre-prepared, but the audience decide the order in which they want you to examine various perspectives to this message.

A useful guide for structuring a business message is *Made to Stick: Why Some Ideas Survive and Others Die* by Heath and Heath (2007).[6]

Understanding the emotional core of storytelling

At the heart of storytelling is the ability to tap into people's emotions. Over 100 years ago, psychologist William James highlighted the power of being able to 'transmit powerful psychological messages'. He argued that storytelling should convey deep psychological truths to influence how people think and feel, highlighting that emotion often outweighs reason.

This places the emphasis on using storytelling techniques that evoke emotions. For instance, in a presentation about electric cars, instead of presenting aggregate statistics about electric car drivers' battery anxiety, rather tell the story of an individual stranded late at night due to a dead battery. This personal approach resonates more deeply with the audience.

Example: The UK Post Office Scandal

The UK Post Office Scandal, which we mentioned earlier, is a good illustration of the power of emotional storytelling. More than 700 postmasters were wrongly prosecuted due to a faulty computer system, leading to wrongful imprisonments. Despite numerous enquiries, little action was taken until a compelling TV drama based on the true story aired in December 2022 (*Mr Bates vs The Post Office*). This emotional and vivid portrayal prompted swift acknowledgement and action, intensely highlighting the impact of storytelling on public perception.

AI's role in story structuring

The good news is that today AI can be our creative assistant for identifying the most powerful story structure. Let's look at some ways it can help.

Supplying us with story structures

AI can help your story structuring – for instance, by using ChatGPT to provide you with a whole raft of different story structures that you may wish to consider adapting and using for your specific purposes.

Prompting new ideas

The better you get at playing the role of creative prompter by submitting different story structures with prompts on the twist and turns you'd like to see introduced, then the better the end result.

Let's consider a university project aimed at examining the student customer experience, from initial enquiry to application, arrival, registration and the first weeks of term.

Feedback from student surveys reveals that their experiences varied widely. Some students had great experiences when first enquiring about the university, but their satisfaction plummeted during the application process. However, their experiences improved again during registration.

An analyst might start by presenting all the data, detailing the highs and lows of the experience with various statistics. While factually accurate, this approach is uninspired.

But by using AI for creative prompting, we can find more imaginative ways to illustrate the ups and downs of the university's performance. For example, framing the student journey as a game of 'snakes and ladders' could be effective. Students climb the ladder with high expectations, only to slide down the snake when doubts about their university choice arise during the less satisfactory stages.

You get the idea. AI can help you think outside the box, acting as a creative partner in offering imaginative ways to tell your story.

So enjoy the way AI can be your critical friend and provide you with some fantastic twists and turns to help you become a great storyteller.

Storyboarding

AI support extends to helping with storyboarding applications to experiment with different story flows. Tools like *Miro* offer a virtual whiteboard platform that replicates the traditional method of using Post-it notes on a whiteboard, allowing you to play around with and determine the best story structure. These tools offer a powerful way to visualise and refine your storytelling process.

Assessing sentiment

AI applications can also analyse sentiment scores for different story structures, predicting audience reactions.

Several AI tools can analyse the sentiment of audiences when presented with different story structures. Here are some examples.

MonkeyLearn: This tool offers sentiment analysis through machine learning, helping you understand how different story structures might be received by your audience.

IBM Watson Natural Language Understanding: This AI service can analyse text to determine sentiment, providing insights into how your audience might react to various story structures.

Google Cloud Natural Language: This tool can analyse the sentiment of your stories, offering detailed sentiment scores and insights based on the text you provide.

Lexalytics: This platform provides sentiment analysis and text analytics, helping you gauge audience reactions to different storytelling approaches.

Brandwatch: While primarily a social media monitoring tool, Brandwatch uses AI to analyse sentiment in text, which can be useful for understanding audience reactions to different story structures.

Hugging Face's Transformers: With pre-trained models for sentiment analysis, this tool can help analyse how different story structures might be perceived by your audience.

Combining human experience with AI

The synergy between humans and AI creates a powerful storytelling combination. Business analysts, with their years of experience, understand effective story structures and the importance of emotional intelligence in connecting with audiences. They know that stories have always been a way for humans to make sense of the world.

However, generative AI also has a vast knowledge of story structures and via creative prompting can offer fresh storytelling angles, informed by what it is able to tell us about audiences' likely emotional engagement with alternative formats.

In summary, the combination of human experience and AI makes for powerful storytelling. Experienced storytellers understand the emotional nuances, while AI offers fresh perspectives. This synergy can lead to truly imaginative story structures.

The Narrative tool

Now, let's explore the next tool in our kit: the Narrative tool.

Creating powerful narratives

Our Narrative tool is designed to address three key aspects of storytelling: creating a theme, selecting words with care and ensuring consistency of words, stats and images by applying the 'Rule of Three'.

Creating a theme

The Narrative tool ensures your story has a clear and distinct theme, setting the tone for your communication. Audiences appreciate knowing the overall direction of a presentation or document early on.

It's crucial to signal your overall theme and central message in advance, preparing your audience for what is to come. Is this presentation going to be a dramatic rollercoaster ride, full of anxiety and potential disruption of current practices? Or will it be a calm journey through familiar territory, affirming that the organisation is mostly on the right track with only minor adjustments needed?

Reflecting on your overall theme will also help you develop communications strategies to ensure you achieve your purpose and land your message. For example, if you anticipate there will be resistance to your narrative, then consider using the 'connections, not alternatives' technique.

Rather than presenting starkly different alternatives that may be met with resistance, start by highlighting the aspects of the organisation's current practices that are working well. Then, demonstrate how these existing practices serve as a foundation that can be connected to the introduction of new methods.

By framing existing practices as a springboard for improvement, the audience is more likely to see how their own ideas provided the platform for a new way of thinking and therefore be more receptive.

Care with words

Respecting the power of words is crucial. Here are a few examples illustrating the impact of careful word choice.

Franklin D. Roosevelt: In a speech after the sudden attack on Pearl Harbour, he revised 'December 7th 1941 . . . a date that will live in world history' to 'a date that will live in infamy', evoking a stronger sense of betrayal and galvanising the American people's support for entering World War II.
Winston Churchill: In his famous speech following the Battle of Britain (1940), he shifted the focus from a metaphor about the loss of RAF pilots (*These were our finest flowers*) to one of triumph and heroism (*This was their finest hour*). The new phrase underscored the courage and resilience of the RAF pilots and motivated the country for the challenges ahead.
Edward Heath: The UK Prime Minister in a 1973 speech changed 'the unacceptable facet of capitalism' to 'the unacceptable face of capitalism', transforming a technical critique into a more powerful human criticism of corporate excesses.

The Rule of Three: words, images and data

The Narrative tool also ensures consistency between the words used, supporting images and metaphors and the data presented. This Rule of Three creates a cohesive and powerful message.

Example on Climate Crisis

Headline: Sea levels are rising – act now.
Image: A striking image of a melting glacier.
Data: Global temperatures have risen by 1.2°C since pre-industrial times.

How AI can support the crafting of narratives

With AI tools, our goal is to emphasise the importance of word choice and encourage careful reflection on the words used. In today's fast-paced, social media-driven world, the craft of writing is more important than ever. By combining human instincts and AI support, we can create impactful and purposeful communications.

Six ways AI enhances our narrative creation

Editing and refinement: ChatGPT and similar tools serve as excellent writing assistants for refining drafts. By setting the context and specifying the desired writing style, AI can provide fantastic alternatives through iterative prompts, elevating your initial output.

Evaluating clarity: AI tools like *Jasper* and *Persado* can assess the clarity, tone and style of your drafts, suggesting changes to enhance impact based on your audience. Other tools to explore include *Writesonic*, *StoryChief* and *Narrato*.

Bringing your writing alive: Beyond editing, AI can prompt you to take your writing in more creative directions. Your AI writing partner might suggest:

- Including anecdotes and personal stories to make your presentation relatable – dial up your unique 'original voice'
- Being bolder in presenting your point of view by using more powerful and varied metaphors and analogies
- Role-playing as your audience to evaluate the impact and compelling nature of your message

Improving emotional impact: AI tools with neuro-linguistic programming backgrounds can help gauge if you are effectively tapping into your audience's emotions. These tools can assess performance on key emotions like joy, anger, sadness and excitement.

Enhancing delivery: For verbal presentations, AI tools can help you reflect on your pace, voice modulation and overall tone. These tools provide insights to improve your delivery style, whether face-to-face or online.

Optimising overall communications effectiveness: ChatGPT for example can suggest alternative ways to juxtapose headlines, images and data, enhancing the effectiveness of your communication. This helps ensure a cohesive and impactful narrative.

In sum, AI is increasingly capable of supporting a wide range of tasks to help craft and deliver impactful narratives. And as AI continues to improve, it will offer even more sophisticated tools for narrative creation and presentation. Also, increasingly chatbots are being used effectively for one-on-one tutorials, showcasing the evolving role of AI in education and communication.

The Impact tool

Let's conclude our overview of our story tools framework by examining the Impact tool. This tool was included to emphasise the importance of infusing business communications with the personality and personal experiences of the presenter.

We've acknowledged that the presenter's experience is a vital part of the evidence supporting the storyline. Personal anecdotes and stories can tap into the audience's emotions, enhancing the communication's impact – something AI currently lacks.

AI can provide broad advice on how to introduce personality into business communications, but the final judgement depends on the communicator's personality and the audience's nature.

Here are some guiding principles when it comes to making an impact.

Engage your audience on three levels

The key to crafting a message that will 'stick' with your audience and encourage them to share it with others is to engage at three levels.

Thinking: Make the audience think about your message.
Feelings: Tap into the audience's emotions.
Involvement: Involve your audience through questions and relate your message to their experiences.

Provide hooks, twists and turns

Great communicators start with a hook that draws in the audience, for example:

George Orwell begins his novel *1984* with 'It was a bright cold day in April, and the clocks were striking thirteen'. (Written mainly in 1948.)
Albert Camus starts *The Outsider* (1942) with 'My mother died today. Or maybe yesterday; I can't be sure'.
Bob Dylan starts his song *All Along the Watchtower* with 'There must be some way out of here said the joker to the thief' (Released in 1967).

These openings make us want to know more.

Create craft memorable sound bites and surprise

Why not add in memorable sound bites – these increase the likelihood that your message will be actioned.

So from the world of politics many will remember the powerful call to action that inspired the patriotic taking of responsibility from JFK, 'Ask not what your country can do for you, ask what you can do for your country' (1961 Presidential Inaugural Address).

And from the world of business 'Think different', first used in 1997, neatly encapsulates Apple's brand identity and philosophy of always distinguishing itself from its competitors.

And 'The Happiest Place on Earth' brilliantly captures the essence of Disneyland's promise to provide a magical experience that exceeds expectations.

Throughout your presentation, include moments that surprise your audience, prompting them to lean in and stay engaged. Use various techniques and devices to create these engaging moments and enhance your presentation's impact.

Switch from the aggregate data to telling the hero's tale

We've discussed the power of presenting an argument through the story of an individual hero or villain rather than relying solely on aggregate statistics.

While this approach is powerful, it's important to ensure the story reflects the typical experience shown by the overall data. Using an extreme, non-representative case can be misleading, but if the story mirrors the general trend, it's a valid and impactful technique.

Introduce personal storytelling

When the presenter shares their personal experiences and feelings upon first encountering the evidence, it can be a legitimate way to connect with the audience. However, the presenter must ensure these personal stories resonate with the audience and avoid self-indulgence.

Provide the third corner perspective

Involving the audience in a presentation can sometimes elevate the discussion above a binary argument. For instance, a debate on private healthcare could be framed as a balance between two equally honourable perspectives:

equality in healthcare access and the right to choose how to spend one's own money. This approach can elevate the conversation, but it must be done carefully to avoid appearing overly abstract.

Use humour

Humour can be a powerful communication tool that AI cannot easily replicate. However, it must be used carefully. Effective humour demonstrates an ability to understand and engage in an authentic way with your audience and to grasp the wider context.

For example, when the then-elderly comedian Bob Hope, who lived to be 100 (1903–2003), was asked in a TV interview if he would prefer to be cremated or buried, he replied, 'Surprise me!' Such wit is difficult for AI to match.

Political figures often try to use humour to connect with their audience, but you have to get it right. For example, Denis Healey, the UK Labour politician, was dubbed the 'Moses of the Labour Party'. The speechwriters for the UK PM Margaret Thatcher, proposed a witty retort, 'Keep taking the tablets', playing on the biblical reference. Allegedly, Thatcher misunderstood the joke and altered it to 'Keep taking the pills', which diluted the humour!

Risk-taking: sticking to the script versus responding to the moment

Many politicians and business leaders are trained to stick to a script, often repeating a bland message. To have a real impact, it's sometimes necessary to deviate from the script and show genuine humanity. This requires careful judgement.

One author recalls interviewing disadvantaged youths and deciding to ask a young man with severe facial scars, 'May I ask what happened to you?' This direct question led to a meaningful conversation about parental violence in his childhood. This intervention provided more powerful insights than working through the official interview script.

So we've reviewed the seven story tools, highlighting the strengths of human storytelling and the support AI can provide. Let's now summarise actions to enhance the ability to inspire through business narratives.

Actions to stand out as an engaging business storyteller in the AI era

Here are some actions you can take to cultivate the storytelling habit while working alongside AI.

Enhance emotional sensitivity, empathy and emotional intelligence

Humans excel at conveying powerful psychological messages that resonate with the audience. Our emotional intelligence is a key advantage over AI.

Remember Maya Angelou's words: 'People will forget what you said, they'll forget what you did, but they will never forget how you made them feel'. This is often quoted from her interviews in the 1980s and 1990s.

Focus on authenticity, genuineness and kindness

Authentic and kind communications will always triumph over sterile, algorithm-generated messages. Aldous Huxley, being interviewed in the early 1960s, concluded, 'It's a little embarrassing that after 45 years of research and study, the best advice I can give people is to be a little kinder to each other'.

Tap into collective consciousness

Effective communicators understand and connect with the collective consciousness, sensing what resonates deeply with people.

For example, whilst undertaking a business challenge about France on the UK *Apprentice* TV programme, a contestant naively and amazingly asked, 'Do the French love their children?' This illustrates an alarming lack of connection to the collective understanding (Season 6, Episode 2, 2010).

It may be that the then British Prime Minister Rishi Sunak now regrets his inability to tap into the mood of the national collective consciousness when, in 2024, he prematurely left the eightieth D-Day Landing commemorations to record a TV interview back in London upsetting veterans and their families.

Capitalise on mental time travel

Humans can learn from past experiences and imagine future scenarios. Use this ability to craft stories that shape a desirable future.

Cultivate the art of mental time travel to paint vivid future histories.

Develop a detective-like observational eye

AI is powerful in many tasks, but humans excel at noticing small details that reveal much about human behaviour.

For example, the writer David Sedaris, in an essay titled *Laugh, Kookaburra*, first published in *The New Yorker* in 2009, shares a story about his efforts to stop environmental littering. He recounts collecting litter from a nearby natural beauty spot and noticing a sweet wrapper meticulously folded and placed inside a soft drink bottle, with the cap screwed back on, before being thrown onto the grass. These small details reveal a lot about human behaviour!

Remember AI is an ally in storytelling

To conclude, AI won't replace the unique human ability to convey the essence of the human condition. But AI can enhance your storytelling skills, providing valuable insights and knowledge.

So embrace AI to augment your storytelling capabilities and harness its power to become a more well-rounded communicator. Engage with AI to complement your creativity and imagination, elevating your storytelling to new heights.

Summary

In this chapter, we emphasised the importance of storytelling in a business context. Storytelling is a crucial skill for knowledge workers, showcasing the immense potential of humans working alongside AI to create compelling communications.

We explored our seven story tools framework, demonstrating how AI assists and enhances our natural storytelling abilities.

In the next chapter, we will address the challenges of introducing the polymath concept into organisations, focusing on ensuring the right organisational fit and leadership style to maximise this technology's potential.

Notes

1. Pink, D. (2005). *A Whole New Mind: Why Right-Brainers Will Rule the Future*. Riverhead Books, a division of Penguin Group.
2. Godin, S. (2012). *All Marketers Tell Stories*. Penguin Group.
3. Gallo, C. (2009). *The Presentation Secrets of Steve Jobs: How to Be Insanely Great in Front of Any Audience*. McGraw-Hill Education.
4. Smith, D. V. L. (2019). *The High-Performance Customer Insight Professional: How to Make Sense of the Evidence, Build the Story and Turn Insights into Action*. Amazon Publishing.
5. Orwell, G. (1946). *Politics and the English Language*. Horizon, 13(76), 252–265.
6. Heath, C., & Heath, D. (2007). *Made to Stick: Why Some Ideas Survive and Others Die*. Random House.

13

THE GALVANISING LEADER

The advent of AI demands a new approach to team leadership. This chapter explores the strategies and techniques that leaders must adopt to effectively guide knowledge workers through the AI era.

We examine various sensitive employee and workplace issues that leaders must be aware of to manage teams successfully, even before the introduction of AI. We then emphasise the importance of leaders in the AI era acting as linchpins showing high productivity, energy and efficiency to achieve results. Next, we discuss the role of leaders in presenting a vision that highlights AI's potential to their teams.

Also, we highlight a new dimension of leadership in the uncertain and disruptive AI era: the need for sensitivity, emotional intelligence, compassion and fostering a collaborative environment. This is crucial as some will benefit significantly from AI, while others may feel anxious, threatened, or disadvantaged by its arrival.

DOI: 10.4324/9781003514879-14

We address the importance of leaders cultivating adaptive management styles to create the organisational structures, procedures and techniques necessary for integrating AI.

The commitment of leaders to providing lifelong learning opportunities, ensuring their teams receive continuous education to keep pace with the relentless advancement of AI technology is addressed. And we conclude with a profile of the Galvanising Leader.

In this chapter, we examine the key dimensions to leading a team in the AI era. These include being sensitive to what it is to lead and manage in today's workplace environment together with the need to provide visionary pathways to help teams work with rather than against AI.

We also focus on the importance of team leaders being 'can-do' linchpins who can seize the productivity advantages offered by AI. Then we then stress the need for team leaders to provide sensitive, collaborative, compassionate and adaptive leadership in an era that will be characterised by uncertainty and disruption. Finally, we look at the issue of team leaders providing ongoing learning and support for their teams.

Providing sensitive leadership in a complex workplace

Team leaders understand that, even before AI, the workplace was undergoing significant changes driven by cultural, social and economic factors. They recognise the importance of being sensitive to the responsibilities involved in managing people's careers and working lives.

Today's leaders must respect individual rights related to fair wealth distribution, equality, diversity and inclusion, mental health, hybrid and flexible working and work–life balance. With the arrival of AI, three key issues have become more pronounced.

As anxiety about job security rises, with the potential for AI to evolve from an enabling tool to one that can replace certain job functions, leaders must address these inevitable concerns.

There are also ethical considerations. Leaders need to tackle ethical questions regarding AI use in various scenarios, including its impact on environmental sustainability.

Then there are societal implications. Ideally, employers and leaders should, notwithstanding the challenges, consider the broader societal effects of their employment decisions, recognising that AI may exacerbate social polarisation by creating both 'newly advantaged' and 'newly disadvantaged' groups.

All this calls for the need to demonstrate high levels of empathy. Actively listening and respecting individual concerns are crucial traits for leaders. In addition, it is important to communicate genuinely, transparently and sensitively. Leaders need to guide individuals through the AI transition, highlighting opportunities and setting motivational milestones.

To manage these issues, team leaders in the AI era will benefit from cultivating a polymath mindset. Understanding the interconnectedness between work, individual mental health, well-being and societal implications is increasingly important.

Delivering with an action-orientated management style

Beyond sensitivity to workplace issues, AI team leaders must master fundamental management and leadership skills – timeless qualities that turn ideas into action and achieve results. Let's focus on three essential aspects of effective leadership.

Be a winning linchpin

Seth Godin (2010)[1] emphasises the need for effective leaders to be 'linchpins' who can bring order to chaos. These individuals simplify problems rather than complicate them, making intelligent decisions to eliminate unnecessary confusion whilst addressing genuine complexity.

Linchpins radiate energy and positivity, solving problems with a can-do attitude, unlike energy drains who sap enthusiasm. They possess strong management and leadership skills, and whilst AI can assist with administrative tasks, their core human-centric qualities remain the crucial ones.

The motto of many business leaders who have mastered the art of making things happen is 'Don't let the process kill the big idea'. They always start with the end in mind and are skilled at turning ideas into actions. They resonate with a comment attributed to Steve Jobs that 'Ideas without action aren't ideas, they're regrets'. This unique ability to make ideas happen ensures that linchpins will remain irreplaceable by AI.

Embracing the entrepreneurial mindset

To thrive in the AI era, team leaders will also benefit from adopting an entrepreneurial approach to managing change and achieving success. Effective team leaders understand that the key to success is taking massive, determined action – they always get started!

This involves effectual reasoning – starting an adventure even if all elements of the plan aren't finalised. By setting off in the right direction, adjustments can be made along the way, akin to 'building the plane as you fly it'.

For a review of entrepreneurial best practice, see *The Entrepreneur Mindset* (DVL Smith, 2023).[2]

Inspiring confidence

A crucial leadership skill is the ability to inspire confidence in others, as well as in themselves. This has always been important, but in the AI era, filled with uncertainty and disruption, the ability to build team confidence and engage with AI is invaluable. Galvanising Leaders understand the confidence–competence virtuous circle and know how to leverage it for their team's success.

Responding to the new AI environment

Let's now look at three elements of what constitutes a visionary AI-fluent team leader.

The AI vision

A crucial AI leadership skill is the ability to create a compelling vision of AI's future that energises and motivates the team. In today's fast-paced environment, many are uncertain about AI's trajectory and look to their leaders for clarity. Leaders must translate this vision into clear, constructive pathways, helping team members develop the skills needed to work alongside AI.

A visionary leader sees the big picture and identifies the exciting opportunities AI offers. They present AI as a catalyst for positive change rather than a threat. Such leaders understand where their industry is heading, how their company fits into this future, and the strategies and tactics needed to maximise AI's benefits.

These leaders also have to have the honesty to share any downsides of AI's impact on their business. There may well be implications for headcount or the types of employee profile that the business will be looking to push forward, and this may mean that some individuals may not progress as they thought they would or indeed not have a role. It is incumbent on leaders to share this vision honestly and then support people through this process.

In addition, a visionary leader not only sees the long-term benefits of AI but also breaks down the journey into manageable steps. They will outline a series of achievable milestones that guide the team towards realising the vision and enjoying its benefits.

Moreover, effective leaders articulate their vision and milestones in a motivational manner. They help team members understand their roles in the future and how they can contribute. As leaders, they will map out a journey that team members will recognise as both accessible and rewarding.

Building personal AI proficiency

As AI becomes integral to key tasks, team leaders must assess their own AI proficiency to effectively lead and maintain credibility. A proficient AI team leader will have a solid understanding of basic AI concepts, and how AI is likely to evolve.

They will understand key applications such as natural language processing (e.g. ChatGPT), image and speech recognition, as well as basic data and business analysis tools, but additionally they will have an appreciation of some of the foundational technologies such as neural networks and deep learning.

Here the critical question is how much AI knowledge is necessary for a team leader to lead effectively and maintain credibility. This depends on the business context and the team's dynamics, but there are general principles to consider:

Information curve principle: Acquiring 80% of the necessary knowledge to understand AI applications is relatively straightforward. It is the remaining 20% that requires extensive experience. So the good news is that, with a modest time investment, you can, as a team leader, quickly understand a wide range of AI applications.

Credibility test principle: It is important to determine the depth of knowledge required to be credible in guiding AI strategy. For example, a CEO is expected to know themself the total number of employees in their company, but it is legitimate for them to refer specific queries about employees' qualifications to their HR team without losing credibility. Following this point, an AI team leader must know enough to guide the overall AI strategy effectively but can delegate highly technical details to specialists.
Self-monitoring: Regularly and honestly assess whether you really understand AI tools in sufficient depth to lead your team ethically and effectively. A superficial grasp can undermine your credibility, whilst a solid understanding of key principles without necessarily delving into detailed technicalities will be still seen as a professional and strategic approach.

By following these principles, an AI-fluent team leader can balance the breadth and depth of knowledge to lead effectively and maintain the trust of their team.

AI and ethics

Another aspect of being an AI-proficient team leader is promoting the ethical use of AI. Leaders must ensure their team understands and adheres to strict professional standards in AI deployment. This involves being aware of relevant legal and ethical boundaries within their specific knowledge sector.

Let's explore a critical aspect of AI team leadership that extends beyond fundamental management skills: the need for compassionate leadership in the current era.

Leading with a compassionate management style

We have discussed the importance of visionary AI leaders who respect employee rights and expectations and who are proficient in guiding their teams through AI integration. Now, let's focus on an increasingly important leadership skill needed in today's era. This is the adoption of a compassionate, human-centred approach to leadership.

Compassionate leadership involves understanding and empathising with the personal and professional challenges faced by team members. This approach creates a supportive environment, promoting team well-being and building collective resilience in dynamic, volatile and uncertain environments. Prominent advocates of compassionate leadership include:

> The Dalai Lama, who champions compassion, kindness and empathy to foster collaboration and harmony.
> Rasmus Hougaard and Jacqueline Carter (2018),[3] authors of The Mind of the Leader, which highlights compassion as a vital leadership quality.
> Jane Dutton and Monica Worline (2017),[4] authors of Awakening Compassion at Work, focusing on compassion's impact on organisational behaviour.

Compassionate leadership is grounded in emotional intelligence and empathy and understanding team members' well-being concerns, but it goes beyond 'just' empathy by taking actionable steps to support employees with their challenges.

A compassionate team leader:

- Establishes a clear AI vision for their team
- Creates a supportive and resilient team environment
- Demonstrates understanding and empathy for team members' personal and professional challenges
- Takes actionable steps to address team members' struggles and promote well-being

Let's now delve deeper into the specific behaviours and actions that define a compassionate team leader in the context of AI integration.

We begin by looking at the profile of the compassionate team leader – how they will behave, having set up the AI vision for their team.

Profile of the compassionate AI team leader

Address compassionate issues: Compassionate leaders openly discuss concerns like job security, work–life balance and the mental toll of rapid technological change. They create transparent plans to help team members through transitions.

Empower team members: They empower their teams to take personal responsibility for solving problems and for their own personal and creative development.
Promote collaboration: They build teams that value collaborative efforts, encouraging members with diverse skills to respect and leverage each other's strengths for the collective benefit.
Foster inclusive team dynamics: They ensure that both technical and non-technical members feel valued and understand their role in achieving the overall AI goals.
Listen and act: They genuinely listen to team members and take authentic actions to address issues like career burnout and AI-related anxiety.
Ensure clear communication: They maintain clear, transparent communication, demonstrating how AI is being integrated and providing opportunities for everyone to progress while ensuring accountability.
Balance pragmatism and ethics: Compassionate leaders take practical and effective actions to achieve goals while operating responsibly and ethically with AI technology.
Encourage innovation: They foster a culture of creativity and experimentation, celebrating collective successes without highlighting individual winners or losers, and accepting failure as part of the learning process.
Prioritise upskilling: They focus on upskilling team members with personalised development programmes that address specific concerns, acknowledging the disparities created by AI advancements.
Commit to lifelong learning: They are dedicated to lifelong learning for their teams, implementing programmes to help them cope with the pace of AI change.

The compassionate team leader inspires and motivates their team. They listen actively, paying attention to team members' concerns and feedback. They provide support, offering help and resources for personal and professional challenges.

Also, they foster a positive environment, creating a workspace that promotes well-being and collaboration. And the compassionate leader encourages growth, supporting team members' development and career progression.

In addition, compassionate leaders build resilience, helping the team develop strategies to cope with and overcome difficulties. By adopting these practices, compassionate leaders can effectively inspire and motivate their teams.

Adopting an adaptive leadership style to drive AI change

To drive the change, AI team leaders will benefit from following the principles of adaptive leadership pioneered by Heifetz, Grashow and Linsky (2009).[5]

Adaptive leaders excel in complex and uncertain environments where solutions are not straightforward. It is a management style that is comfortable with constantly adjusting and remaining flexible to navigate the moving parts of complex challenges in the AI era.

These leaders create a shared vision for their teams, empowering them to foster innovation and flexibility. Given AI's trajectory, they expect and embrace discontinuous change, respecting individuals' concerns and anxieties during the change process while staying committed to long-term organisational change.

Adaptive leadership involves making short-term adjustments while keeping an eye on long-term goals, ensuring a balanced approach to change. It is a leadership style that is characterised by a bottom-up approach, encouraging team collaboration to find solutions. This contrasts with transformational leadership, which is more top-down and driven by a high-level strategic vision from the organisation's top leader.

Summary of the key characteristics of adaptive leadership

Problem crystallisation: Adaptive leaders focus on the core problem rather than symptoms, identifying fundamental external factors and internal constraints crucial to finding a solution.

Flexibility and forward movement: They embrace ambiguity and imperfect information, constantly moving forward with a solution despite these constraints.

Resource utilisation: At the problem diagnosis phase, adaptive leaders are adept at discerning issues that can be addressed with existing resources versus those requiring new systems and learning.

Team mobilisation: They excel at bringing people on board from all levels within the organisation, fostering a collaborative environment where team members take shared responsibility and credit for solutions.

Influence and credibility: Adaptive leaders lead through influence and personal credibility rather than relying solely on authority.

Empowerment: They empower team members, encouraging collaboration and experimentation.
Demonstrate compassion: They work sensitively to inspire and help team members overcome any overwhelm caused by change, thereby building their motivation to take on new tasks.

Below, we outline the kind of action plan that enterprising AI team leaders might have in place to drive AI change.

A programme for successfully introducing AI

Retooling your organisation and its people to make it AI-enabled should be viewed as a major change management exercise. There are no quick fixes or an hour-long training course that people can take, to get ready for this. It will require prolonged effort and focus, with leadership from the top. Within this context, here are seven steps to get you started.

Step 1: Educate and demystify AI

Start with educational workshops and training sessions to help the team understand AI. *Google AI* and *Coursera* courses provide foundational knowledge of AI. Set learning goals and expectations for the team.

When introducing AI, emphasise that it will augment, not replace, many roles. Provide simple examples such as using *IBM Watson's* suite of AI tools to enhance customer service, HR, or marketing functions. This can free up time for team members to engage in more creative tasks.

Step 2: Practical demonstrations to highlight AI's value

Showcase the benefits of AI in improving processes and decision-making. Highlight both personal and professional advantages of embracing AI.

For instance, demonstrate how *Microsoft Copilot* can support your decision-making and how AI tools like *Tableau* can create interactive visual dashboards.

Step 3: Implement systematic change management

Involve employees in the AI implementation process to increase buy-in and reduce resistance. Foster an inclusive change management approach to ensure team members feel included and less likely to resist AI. Use collaborative platforms like *Miro* and *Trello* to illustrate this inclusiveness.

Step 4: Gradual AI integration

Introduce AI gradually to avoid overwhelming team members. Phase the integration to showcase AI benefits without causing stress. There are tools within *Zapier*, which automate numerous routine tasks, including email management and social media posting that can demonstrate the immediate advantages of AI.

Step 5: Foster a supportive, cross-disciplinary culture

This approach focuses on tackling priority challenges by working across traditional boundaries encouraging teams to work in a collaborative way. Utilise applications like *Slack* and MS *Teams* to facilitate smooth communication.

Step 6: Establish continuous support, training and learning programmes

Implement a robust support programme and allocate resources for regular AI skill updates. Team leaders should consider the most effective training methods for their team, including:

Lectures and tutorials: Use lectures, webinars and one-on-one tutorials for topics like AI ethics and governance.

Hands-on workshops: Offer simulations and practical exercises with AI tools to give team members first-hand experience.

Case studies: Present best practice examples from other parts of the organisation or other companies to demonstrate successful AI integration.

Role-specific training tasks: Assign tasks that show how AI tools can improve major job functions, making the benefits of AI tangible.

Collaborative projects: Engage teams in AI-enhanced projects to highlight the synergy between human intelligence and AI, benefitting those who prefer collective problem-solving.

Continuous learning: Implement step-by-step learning with feedback loops, such as monthly update sessions, to track and reinforce skill development over time.

Step 7: Implement a monitoring and evaluation system

Set up a system to assess the effectiveness of the AI introduction programme. Use feedback loops to inform and adjust the ongoing AI implementation strategy.

A commitment to lifelong learning and training

With the rapid advancement of AI technology, continuous training has become even more crucial. Thus, effective AI team leaders will provide access to training resources and opportunities for developing AI-specific skills.

This builds on the concept of 'servant leadership', introduced by Robert K. Greenleaf[6] in 1970. He emphasises that effective leaders achieve organisational goals while helping others grow. These leaders empathise with their employees' needs and prioritise ongoing training to enhance their team's capabilities.

Our Galvanising Leader will ensure that this training is integrated into daily practices rather than being a token effort. They are dedicated to continuous skills training for their team members. They foster a culture of lifelong learning and development, recognising its importance in personal and professional growth.

Today's leaders cultivate a team culture of continuous learning by acting as mentors, promoting curiosity and the exploration of AI's potential. They enjoy sharing their knowledge, helping team members reach higher levels of critical and creative thinking in collaboration with AI.

Profile of the Galvanising Leader

Let's sum up by providing a profile of the Galvanising Leader able to drive change in the AI era.

Deep AI knowledge

Possess a strong understanding of AI capabilities, limitations and applications to make informed decisions on its deployment in various business processes.

Strategic vision

Have a clear strategic plan for integrating AI into the organisation to transform operations. They learn from other visionary leaders, experiment with new ideas and understand that a broad knowledge base is key to driving creativity and innovation.

Ethical awareness

Understand the importance of adhering to ethical standards concerning privacy, security, fairness and transparency in AI use.

Resilience and mental strength

Demonstrate resilience and mental strength, along with the energy to manage the disruptions and challenges that come with AI deployment.

Flexibility and adaptability

Adopt a flexible and adaptable approach to organisational and systems change, ensuring smooth transitions and maintaining employee morale. They recognise the importance of building collaborative cross-functional teams and value interdisciplinary problem-solving.

Compassionate leadership

Exhibit a human-centred, compassionate leadership style with emotional intelligence, self-awareness and empathy, managing interpersonal relationships sensitively during periods of change.

Transparent communication

Excel in transparent communication, keeping teams informed about AI initiatives and their impacts, minimising uncertainty and reducing resistance to change.

Summary

In this chapter, we emphasised that a successful transition to AI requires team leaders with a deep understanding of AI technology, strategic foresight, ethical rigor and a commitment to human-centred leadership. These leaders are able to navigate the technical complexities of AI integration while possessing the entrepreneurial skill to turn ideas into action effectively. They see the merit of adopting an adaptive leadership style that acknowledges and addresses team sensitivities and anxieties about AI.

In summary, the AI-fluent leader combines technical expertise, the ability to execute and a compassionate approach to fostering a collaborative team culture.

So you can see why we opted to use the label Galvanising Leader to sum up this role and power skill. This is because these leaders will have the wherewithal to 'galvanise' everyone around them into seeing and enjoying the opportunities that AI presents coming down the track. These leaders will know how to take their team with them on a successful journey towards the era of collaborative human AI initiatives.

Notes

1. Godin, S. (2010). *Linchpin: Are You Indispensable?* Portfolio.
2. Smith, D. V. L. (2023). *The Entrepreneur Mindset: The Art of Making Ideas Happen*. Amazon Publishing.
3. Hougaard, R., Carter, J., & Coutts, G. (2018). *The Mind of the Leader: How to Lead Yourself, Your People, and Your Organization for Extraordinary Results*. Harvard Business Review Press.
4. Dutton, J. E., & Worline, M. C. (2017). *Awakening Compassion at Work: The Quiet Power that Elevates People and Organizations*. Berrett-Koehler Publishers.
5. Heifetz, R. A., Grashow, A., & Linsky, M. (2009). *The Practice of Adaptive Leadership: Tools and Tactics for Changing Your Organization and the World*. Harvard Business Press.
6. Greenleaf, R. K. (1970). *The Servant as Leader*. Greenleaf Center for Servant Leadership.

14

COLLABORATING WITH AI

In this chapter, we begin by recapping the overall aim of this book and summarising the core power skills at the heart of our message. Specifically, we reinforce the importance of thinking in an interdisciplinary way like a polymath. We then discuss the best ways to apply these power skills individually and as a team. Finally, we explore how AI is leading us towards a world of collective intelligence.

With this book, the authors aim to ensure that knowledge workers are aware of the rate at which AI is likely to change their world and society. Specifically, we want to clarify how AI impacts fundamental knowledge worker skills and provide the seven key power skills we believe are essential for successfully collaborating with AI.

With this in mind, we begin our final chapter with a brief recap of the seven power skills and a review of how best to apply them in practical situations. We then discuss how AI could affect humans' everyday thinking

DOI: 10.4324/9781003514879-15

patterns and briefly explore expert perspectives on the likely arrival of collective intelligence – the journey towards the 'supermind'.

A recap of our seven power skills

For the sake of clarity, we explained each of our seven power skills in a linear way, dealing with one skill at a time. However, in practice, a knowledge worker will apply these skills fluidly and interrelatedly when faced with challenges.

We have made the point that certain knowledge workers may focus on some power skills over others, but, in the spirit of interdisciplinary thinking, all team members will have some basic level of proficiency across all the skills. In this context, it's helpful to provide a summary of the power skills that begins to demonstrate how they work together in tackling an assignment.

At the heart of the power skills is the AI interface skill set. This involves understanding how to interact effectively with AI systems to leverage their capabilities to their fullest potential. Being a human-AI interface expert requires knowing how to use AI tools, interpret AI outputs correctly, and provide meaningful feedback to improve AI performance. This skill ensures that collaboration between humans and AI results in robust, ethical, actionable and relevant outcomes.

Next, we consider three power skills – the Sensemaker, Critical Thinker and Audacious Creator – as inputs that lead to contextually sound, well-thought-out and creative business solutions.

The Sensemaker involves interpreting and understanding complex and ambiguous information. AI is powerful at analysing massive amounts of relevant data and identifying patterns but often lacks the ability to understand the nuanced context in which these outputs are generated. Human sensemaking becomes invaluable in teasing out solutions that may have escaped AI.

The Critical Thinker focuses on abductive reasoning, arriving at the best possible judgements in situations of high uncertainty and imperfect information. This involves exploring the underlying causes of observed phenomena, which can be beyond AI's capabilities, given humans' subtle understanding of the human condition.

The Audacious Creator acknowledges the collaborative role AI plays in creativity but recognises that human creativity – insights, emotional intelligence and application – provides the final touch that is still beyond AI.

We then moved to the power skills around communication and future planning: Forward Thinker and Inspiring Communicator.

The Forward Thinker involves envisioning plausible future scenarios, aiding in long-term strategic thinking and preparing for future challenges and uncertainties. AI plays a significant role in predictive analytics and trend forecasting, but humans uniquely engage in forward mental time travel, recalling visceral and emotional experiences to envision future possibilities in ways more sensitive to human needs than AI.

The Inspiring Communicator acknowledges AI's powerful role in business communications but emphasises that storytelling in business hinges on tapping into human emotions in ways AI has yet to master fully.

Our final power skill is the Galvanising Leader, a new form of compassionate leadership fostering a supportive and inclusive environment. This skill is crucial for the ethical and robust integration of AI into human working patterns, addressing concerns about AI's impact and promoting a culture of empathy, transparency, collaboration and trust. See Figure 14.1 below.

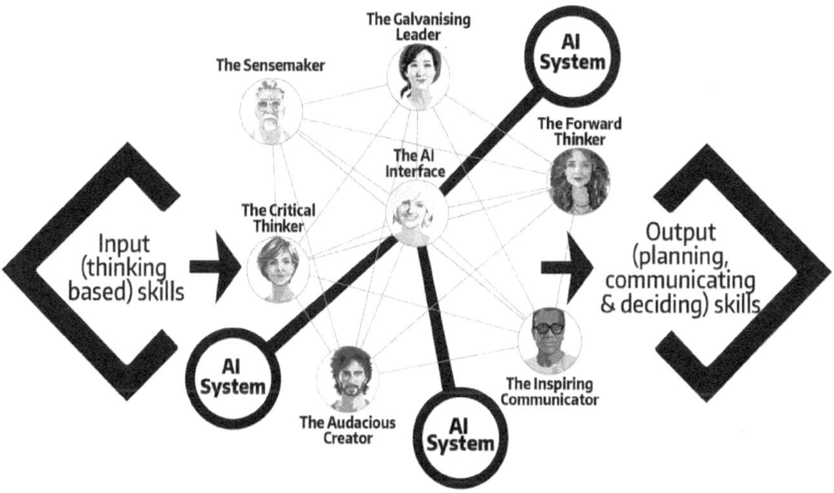

Figure 14.1 The seven power skills

Mastering our seven power skills

Having reviewed our seven skills, we are often asked whether a typical knowledge worker needs to master all seven power skills or if they can selectively focus on some. A central theme of this book is the argument that, in collaborating with AI, knowledge workers would benefit from adopting a polymath approach, embracing diverse ways of thinking.

Our argument is that AI will increasingly handle much of the heavy lifting in specific knowledge-based areas. The added value humans bring will revolve around our ability to see connections between different subjects, draw together nuanced contextual issues and understand the bigger picture.

By enhancing their range of skills, knowledge workers will improve their ability to collaborate with AI, ensuring that AI serves as a tool for augmenting human potential rather than replacing it. Therefore, it would be sensible for knowledge workers to have an appreciation of the fundamental principles underlying each of the power skills described in this book.

In practical terms, we envision knowledge worker teams comprising individuals who are more adept at certain power skills than others. However, it is important for all team members to see the overall picture. Many readers will be familiar with the concept of the T-shaped team, where all members have a broad awareness of what everyone else is doing while some specialise in particular areas. This model is recommended for knowledge workers working as a team, focusing on the power skills identified in this book.

The impact of AI on our cognitive structures

As this book focuses on human-AI collaboration, we need to address how the integration of AI into our daily lives and work environments might influence human brain function and evolution.

As the symbiotic relationship between humans and AI evolves, with each enhancing the capabilities of the other, there could be a shift in the human cognitive landscape. This process, often called extrospection, involves external tools and systems aiding our cognitive processes. Over time, humans may increasingly rely on AI for certain types of thinking, allowing us to focus on areas where we have a distinct advantage.

Noam Chomsky is reported as saying, 'Much of what is distinctive among human beings is a specific manner in which a variety of shared cognitive structures develop'. This is a recurring theme in his work and is discussed in his book *Language and Mind* (1968).[1]

The idea that new technology will change how we think and need to think is not new. Technology has always shaped our consciousness, from 40,000-year-old cave paintings to the written word, the printing press, the phone, fax, email and internet-enabled social media. Each innovation has influenced how we interact with and process information. The question now is how we will evolve with these latest powerful information technologies.

This is a vast topic, but it's important to conclude with some expert observations about the overall direction of this evolution. Information technology is reshaping human thought processes, expanding our horizons, both internally and externally. On the subject of consciousness: in his book, *The Origin of Consciousness in the Breakdown of the Bicameral Mind* (1976),[2] Princeton University psychologist Julian Jaynes argued that consciousness, as he defines it, is a learned process that developed around the second millennium bce. It is not a foundational building block of the species but an evolutionary outcome. Here, we define consciousness simply as an awareness of our internal and external existence.

Tapping into our internal and external worlds

This consciousness relies on the 'sensors in the ground' we have to tap into our internal and external worlds. The feedback from these sensors has been expanding for a long time, and the pace of this change is accelerating. As our context and environment change, we will continue to evolve.

The brain never stops changing in response to learning, experience, or memory formation, a process generally known as neural plasticity, see Chen et al. (2020).[3] Neural plasticity involves adaptive structural and functional changes to the brain, allowing it to respond to both internal and external stimuli by reorganising its structure, functions, or connections.

As more data, information, knowledge and insight become available, it's interesting to consider how the balance of our 'sensors in the ground' might change. We may place greater weight on external rather than internal cues, emphasising extrospection – the observation of things external to one's own mind – over introspection. In *Philosophical Investigations* (published posthumously in 1953), Ludwig Wittgenstein[4] said, 'An inner process stands in need of outward criteria', highlighting the need for external reference points.

In searching for an illustration of extrospection, we found a sporting example: introspection can be dangerous for a closing pitcher in baseball, whilst extrospection helps keep the pitcher's focus attuned to the game unfolding around him. This illustrates how focusing on external cues can be more beneficial than internal reflection in certain contexts.

Outsourcing our thinking

An interesting thought piece from the Commonwealth Scientific and Industrial Research Organisation argued that outsourcing information management to AI has consequences. It can influence not only what we think but also how we think (Bentley, Mason & Grimberg, 2023).[5] Studies have shown that access to the internet has changed our cognition, memory and creativity. Whilst having access to vast amounts of information increases our collective meta-knowledge and ability to find information, it also reduces our memory of what that information was (Pilat & Sekoui, 2021).[6]

Offloading our thinking to search engines might free up mental reserves for problem-solving and creative thinking, but it is also associated with increased distraction and dependency (Sparrow & Chatman, 2013).[7] Regardless of the quantity or quality of information retrieved, this process increases our cognitive self-esteem – our belief in our own 'smarts' (Bentley, Mason & Grimberg, 2023).

The latest AI models do more than catalogue and present search results. They can locate, evaluate, synthesise, structure and present information, mimicking knowledge and insight. How will our cognitive processes react to this? Does this change the balance between our internal sensemaking and the external cues provided by technology, requiring more acute extrospection skills? This ongoing evolution of our cognitive structures is a critical area for further exploration as we continue to integrate AI into our lives.

And this discussion about how we create meaning through a combination of extrospective and introspective thinking leads us to a brief review of the concept of collective intelligence and the journey towards the 'supermind'.

Collective intelligence and the Supermind

Keith Richards, the Rolling Stones guitarist, is reported as saying that 'Good music comes out of people playing together, knowing what they want to do and going for it'. This brings us to the concept of collective intelligence. This requires us to be more extrospective than introspective, as much will come from the collective rather than from within.

Earlier in this book, we touched on the 'technological singularity' popularised by Vernor Vinge (1983) and Ray Kurzweil (2005) – the point at which technology becomes self-aware or humans biologically integrate with machines to evolve. Vinge famously stated, 'Within 30 years we will have the technological means to create superhuman intelligence. Shortly after, the human era will be ended'.[8]

We are not arguing for or against this notion of a hard singularity but rather using the idea of a 'soft singularity' developed by anthropologist Professor Matthew O'Lemmon (2020).[9] This concept describes 'the impact AI is having on the increase in speed of communication, rates of connectivity, and time spent online, all of which have hastened the convergence to a collective consciousness'. AI is seen as the latest in a long line of information technologies pushing us towards some form of collective consciousness by closing the cognitive gap between individuals and levelling the playing field through access to information.

Kevin Kelly, founding executive editor of *Wired Magazine*, pointed out that it might be challenging to understand what happens once we have a global connection of seven billion people and seven trillion machines and AIs all connected together (2016).[10] This scenario suggests that events at that level may be beyond our current understanding.

The power of collective intelligence

Collective intelligence is a complex adaptive system defined within organisational psychology as groups of individuals capable of acting collectively in ways that seem intelligent and cannot be explained by individual intelligence alone. Individuals in this system see themselves as autonomous but actively participate as 'interacting agents'. The interaction between these agents gives rise to intelligence that cannot be predicted by aggregating individual intelligences – the process of interaction adds something unique.

Edwin Hutchins, in his book *Cognition in the Wild* (1995),[11] writes that 'Humans create their cognitive powers by creating the environments in which they exercise those powers'. Groups must have cognitive properties not predictable from the individuals alone. Collective intelligence arises from the synergies between different skill sets and mental models, an emergent phenomenon from the interaction of diverse agents.

By collaborating, the collective achieves a level of 'super-intelligence' that surpasses individual capabilities. Salons, clubs and societies, beloved by polymaths, are forms of collective intelligence, offering mind-expanding and enhanced problem-solving capabilities.

The hive mind

Parallels are often drawn between human collective intelligence and the natural world, such as colonies of ants or bees. Howard Bloom's *Global Brain* (2000)[12] depicts collective intelligence in bacterial colonies and insects, drawing parallels with human societies. He describes the network of life on Earth as a 'complex adaptive system', a global brain in which each of us plays a role.

In literature, H. G. Wells depicted an alien hive society in his 1901 novel *The First Men in the Moon*. The term 'hive mind' came into popular culture in the 1950s, coined by science fiction writer James H. Schmitz in his short story *Second Night of Summer* (1950). The hive mind is an awareness formed from the communication of individual minds, different from each of its constituent minds, and not defined by their separateness (James Sirois, 2020).[13]

We are not discussing science fiction or neural implants but basic human-to-human cooperation in pursuit of common goals. How we form and operate as a group, share knowledge, and extend individual capabilities are central to collective intelligence.

In a business context, the 'hive mind' has been used negatively to describe groupthink and positively to describe the benefits of collaboration and networking that drive up 'organisational IQ'. Dr Thomas Seeley's *Honeybee Democracy* (2010)[14] provides a framework for group decision-making: creating groups with mutual respect and shared interests, minimising leaders' influence, seeking diverse solutions and aggregating group knowledge through debate.

Collective intelligence feels different from the hive mind because it requires the interplay of different perspectives, perhaps an element of healthy debate, leading to better outcomes. In the 1980s, Bruno Latour et al. developed 'Actor-Network Theory (ANT)' (2005),[15] which sees objects, ideas and processes as just as important in creating social situations as humans. Somewhat controversial at the time, it does have parallels with Thomas Malone's Superminds, in that humans and machines are inseparable, all playing roles in thinking networks.

The Supermind concept

In *Superminds* (2018),[16] Thomas Malone outlines the potential power of intelligence exhibited by groups of people and computers working together in a hybrid model. Instead of computer agents solving problems alone, cyber-human systems allow humans and machines to work together. This approach leverages human general intelligence and specialised skills with the knowledge and capabilities of machines.

In his book *Big Mind* (2018),[17] Geoff Mulgan develops a similar idea that collective intelligence is:

> The capacity of groups to make good decisions through a combination of human and machine capabilities [and that] collective intelligence depends on functional capabilities: distinct abilities to observe, analyse, remember, create, empathize and judge – each of which can be enhanced by technologies.

Douglas Englebart, one of the pioneers of human computer interactions, argues that:

> Regardless of the end goals, Collective IQ comes down to how quickly and intelligently the group can iteratively assess a situation, identify needs and opportunities, realize desired outcomes, and incorporate lessons learned, while continuously adapting to changing conditions until the goals are met.
>
> (*Augmenting Human Intellect: A Conceptual Framework*, 1962)[18]

Staying with this idea, Marvin Minsky encouraged thinking of networked intelligence as a 'society of mind',[19] viewing natural cognitive systems as vast societies of individually simple processes. These processes are the fundamental thinking entities from which collective intelligence is built, with diversity being key to their power.

> What magical trick makes us intelligent? The trick is that there is no trick. The power of intelligence stems from our vast diversity, not from any single, perfect principle.
>
> (*The Society of Mind*, 1987)[20]

For collective intelligence to flourish, interacting agents must exhibit diversity, bringing different skills, experiences and perspectives to the group. This heterogeneity catalyses the group's 'super-intelligence'. Decentralised thinking is also crucial – forcing decision-making through a single control point restricts the free flow of ideas. Collective intelligence requires leadership without a single leader, a 'let a thousand flowers bloom' approach.

Coordination, collaboration and communication are cornerstones of collective intelligence. Don Tapscott's four principles for an open world (2006)[21] include collaboration, transparency, sharing and empowerment – parallel collective intelligence. His 'Ideagora' concept, a marketplace for minds, allows organisations to tap into collective knowledge and innovation.

In the 21st century, human intelligence can be augmented with AI, creating a human-computer hybrid system. This integrative framework combines human power skills and emotional intelligence with AI capabilities, achieving greater synergies and pushing the boundaries of collective intelligence.

Malone raises the prospect of organisation superminds being more than just collective intelligence – he asks if they can be conscious too. He uses the example of Apple, describing it as 'aware, self-aware, goal-directed, and integrated in complex ways'. He shares a conversation with Apple CEO Tim Cook, who agreed that Apple, like a person, has values, goals and consciousness.

Of course, we cannot objectively measure consciousness. And maybe it is a stretch to leap from the ideas of the collective intelligence of networked power skills to a sort of human intelligence – AI cyborg – to the 'conscious organisation'. In this chapter we are simply musing on the possible evolutionary paths and how these networked power skills may relate to and interact with the current and future AI models and technology more broadly.

> Does this mean you have to agree that groups are conscious in order to understand and take advantage of . . . collective intelligence. No, you don't. But especially as new information technologies allow us to

> build more and more intelligent combinations of people and computers . . . it will become more and more useful to think of many kinds of superminds as conscious.
>
> (Thomas Malone, 2018)[22]

Harnessing the power of diverse thinking

To conclude, our argument is that AI will transform the working lives of knowledge workers more quickly than many anticipate. Therefore, it is sensible to begin acquiring the skills that best equip us to collaborate with the extraordinary new thinking that AI offers.

Much of the knowledge, information and detailed analysis once believed to be the sole domain of humans is now handled with ease by AI. This shift underscores the need for us to develop polymath skills – working across diverse information streams, applying emotional intelligence, empathy, compassion and nuanced insights that AI might miss. These human qualities are essential for adding value to the new human–AI partnership.

We've been handed a powerful F1 racing car to replace our old family saloon, but we now need to learn how to become better drivers to do justice to this fantastic new technology. By embracing polymath thinking, we can maximise the potential of AI, ensuring that it augments human capabilities rather than replacing them.

Notes

1. Chomsky, N. (1968). *Language and Mind*. New York: Harcourt, Brace, Jovanovich.
2. Jaynes, J. (1976). *The Origin of Consciousness in the Breakdown of the Bicameral Mind*. Houghton Mifflin, Mariner.
3. Chen, Q., Yang, H., Rooks, B., et al. (2020). *Autonomic Flexibility Reflects Learning and Associated Neuroplasticity in Old Age*. Human Brain Mapping.
4. Wittgenstein, L. (1953). *Philosophical Investigations*. Oxford Blackwell.
5. Bentley, S., Mason, C., & Grimberg, E. (2023). *Wising Up: How Generative AI Could Change the Way We Think*. CSIRO.
6. Pilat, D., & Sekoul, D. (2021). *Google Effect*. The Decision Lab. Retrieved July 2, 2024, from https://thedecisionlab.com/biases/google-effect
7. Sparrow, B., & Chatman, L. (October–December, 2013). *Social Cognition in the Internet Age: Same as It Ever Was?* Psychological Inquiry, 24(4), 273–292.
8. Vinge, V. (1993). *The Coming Technological Singularity: How to Survive in the Post-Human Era*. VISION-21: Interdisciplinary Science and Engineering in the Era of Cyberspace, NASA Conference Publication 10129, pp. 11–22.

9. O'Lemmon, M. (2020). *The Technological Singularity as the Emergence of a Collective Consciousness: An Anthropological Perspective.* Bulletin of Science, Technology & Society, 40(1–2), 15–27.
10. Kelly, K. (2016). *The Inevitable: Understanding the 12 Technological Forces That Will Shape Our Future.* Viking.
11. Hutchins, E. (1995). *Cognition in the Wild.* MIT Press.
12. Bloom, H. (2000). *Global Brain: The Evolution of Mass Mind from the Big Bang to the 21st Century.* Trade Paper Press.
13. Sirois, J. (August 2020). https://philosophynow.org/issues/139/The_Singularity_of_the_Human_Hive_Mind.
14. Seeley, T. D. (2010). *Honeybee Democracy.* Princeton University Press.
15. Latour, B., Callon, M., Law, J., & Akrich, M. (2005). *Reassembling the Social: An Introduction to Actor-Network-Theory.* Oxford University Press.
16. Malone, T. W. (2018). *Superminds: The Surprising Power of People and Computers Thinking Together.* Little Brown Spark.
17. Mulgan, G. (2018). *Big Mind: How Collective Intelligence Can Change Our World.* Princeton University Press.
18. Engelbart, D. C. (1962). *Augmenting Human Intellect: A Conceptual Framework* (Summary Report AFOSR-3223). Menlo Park, CA: Stanford Research Institute.
19. Minsky, M. (1987). *The Society of Mind.* Simon & Schuster.
20. Minsky, M. (1986). *The Society of Mind.* New York: Simon & Schuster.
21. Tapscott, D., & Williams, A. D. (2006). *Wikinomics: How Mass Collaboration Changes Everything.* Portfolio.
22. Malone, T. W. (2018). *Superminds: The Surprising Power of People and Computers Thinking Together.* New York: Little, Brown and Company.

INDEX

Note: Page numbers in *italic* indicate a figure on the corresponding page.

FSC
www.fsc.org
MIX
Papier | Fördert gute Waldnutzung
FSC® C083411

Kolibri 360 GmbH
Ferdinand-Jühlke-Straße 7
99095 Erfurt, Deutschland
produktsicherheit@kolibri360.de